Detroit
City of Champions

THE STORY OF THE MOST IMPORTANT SEASON IN DETROIT SPORTS HISTORY

To sign the petition "Bring Back Champions Day."
Please visit: www.DetroitCityofChamps.com

From one Detroit Sports fan to another, I hope you enjoy this first edition copy. Best Wishes and Long live Champions Day!

DIOMEDEA PUBLISHING

Copyright © 2008 Charles Avison

Published by Diomedea Publishing
www.diomedeapublishing.com
www.detroitcityofchamps.com
www.myspace/detroitcityofchampions.com

ISBN: 978-0-9817434-0-0

Interior design by Sans Serif Inc., Saline, MI
Cover design by Curtis Avison
Pictures on cover by permission of *The Detroit News*

Printed in the United States

OMNIUM RERUM PRINCIPIA PARVA SUNT

The beginnings of all things are small

—Cicero

TO THE READER:

In attempting to bring the sights, sounds, and feelings of this story to the modern day it was necessary to use quotes from this time. Included in some of these quotes are words and feelings from an era that was different from our own. In the beginning it was difficult to decide whether or not to include these words, eliminate sections of a quote, or simply pass up on the quote in its entirety. I made a decision however, that I would never lie to you the reader, I would never cover up certain realities, I would never "bend" the truth in order to make this story more palatable to all readers' tastes. It must be understood that any words, phrases, or quotes, especially regarding race are a reflection of this era and not a reflection of the author.

I also wish to briefly discuss the types of photos that I chose to use. I wanted to do something a bit different than other sports books in order to enhance some of the moments of this story. Since many of the original pictures have been lost to the sands of time; I had to turn to the original copies of the newspapers. The modern age allows for an increased ability to reproduce these images, and many of them turned out more spectacularly than I could have hoped. Many however, may appear "grainy" or less perfect than a traditional publishing house would allow. It was not a difficult decision to include these because they truly help enhance this story, and my way of thinking is that less quality is better than no quality at all.

Finally, the facts presented in this book were cross referenced with a variety of sources. The seasoned Detroit sports reader may notice small variations between the statistics and facts in this book and those of other authors. The reason, is that whenever I was in doubt, I used primary source information often times straight from the newspapers. I have always taken pride in my attention to detail and will stand by my work should any argument come my way. For you, the reader, deserve nothing less.

Sincerely,

CONTENTS

PREFACE

It was late that night in Kalamazoo, Michigan, 2005. Jeremy Hunter, Kevin Bush and I were up late entertaining ourselves with a combination of beer and a Detroit Tiger statistics guide. It was Jeremy who was reading off stats and interesting highlights of our favorite team. I asked him to read the section on the 1935 team and how the Tigers had won their first championship. After reading it, he came to an asterisk at the bottom of the page which said "in 1935, Detroit became the City of Champions after the Tigers, Lions, and Red Wings all won their championships." The three of us were astounded, as none of us had ever heard of that before. It definitely peaked my interest. As a senior at Western Michigan University at the time; I was taking a sports history class and decided that I would make this the subject of a paper that I was about to write. I was more than a little frustrated when I went to the library and found no books on the subject. I then turned to the internet and found an online Detroit News article by Patricia Zacharias, but little else. Scraping together enough information for the two page paper and giving a short presentation on it in class convinced me that this was a subject which needed more investigation.

Later that year I approached Linda Borish, the professor who had taught the class, about making this topic the focus of my bachelors degree thesis. I figured I was "killing two birds with one stone" because I needed a topic and I also wanted to know more. My concern, however, was finding enough information to write a thesis that would have to be thirty pages long. I need not have worried because when I started looking at newspaper articles from this time I was amazed at how much information there was. In fact, I had to trim off eight pages to come under the maximum page limit. The original thesis was focused on the "impacts of the City of Champions," and didn't really delve much into the story. At one point while travelling abroad for a couple of years I picked up a copy of my thesis and reread it, thinking to myself "this story really is too good to keep on the shelf," especially since no one that I had ever spoken with had heard of these events. I decided to revisit the subject in early 2007 with a couple of trips to the Detroit Public Library. What I was looking for was an old newspaper that I never knew existed called the Detroit Times. For my original thesis I had used primarily *The Detroit News* and *Detroit Free Press*, but the information I found in the Times almost knocked me off my feet. Apparently the Times had taken the lead in covering the story of "City of Champions," and the wealth of information contained within, was absolutely incredible. So much information, that I decided it was time to write my first book.

As a Detroit sports fan, I not only love to watch the games, I also enjoy reading the papers. Since there were no other books on this subject I had to go directly to the original newspaper sources to find the information. It was as a fan and as a researcher that I poured through the countless newspaper articles to bring this story up-to-date. As I read these newspapers, what I realized, was that the people of this time had their own story to tell and that if I was going to communicate the real essence of these events, I had to let these people speak for themselves. This is why I have used quotes of their sights, sounds, behavior and feelings; wherever possible.

I have three goals for this book. The first was mentioned above; to dust off this story and bring it back to the modern day. So that everyone, especially fans of Detroit sports have a concise reference for the story of their teams' first championships. My second goal is to try and understand why this story is so little known? How is it that such an amazing story has been all but forgotten? My third goal is a bit more ambitious. When I first did a search on the internet under the title "City of Champions," the computer came up with 45,100,000 hits, with cities all over the world cluttering up the web with frivolous claims. I want to put forth the argument that Detroit is the only "City of Champions." While other cities may have had championships and have champions in their city, Detroit is the only city that can claim this title. Let it be enough for now, to say that Detroit captured this title through the highest level of athletic achievement, and then proclaimed it from the highest building. No city argued back then; and no city has put forth a better case since.

I hope you enjoy reading this book as much as I enjoyed writing it. As a fan it was a real pleasure to research and write about a topic that I found so incredibly interesting.

Impressive towers began to define the skyline of modern Detroit in the early twentieth century. Here, a "worm's eye view" shows the original Buhl, Ford, Penobscot, and Union Trust buildings.

—Photo Courtesy of *The Detroit News*

INTRODUCTION

At the beginning of the 20th century, Detroit was a city on the rise. Being well placed along the Great Lakes to make river transport easily accessible, it was an early hub of moving goods and raw materials. With the invention of the automobile and the ensuing manufacturing refinements, Detroit became the capital for the production of motor vehicles and quickly gained its reputation as "the motor city." By 1920 the population of Detroit had risen to one million people. Between 1921 and 1927 the downtown took on the look of a major American city as many high-rise buildings were built. The 24-story First National Bank, the 36-story Book-Cadillac, and the 47-story Penobscot building to name but a few. These and other new buildings created a skyline of impressive towers that indicated the boom Detroit was experiencing.

Detroit was also on the upswing with regards to its social and cultural aspects. The Detroit Public Library was built in 1921, followed by the Detroit Institute of Arts in 1927 and the Fox Theatre in 1928. Improvements made to the public school system, and the building of many other theatres gave residents of Detroit; education and entertainment, which could rival any city in the world. The rising boom of auto production in Detroit, and the introduction of the $5.00 workday left the rising population of the city with more disposable income. When Henry Ford initiated the 40-hour workweek in 1922, they had more free time as well. These were very important events for the history of Detroit sports because of the concept that more time and disposable income allows people to seek recreation and leisure activities.

Long lines for food and work were common after the stock market crashed.

By 1929 the production of automobiles peaked when 5,337,000 vehicles were built. However, all of this prosperity ended with the stock market crash of October 29th 1929, a day which would be forever called "Black Tuesday." This of course was the first day of the Great Depression. By 1930, car production had dropped down to 3,363,000, and by the following year to 1,332,000. On September 25th, unemployment registration offices opened and 19,412 people registered. By September 29th the number had grown to 75,704. January 2, 1931 saw an unemployment demonstration outside of city hall. By the end of the month 223,568 people were unemployed and Detroit was declared (by the U.S. census) to be the hardest hit city; followed by Cleveland, Chicago, Buffalo, and Philadelphia.

On March 7th, a hunger march was organized by a communist candidate for mayor named John Schmies. The march was planned to go from Detroit to the suburb of Dearborn. A riot was sparked during the march when Dearborn police tried to stop them at the border. After four were killed and hundreds injured; 15,000 people walked in a funeral procession. Following this procession 30,000 people massed at the cemetery to hear the song "The International (communist workers anthem)."

In addition to these rough economic times, the world was full of uncertainty. In Europe, a growing menace was taking shape in the form of the Nazi party, and its leader Adolf Hitler. Italy had launched an aggressive military campaign against Ethiopia under the leadership of Benito Mussolini. War was most certainly threatening and in most people's minds it was less a matter of if—and more a question of when.

In the midst of all these troubling times, Detroit began to celebrate. A young boxer named Joe Louis had recently turned professional, and in 1935 he began his rampage through the physical and racial barriers of the boxing world. The rise of Joe Louis was as rapid as it was inspiring. His 24 stunning knockouts in this year would propel him from the realm of the unknown—to being universally regarded as the "uncrowned champion" of the world. His brutal beatings of two of boxing's finest fighters began a period of celebrations that no city in the history of the United States has ever witnessed—before or since.

On the heels of Louis' triumphs, the city's beloved baseball team the Detroit Tigers, had clawed their way through the Chicago Cubs to bring home the City's first World Series Championship. But the city was far from finished with its celebrations; over the next seven months the Detroit Lions and the Detroit Red Wings would add their first championships to the city's mantle. This period of dominance remains unsurpassed in the annals of American professional sports, and no other city has since won three major professional sports championships in the same sporting season. If Joe Louis' remarkable rise to the peak of boxing success is added to these three championships, it is easy to see how Detroit could proclaim itself *the* "City of Champions."

The end of prohibition did much to improve the "spirits" of depression era fans. Here, two women work a concession stand at Navin Field.

Life was incredibly difficult for people during the Great Depression. This family was photographed in Detroit after an 800 mile hitch hike, in which they were simply looking for work.

"No other city—no, nor no other state could ever boast, as Detroit can Boast today, that it is the home of the National League and Stanley Cup champions in hockey, the home of the American League and World Series champions in baseball, the home of the National Professional League champions in football, the home of the uncrowned champion of pugilism, the home of the National League record-holder for speed on water, and the home of the numerous other world or national achievers and achievements.

—Harry Leduc, *The Detroit News*, 4/13/36

JOE LOUIS

Joe Louis Barrow was born on May 13, 1914 in the Bucalew Mountains of Alabama. He was the seventh of eight children born to sharecroppers Monroe and Lillie Reece Barrow. As a youngster, the family went through a very difficult period of instability on account of the serious mental illness of their father, who would end up being committed for the rest of his life to a mental asylum. His mother re-married to a man named Pat Brooks, who himself brought several children to an already large family. Looking for more opportunities, the family moved north to Detroit when Joe was 12; in order to find work in the booming Detroit auto factories. As a child, the future heavyweight champion had a stutter which contributed to the quiet nature and soft-spoken demeanor that would characterize him throughout his life. His first steady job was to deliver ice blocks for refrigerators. In the days before electric refrigeration, these 60 pound blocks of ice had to be hand delivered, oftentimes up many flights of stairs. The arduous workouts, later credited by Joe himself, helped him develop his athletic physique.

There are several different legends as to how Joe Louis Barrow became just Joe Louis. The first was that he had been trying to hide his afternoon boxing expenses from his mother, who had thought she was paying for violin lessons. Another legend has it that several early amateur losses prompted

the change so that he could start over with a fresh record; under a new name. The most likely reason however, was that Joe Louis Barrow was too much of a mouthful for ring announcers, and it was shortened to a more concise, boxing name.

Joe Louis' first recorded amateur bout came in 1932 against Johnny Miller, a fighter who was on his way to the U.S. Olympic boxing team that year. Still a novice in the sport, Louis was knocked down seven times and lost the fight by technical knockout (T.K.O.). Disheartened by this loss, he took a job at the Ford River Rouge plant while he worked on improving his technique.

In 1933, the 19 year-old returned to the ring and recorded 13 straight knockouts on his way to winning the light heavyweight Gold Glove tournament in Detroit. Though he lost a couple of fights in 1933, he had also caught the eye of a man named John Roxborough. As a wealthy and influential member of the black community, Roxborough and his partner Julian Black, could offer greater exposure and training expenses to the up and coming fighter; allowing him to concentrate solely on boxing. However, Roxborough was not exactly the most legitimate businessman in Detroit. He officially called himself a "real estate investor," but he actually ran the numbers racket in Detroit and was also involved with other unsavory activities. Joe Louis knew about these "under-world" connections and figured

Joe Louis' "Brain Trust." Pictured are (from left to right), Assistant Manager Julian Black, trainer Jack Blackburn, Louis, Manager John Roxborough, and tutor Cowan.

—Associated Press Photo

that they actually helped him. He recognized the fact that there was a sinister side to boxing and that a fighter who was naive or "unprotected" would be like a lamb amongst wolves, and could really be taken advantage of,

> *"I figured this way: the fight game is a tough game. They knew their way around. They could protect me from racket guys because they knew the angles."*

In February, 1934, Joe Louis won the Detroit Golden Gloves for the second year in a row. He followed this up a month later in Chicago by winning the National Golden Gloves. He further demonstrated his dominance at the amateur level by winning the AAU light heavyweight championship in St. Louis that April. Reaching the pinnacle of amateur boxing, Louis set his sights on a professional career.

In mid-1934 Louis became acquainted with the man who would become his trainer, Jack Blackburn. A tough former fighter, Blackburn was now in his fifties and knew the sport of boxing as well as anyone. In Louis, Blackburn saw a fighter with the athletic ability to become champion; however the question was whether America's segregated society would even give him the chance at the title,

> *You were born with two strikes on you, that's why I don't fool with colored boys! They're too hard to sell since Jack Johnson went and acted like he did. I can make more sugar training white fighters, even if they're only half as good.*

> —Jack Blackburn to Joe Louis

He had reason to wonder because there had not been a black heavyweight champion since Jack Johnson twenty years before. In fact no black fighter had been even given a chance at the title since that time. Besides the prevalent racism in America at that time, a major reason black fighters had not been given a chance was because of Jack Johnson. When Johnson had won the heavyweight title in 1908 he became brash and arrogant; *"taunting his opponents, gloating over his victories, fraternizing with and marrying white women of low reputation."* After he had won the championship, race riots and lynchings had occurred leaving many people dead. Johnson held the title until 1915, but the ramifications of his behavior lasted for many years. He had embarrassed many people, black and white with his scandals; and though he did break the boxing color

Quiet and soft-spoken outside the ring, Joe was quick in becoming a terror inside of it. The fierce look he displays here would often times be the last thing his opponents would see before the back of their heads hit the canvas.
—*Detroit Times* photo/Courtesy of *The Detroit News*

barrier, he also left a very poor legacy for other black boxers to follow. It was with this poor legacy in mind that the managers and trainers prepared Joe Louis for. Louis had to be taught to behave unlike Johnson outside the ring so that he could become champion inside the ring. A naturally shy and genuine person anyway, the rules installed by Roxborough and Blackburn came easy for him,

> *He would always be soft-spoken, understated, and polite, no matter what he accomplished. He would not preen or gloat or strut in the ring. If he needed*

Though he was an outstanding fighter and the first African American heavyweight champion. Jack Johnson (right) left a poor legacy for future boxers of color to follow.

his teeth capped, it would not be done in gold, as Johnson had done. He would always conduct himself with dignity and not, as Louis once put it, like one of those "fool nigger dolls" with wide grins and thick lips. When it came to women, he would stick to his own kind, and platonically at that, at least for now. He would never fraternize with white women, let alone be photographed with them. He would not drive fast cars, especially red ones. Anyone wishing to hold Louis back would get no help from Louis himself. The press would be saturated with stories of Louis' boyish goodness, his love for his mother, his mother's love for him, his devotion to scripture, his abstemiousness and frugality.

—David Margolik in Beyond Glory

As an amateur fighter, Louis had relied mainly on raw power to pound his way through the ranks. As a professional, Blackburn had to teach him many fundamentals of fighting heavyweights. Defense, punching without leav-

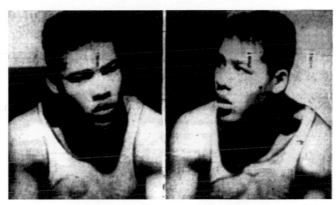

Joe Louis would eventually go on to become a legend. But at the beginning of 1935 he was relatively unknown.
—*Detroit Times* photo/Courtesy of *The Detroit News*

ing an opening, feints (fake punches), and balanced footwork were all taught to the young fighter. The one thing that Blackburn really had to drill into Louis was that his ultimate goal was the knockout, because the trainer had worried that the "nice-guy" Louis might lack the instinct to brutalize an opponent. As Blackburn would later say, "*Joe Louis ain't no natural killer, he's a manufactured killer.*"

The first few fights of Joe Louis' professional career were one sided in the extreme. His debut came on July 4th 1934, against Jack Kracken and ended in the first round with Kracken lying on the ground outside the ring. His second fight in October ended with Art Sykes' taking an ugly head-first bounce off of the canvas. His fight on November 14th could not officially be ended until Stanley Poreada was removed off of the timekeepers lap! Later that same month he left Charlie Massera unconscious, and hanging on the ropes "like a sack of wheat."

It was after these first few fights that people started to realize how powerful Louis' fists were, but it was after he had gone undefeated in his first 12 fights, that he really started garnering national attention as an up-and-coming boxer. The rise of Joe Louis in the boxing world also paralleled the rise of the black man in America. It was at this point that the NAACP became more organized and started filing lawsuits against racist institutions. Black culture saw its renaissance, in the new jazz music scene and night clubs. Black leaders and politicians were entering public service while businessmen were emerging and creating opportunities for themselves and others. Black newspapers such as the Chicago Defender, Pittsburgh Courier, and Detroit Chronicle echoed the voice of black America which became more outspoken and began to

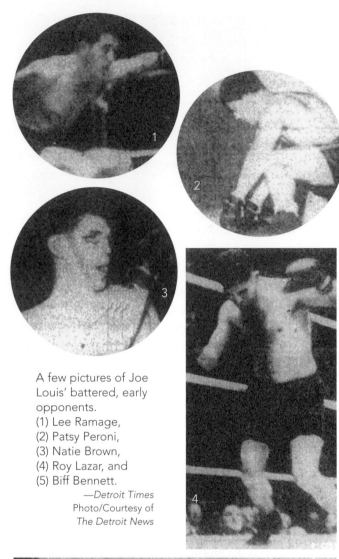

A few pictures of Joe Louis' battered, early opponents.
(1) Lee Ramage,
(2) Patsy Peroni,
(3) Natie Brown,
(4) Roy Lazar, and
(5) Biff Bennett.
— *Detroit Times* Photo/Courtesy of *The Detroit News*

demand that the country take notice. Despite all of these advances however, America and American sport was still heavily segregated. Baseball, football, and hockey still had color barriers. Boxing allowed black fighters to a certain extent, but still labeled fights between black and white men as "mixed bouts." In the midst of the Great Depression survival was tough, but it was even worse for Americans of color who generally took worse jobs for

less pay than white Americans. If ever there was a time when black America needed to celebrate, it was at this time, and now their champion had arrived.

As it was for the rest of the sports in Detroit, 1935 would prove to be a very important year for Joe Louis. He entered the year 12–0 and would end up fighting 14 fights in 12 months. The year would see him rise from an up-and-coming fighter; to a superstar and "uncrowned champion" of boxing. Beginning on January 4th Louis began a cross-country tour, with bouts in Chicago, Pittsburgh, Los Angeles and San Francisco. Returning to Detroit on March 13, 1935; he fought 16 days later before heading off on a Midwest tour, with bouts in: Chicago, Dayton (Ohio), Flint (Michigan), Peoria (Illinois), and Kalamazoo (Michigan). Still undefeated, Louis was becoming highly regarded on the national stage. In fighting anyone who would fight him, at any time and at any place, Louis was making it very tough for the more well-known fighters to dodge him.

His fight on June 25th 1935, however, would be the biggest of his career so far. That this fight against Primo Carnera would happen at all was important because Louis was now entering the realm of title contender. Previous black fighters had been stopped short of this point several times as a result of the segregated nature of America. That he had gotten to this point was due to the wholesome image that he and his managers had created, but it was also due to a fundamental ideal that somehow manages to smash down even the heaviest barriers— Greed. Boxing was suffering during these depression years and Joe Louis' vicious knockouts were becoming a huge draw. He was simply too good a fighter to ignore, with 18 knockouts in 22 contests. Since he had turned pro, Joe Louis had been pounding anyone who stood in front of him, and now it was Primo Carnera's turn.

JOE LOUIS VS. PRIMO CARNERA

Primo Carnera was an Italian born, giant of a man who fought under the nickname "the Ambling Alp." He stood at six foot six inches tall and weighed 265 pounds compared with the 6'1-1/2", 197 pound Louis. Carnera at one point had been the heavyweight champion after beating Jack Sharkey on June 29, 1933; before losing it to Max Baer in June, 1934. The fight took place at Yankee Stadium, and would be the first for Joe Louis in New York, the capital of the boxing world. Among the sixty-four thousand in attendance that night were 15,000 black fans, including Duke Ellington (famous musician), and Jack Johnson. Four other current or former boxing champions were also present: Gene Tunney, Jack Dempsey, Max Baer and James D. Braddock ("the Cinderella Man" who had beaten Max Baer for the championship only two weeks before). Other famous faces in the crowd that night were Mayor Fiorello La Guardia (of New York), J. Edgar Hoover, Babe Ruth and Howard Hughes.

Regardless of race, status, or religion, everyone who was present that night witnessed the power of Joe Louis, as he inflicted a severe beating on Carnera. Blackburn had originally told his fighter to take it slow and work the giant's stomach, which would force him to lower his guard and allow Louis to then target his face. But Louis went right after him and gashed a huge hole in his lip during the first round. As it turned out, the lumbering Carnera was just too slow to defend against Louis, and too stubborn to go down. The result of this was a fearful battering by Louis that lasted through six rounds. When that sixth round came, Carnera tried to grapple with his antagonist, only driving Louis to pound him harder,

Early in the sixth round last night Primo Carnera sealed his boxing doom when he got Joe Louis in a corner, pinioned his arms and tried to rough him against the ropes. Louis made a sudden twist, wrenched himself loose, lashed out with right and left fists, landing both on the wide-open Italian and two minutes later the fight was over, Louis winner by a knockout. Carnera, the Goliath of the ring, was not counted out. The end came with Carnera standing against the ropes, his arms dangling helplessly at his side, his eyes glassy, blood spurting from his mouth. He had been down and up again three times. His face was crimson with the blood that Louis' rapier-like thrusts had brought. As Louis stepped forward to finish him, Referee Arthur Donovan hesitated a moment, then stepped between the two fighters. He waved Louis to his corner and he became officially credited with a knockout. The sixth round had gone two minutes and 32 seconds when Donovan made the last move.

Carnera had brought his usual tactics to play with the start of the gun. He roughed as much as he could and whenever he could and Louis went right on hitting clean, scoring points, fighting with never-changing expression. He never changed his tactics nor his pace until Carnera made his disastrous move in the sixth. As Louis twisted his body out of Carnera's grasp his expression changed. Cold fury now possessed him. He opened up for the first time in the fight. He swung in to the already famous Louis charge; Fast, Furious, Relentless, Whipping in measured punches. Left hooks to the body and suddenly a slashing left and right to the jaw. Carnera fell backwards to the floor, landing on his hips and elbows. Half-sliding, he managed to get up but fell backwards again as soon as he was off the floor.

As Carnera reached his feet, Louis came out of a neutral corner with that panther-like glide of his. He was coming in for the kill. Carnera, bloody and wild-eyed, was flailing wildly with his long, thick arms. He took a left to the body and once more the right swung to the jaw. Again Carnera dropped. Again he got up.

Once more Louis slid out of a neutral corner. He was coming fast now. Around him, in the inky blackness, some 50,000 people stood waiting for the kill. Most of them were shrieking madly. The blood lust was raging.

"Kill him, Joe," came the cry from the blackness about the brilliantly lighted ring. "Knock him out, beat his head off." Joe may have heard; he says he didn't. He moved in fast.

Two light blows, then a blasting left hook to the jaw. Carnera went down for the third and last time. Once more he struggled to his feet.

He was within a foot of the ropes, about a dozen feet from Louis' corner. His arms were dangling helplessly by his side. His legs were quivering, blood gushed from his gasping mouth.

The brown panther was coming at him once more. Carnera did not see him. He was unconscious of everything about him. When Louis was within five feet of the helpless Carnera, Donovan stepped between them and Carnera staggered to his corner.

—H.G. Salinger, Sports Editor,
The Detroit News, 6/26/35

During that sixth round, people in the crowd were heard shouting *"stop it,"* and *"stop the fight."* Despite the battering he had inflicted on Carnera, Joe Louis walked away without a scratch and with a huge $60,000 check. Following this fight were scenes of celebration, especially in black neighborhoods,

When Joe Louis in six short and stinging stanzas made a mole hill out of the man mountain from Italia Detroit's Ethiopia went into a delirium from which it is still in the process of recovery. From Larned street on the south to Holbrook avenue on the north and from John R street on the West to MacDougall avenue on the east, a solid sector of urban population took on an impromptu insanity. Not a mild insanity mind you. It was gargantuan in proportions but glory be it was so packed with good nature that not even the fallen Carnera could have taken offense.

Just as soon as our Mister Louis went to town, so did thousands of his fellow citizens of the dark persuasion and they made it a celebration worth while. Detective Lieut. Wallace Williams, viewing St. Antoine street with a calm dispassionate eye just 15 minutes after Louis had been declared the victor in the Yankee Stadium ring said that St. Antoine street had ever seen anything quite the like of this. And Detective Williams has the background. A Negro himself, he was born less than a block from the scene of the shambles. He has been in on most of the important affairs that have stirred this section of the town over a period of years. But this said Williams," is [different], they're making plenty noise but you can't arrest anybody because they're not doing anything but just that. My, but they're happy and so am I." He went on to tell about the last time his people over on the East Side got so excited. It was that time Jack Johnson beat up on Jim Jeffries back in 1910. This is bigger than that, he said. "Only our people are better humored. They're happier over Louis. They like him better. There was a lot of trouble, bad trouble when Johnson won. Why, I had a battle in a saloon at St. Antoine and Wilkins that lasted an hour and a half." The detective was standing in front of Pathfinder Lightfoots B and C Club (bellman and cooks) at the moment, looking de-

Scenes from the Carnera Fight

—All photos courtesy of *The Detroit News*

The weigh in.

Louis goes after him early.

Carnera goes down for the first time.

Joe swings in the fifth round.

Carnera staggering to his feet for the third and final time.

Carnera's last gasp attempt. Trying to grapple Louis only drove Joe into a fury.

Two different pictures of the same result. A Joe Louis victory in convincing fashion.

—Photos courtesy of *The Detroit News*

The final punch that ended Carnera's night.

—Photos courtesy of *The Detroit News*

(Above) "Louis targets Carnera's stomach, making him gasp." This picture shows the size of "the Man-Mountain of Italia." The former heavy-weight champion Carnera presented an intimidating presence to all who saw him.
—Associated Press Photo

Fans at the Joe Louis Booster Club in Detroit show their joy, moments after the end of the fight.
—Photo courtesy of *The Detroit News.*

Referee Arthur Donovan presenting the victor to the crowd.
—Photo courtesy of *The Detroit News.*

A quick first round Technical Knockout of King Levinsky kept Joe Louis' momentum rolling into September.
—Photo courtesy of *The Detroit News.*

lightedly at the confusion all about him. Inside the club, men and women screamed and shouted and roared for beer and something stronger. Outside the street was bedlam. The great crowd blocked traffic, stormed the headquarters of the Joe Louis Boosters Club across the street. Around the corner, in Big Buffalo's Chicken Shack, there was highjinks. The orchestra went hot right quick. Drummer Price Smith rolled his big bass drum out among the tables, peeled off his coat and vest and really went to work. At the Frog Club, which is Joe Louis' own club there was an aristocratic gathering, plenty of food and plenty of drink, with dancing thrown in. Proudest people there were the kitchen force. They cook for Joe when he's around the club. "He's a steak and chicken man" said Chef Jeff L. Herber. "Specially he's a steak man. Likes em' two inches thick. I should be sizzling his steak for him tonight." All the hot spots blazed far into the morning. That meant the Chocolate Bar, the Plantation, the Harlem, the Waiters and Bellmen. All of them went riding high to town on Joe Louis' smashing rights and lefts. But the streets were mad. Motors honked, people cheered. It was a night to remember. Hastings street on the loose is a sight as well as a sound and this was the tribute of a sound and this was the tribute of a thoroughfare, where flourish the two-bit crap games, to one of its sons on his way to a million-dollar gate.

—George Stark, *The Detroit News*, 6/26/1935

A little over a month after he fought Carnera, Joe Louis arrived in Chicago for a bout against "King" Levinsky. Though this fight would have no where near the hype of his last fight, it was still important. King Levinsky was a consistent, professional boxer, who had fought against every top fighter of his era. In front of 40,000 fans including the governors from six different states (Missouri, Kentucky, Indiana, Illinois, Wisconsin, Michigan), Louis put on a boxing demonstration which lasted all of 141 seconds. During these 141 seconds, Levinsky was knocked down 4 times; the last of which sent him slumping into the corner of the ring where he supposedly told the referee, "*Don't let him hit me again mister!*" The referee didn't and the fight was ended barely two minutes into the first round.

Joe Louis vs. Max Baer

In September of 1935, Joe Louis arrived in New York for what would be his most important fight of the year, and would come to be viewed as one of the greatest fights of his career. His opponent on September 24, 1935, would be the iron chinned Max Baer, a boxer who had enjoyed a very productive career, and had been heavyweight champion from June, 1934, until his loss by decision to James Braddock just a few months before (June, 1935). The fight against Braddock had been one of his worse moments, and now he longed for a shot to take back what he considered "his" title. It is important to understand how good of a fighter that Joe Louis was about to face in Max Baer. Nicknamed the "Livermore Larrupper," he came into the fight with 40 wins, 27 coming by way of knockout. Baer's main weapon was his sensational overhand right, a unique punch that swept down on his opponent like a club. A 1998 article by *Ring Magazine* ranked Baer #20 out of 50 greatest heavyweights and a 2003 article ranked him #22 out of 100 of the hardest punchers of all time. He had, in fact, killed a fighter in the ring, and that event haunted him for his entire career. Baer was a crafty fighter, employing a backhand punch that had no rival in his day or ours.

Baer admitted, after his fight with Braddock, that he had not been as serious in his training as he should have been, but vowed in an interview with Grantland Rice that in this fight with Louis, he would be at his physical best; *"Whatever happens in this fight just put down that I'm in the best condition I ever knew in my life. If Louis can whip me now, he can whip me any time I started."* The reason for Baer's optimistic appraisal of his conditioning was that he had been training out in the woods of Speculator New York, for six weeks. This forest solitude kept him from any of the distractions of wine, women, and song that had hindered his training in the previous fight. Bud Shaver, sports editor of the *Detroit Times* was present at the training ground and described what he saw,

Baer doesn't believe Louis can survive his Sunday punch, that looping overhand right, if he lands it. The records sustain him. Every man Baer has hit with the full power of that right hand has gone down and most of them have gone out. His boxing workouts each day were meaningless as far as

This cartoon by Lew Tower appeared in the Detroit Times and shows the situation of Max Baer heading into his fight with Joe Louis. Braddock had taken "his" title in June of 1935, and his only chance to get it back was to beat Louis.

—*Detroit Times* photo/Courtesy of *The Detroit News*

Joe kisses his new wife Marva (Trotter) Louis, shortly after they were married; mere hours before his fight with Max Baer.

—Photo courtesy of *The Detroit News*

While Max Baer was training in the woods of Speculator, New York, Louis was training in Pompton Lakes. This photo was taken during his training and shows that Joe was also in peak physical condition for his impending bout.

—Associated Press Photo

One of the greatest fighters in boxing history, Max Baer was also one of its most endearing. Loaded with personality, he was an entertainer inside the ring as well as a dangerous, tough fighter. Elements of his engaging personality can be seen in many newsreels from the time and was carried on through his son, Max Baer Jr. who played Jethro Bodine in the original Beverly Hillbillies.

—*Detroit Times* photo/ Courtesy of *The Detroit News*

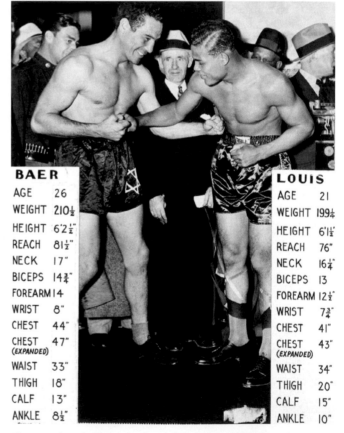

BAER		LOUIS	
AGE	26	AGE	21
WEIGHT	210½	WEIGHT	199¾
HEIGHT	6'2½"	HEIGHT	6'1½"
REACH	81½"	REACH	76"
NECK	17"	NECK	16¼"
BICEPS	14¾"	BICEPS	13
FOREARM	14	FOREARM	12½
WRIST	8"	WRIST	7¾"
CHEST	44"	CHEST	41"
CHEST (EXPANDED)	47"	CHEST (EXPANDED)	43"
WAIST	33"	WAIST	34"
THIGH	18"	THIGH	20"
CALF	13"	CALF	15"
ANKLE	8½	ANKLE	10"

The weigh-in before the fight shows the differences between the two fighters, but it also sheds a little more light on the often misrepresented personality of Max Baer. His antics in this picture have everyone around him smiling including Louis.

—Associated Press Photo

improving his boxing [was] concerned. Not one word of advice or instruction was given Baer in his bouts with sparring partners. He was pummeled unmercifully, made no effort to defend himself. The whole idea seemed to be to toughen Baer until he could stand any punch. He thinks he can because he has taken all the punches of his sparring partners. He is in the best physical shape of his career.

—Bud Shaver, *Detroit Times,* 9/24/35

As the day of the fight drew near, everyone had differences of opinion as to who would win. The big question on most people's minds about Joe Louis was whether or not he could "take a punch." The reason for this question was that in all his fights, he had dominated to such an extreme that no one had really even landed a punch on him. James Braddock, the heavyweight champion of the moment had watched many of Louis's fights and he picked Max Baer to win on account of this idea,

I've never seen Joe Louis receive a good punch. Nobody has ever seen him receive a good punch. Maybe he has been hit hard when nobody was looking. But the fact remains since nobody has seen him take a hard punch; maybe he won't be able to take it when Baer gives it to him. When Louis finds Baer can take his hardest punches, he will become discouraged because Baer doesn't fall down. Then Baer will go to work on him and knock him out. I have no doubt Baer will win.

—James J. Braddock, Universal Service in *Detroit Evening Times,* 9/24/35

Two hours before the fight on September 24, 1935, Joe Louis' trainers announced that he had just been married to his longtime girlfriend Marva Trotter. The marriage between the two had been the subject of much speculation as to when it would occur, and as the fight drew near Marva had said that she wanted to attend the fight as "Mrs. Joe Louis." His trainer, Blackburn wanted to give his fighter motivation for winning the fight quickly, and so the two were married in the New York hotel that Marva was staying in,

Joe Louis was married to a Chicago stenographer tonight, two hours and five minutes before he

climbed into the ring to conquer Max Baer. While a noisy crowd waited outside, the Detroit Negro calmly went through a ceremony that made him the husband of Marva Trotter, of Chicago. Then without a change in expression, he said: "I've got a date with a fellow named Max Baer," and off he rode to the scene of the conflict behind a screaming motorcycle escort.

—A.P. Wire Service in *Detroit Free Press,* 9/25/35

Marva Louis.
—*Detroit Times* photo/ Courtesy of *The Detroit News*

The fight at Yankee Stadium would host a record setting crowd of 83,462 paying fans, though the number of people actually inside the stadium was closer to 95,000 when the numbers of police, firemen, media and gate crashers are included. 35,000 African-American fans were in attendance along with many celebrities

Notable Detroiters watching Baer-Louis fight. (Left to Right) Fred Alger Jr., Frank Roth, Mrs. Alger, and Alfred G. Vanderbilt.

Jack Adams coach of the Red Wings.

Dick Richards Detroit Lions President, and Leo Fitzpatrick.

A look at the setting for the Baer-Louis fight at Yankee Stadium. Oftentimes, baseball parks were used for boxing matches as they could hold far more people than any other venues.

—Associated Press Photo

This cartoon appeared in the Detroit Times on the day before the fight and shows the main weapons of each fighter. Baer and his overhand right or "Sunday Punch." Louis and his straight left.

—*Detroit Times* cartoon/Courtesy of *The Detroit News*

black and white, including: Duke Ellington, Cab Calloway, Jack Johnson, George Burns, Gracie Allen, Edward G. Robinson, Cary Grant, Irving Berlin, James Cagney, and of course the new Mrs. Louis. This fight was the first "million dollar gate" since the 1920's. The million dollar gate had long been the benchmark for how big a fight was, and it meant that the venue had drawn a million dollars or more

in revenue. That this non-title bout could draw so much money in the middle of the depression really shows how big this fight was. People were drawn from all over the country, especially Detroit, where organizations such as the Joe Louis Booster Club were sending bus loads of people to New York. For those who remained in Detroit, a large neon sign anchored on top of the Garfield building flashed the details of the fight at the end of each round. The large crowds of black and white fans who gathered on Woodward Avenue were therefore able to follow the bout.

Going into the fight, the bookies listed the odds at a fairly close 8–5 in favor of Joe Louis. But those who bet on Baer lost their money, as the fight turned out to be completely one sided. Baer had lost contests in the past but he had never been knocked down; that fact changed in this fight as he was doomed from the start.

BAER DOOMED FROM THE START.

NEW YORK, Sept. 25—Max Baer quit last night in the fourth round. A full second after Joe Louis delivered a left hook to Baer's jaw, the recent world's heavyweight champion dropped to the floor, resting his weight on his right knee, his head, bloody and bowed, wagging slowly in resignation and his gloved hands waving a gesture of futility. Baer remained in this position until the referee completed his count of 10 and then he got up.

For three rounds and 2 minutes and 40 seconds of the third round Louis outboxed, outslugged and outfought the former pig-sticker of

Livermore, California. Before the fight was a minute old, Baer's face was cut and bleeding. By the end of the first round he was well covered with gore. He was down twice in the third round, the bell saving him on the second knockdown. When he went out in the fourth he knew the hopelessness of his position and resigned.

At no time during the fight did Baer have a chance. At no time did he make good on any of his promises. He was consistent only in being inconsistent. He did not rush from his corner as he said he would, nor did he crowd Louis, nor did he try to land the long right at the opening of the first round on Louis upper left arm, paralyzing the nerves, as he intended doing before he went into the ring.

He came out carefully and sparred and Louis landed several lefts and rights before Baer ever landed a weak punch. Near the end of the round, when Louis had him backed into a neutral corner, he opened up. For 10 seconds he threw every punch he had at Louis and Louis traded him punch for punch with the difference that Louis' blows hurt and Baer's had no effect on Louis.

It was this exchange in the first round, from which Baer emerged with fresh gashes in his face and a bewildered look, that decided the fight. Baer had given Louis everything he had and Louis had not alone taken it but outslugged him. Baer was a beaten fighter from that moment on. As Louis backed off, Baer waved his glove in a helpless gesture, a pantomimist's "what's the use anyway" expression.

The start of the second round saw Louis with freshly fired confidence, come gliding across the ring. He moved in like a great cat, the left out. Tap-tap-tap. One, two, three, four, five punches flush on Baer's nose without a return. Where was Baer's crushing right? Where was what he has been calling his "Sunday punch?" He was going to turn this loose on Louis right at the start. And here was Louis backing him all over the ring popping lefts, lefts, lefts, lefts, into Baer's face. Punching him in the nose, eyes, and mouth.

Gashing his cheeks, rocking Baer's head with the stinging straight left, a punch that Baer in all his career never learned.

Five lefts to the face and Baer had not returned one. Then came a left hook to the jaw, Baer countered with two light punches. Louis ripped home two rights and then a left. Then a return to the straight left one, two, three, four, five of them.

Baer never saw so many gloves before. He never knew that so many could come from one direction. He could not avoid the punch, could not evade it. He had the longer reach but he wore a bewildered look that explained why he did not take advantage of the reach. He was too dazed. He had had not expected this.

Near the end of the second round, Baer grabbed hold of Louis and tried to wrestle him. Louis whirled the helpless Baer around and tossed him against the ropes. Baer, like Carnera, discovered that Louis is a strong man who can fight any kind of a fight.

As Baer returned to his corner at the end of the second round Jack Dempsey, who had been induced to second him in the hope that he could induce him, in turn, to fight, grabbed Baer and yelled into his ear during the full minute intermission.

As they came together at the start of the third, Baer, following instructions, cut loose with a hard right uppercut. Louis rode the punch and as Baer backed away, Louis half-sneered, half-snarled at him.

Louis, too, had been given instructions, and for the first time he was fighting cautiously. Baer kept cocking his right as Louis stalked him about the ring. He missed two hard rights and Louis landed two lefts and three rights on Baer's jaw.

Baer dropped. He took a count of nine. He got up and backed away. His right was low, his left lower. Louis landed two rights and two lefts on Baer's unprotected jaw. The defenseless Baer went down again. Once more the referee began counting. As he tolled the fifth second, the bell interrupted him. Dempsey rushed across the ring, helped Baer to his feet and led him to his corner.

Baer was wobbly when he came out for the fourth round. Louis moved in faster this time. He landed two rights and two lefts on Baer's jaw, then switched his attack. As Baer's guard came up

Scenes from the Baer-Louis Fight
—All photos courtesy of *The Detroit News*

Another view of the final moments of Max Baer's night.

Louis' straight left catches Baer solidly.

Louis looks on quietly as Baer is counted out, the crowd cheering wildly. Baer was quoted after this fight, "fear is standing across the ring from Joe Louis, and knowing he wants to go home early."

"Magic Eye" shows final combination that finishes Baer.

Louis introduced to the crowd as victor.

Louis smashed home two blows to the stomach. Baer's guard dropped and Louis landed two lefts and a right in Baer's face.

Baer came back with two, one a right in which he put all he had. Both blows glanced off Louis, who stepped inside of them.

Louis switched back to the face. He rocked Baer's head twice. Blood was gushing from Baer's nose. His eyes seemed glassy. Louis landed a left, then a right cross. He smashed a left hook to Baer's jaw. Baer backed away. When he was over near the ropes he went down on one knee. He stayed there until the referee finished counting.

As Dempsey was leading Baer back to his corner, a veteran of the ring wars climbed on top of his ringside chair and bellowed: "Folks, you've looked at the greatest fighter in the history of boxing—Joe Louis.

He could have licked Dempsey the best day he ever saw. He could have licked any man that ever lived."

—H.G. Salinger, Sports Editor of
The Detroit News, 9/25/35

This win by Louis answered any doubts as to who was the man to beat in the boxing world and it ended any discussions about his chances in future fights. Baer was one of the top fighters of this time, and Louis had not only beat him, but he had annihilated him,

We did not anticipate Baer getting such a terrific beating from Louis. The brown lad displayed improvement over his fight with Carnera. If improvement is possible in such an almost perfect bit of ring mechanism as Louis. He was deliberate to an astounding degree. Every move he made was another move toward the complete destruction of Baer.

—Damon Runyon, Universal Services
in Detroit Times, 9/26/35

The final bell that was rung to signal the end of the fight started off a wave of celebrations that radiated from the scene of the fight, through Harlem and New York, Detroit, and along the air waves across the country. In Harlem 200,000 people celebrated in the streets. A quote by the Amsterdam News in New York put it, "why attempt to describe it? You probably were in it!" Back in Detroit, the celebrations bordered on delirium,

The coolest person in Detroit's Negro population Tuesday night was Mamma Lily Barrow, Joe Louis' mother. Surrounded by her immediate family, friends and neighbors in her home at 2100 McDougall Ave. she pressed her right ear to the speaker of her radio, untouched by the ill-concealed excitement about her. Joe evidently inherits his coolness from her. With her right arm draped about the radio cabinet she stared fixedly at the floor in deep study during the whole fight. When it was announced that the referee was holding up Joe's right arm she uttered a deep-seated sigh and muttered "Bless the Lord." At that moment half a hundred jubilant neighbors burst through the front door shouting and threw their arms about Mamma Lily. Others jumped up and down, some shouted with joy and danced about her. Mamma Lily said nothing. She just sat there and beamed.

Meanwhile utter pandemonium burst loose on Detroit's East Side. In a moment the city's main artery shifted over to Hastings St. where for hours after the result became known crowded, hooting, bunting-draped cars wormed their noisy way through the throngs of dancing, shouting, Negroes. Special details of police endeavored amiably and sometimes successfully to keep some sort of traffic movement. There were no hard feelings on Hastings St. It was their night to howl and who would stop them. Groups of tense ecstatic Negroes surrounding radios on sidewalks synchronously shouted their joy with the announcement of the knockout. Hundreds more swarmed from houses, crowded into the streets, beating dishpans, kettles, and jugs. They screamed and danced and sang.

Celebratory parades, starting spontaneously from side streets, converged into Hasting St. causing the most snarled traffic jam that thoroughfare has experienced since Joe's successive victories have made it the Main St. of the City's Negro population. Men and women climbed on tops of automobiles; youths climbed telephone poles and hung their shirts on cross-arms for victory pennants. There were street-corner clog dances with women beat-

A photographer was on hand to capture this image of Lily Barrow with family and friends, moments after hearing the results of the fight over the radio.

—*Detroit Times* photo/Courtesy of *The Detroit News*

Fans turn out to greet their hero as he returns to Detroit.

—*Detroit Times* photo/Courtesy of *The Detroit News*

One of the results of Joe Louis' new found fame, were that people craved information about aspects of his every-day life. Here, Joe sits down to eat with his mother, Lily Barrow (middle) and his wife Marva (right).

—*Detroit Times* photo/Courtesy of *The Detroit News*

ing rhythmic accompaniment on dishpans; frightened children scurrying between houses or standing on curbs, wide-eyed at the bedlam.

The Joe Louis Booster Club at St. Antoine and Benton Sts. was the center of a tumultuous gathering that increased in size and volume from the moment the victory was heralded. In the 30 minutes between the opening of the ringside broadcast and the final count of the referee over Baer, Hastings St. was almost silent. Only the radio noise and the occasional rumble of passing street cars were heard. But with the final count of 10, the jubilation began. Grandmothers, husky young imitators of the Brown Bomber, school children, girls—all joined in a prolonged bedlam of shouting, screaming, cheering and noise-making.

Traffic on Joseph Campau Ave. between Evaline and Caniff Aves in Hamtramck, was blocked for more than 20 minutes when a man, paying a pre-fight bet towed a Negro youth up and down the street in a small cart. Hamtramck's Negro population on Conant Ave. celebrated at Delmont and Trowbridge Ave., on Dequindre between Caniff and Commor Aves. And at Yemans and Evaline Aves.

Joe's nuptials were remembered by a Negro woman at Winder and Hastings Sts. She stood on the corner and pelted paraders with rice which she carried in a large paper bag. "Happy REturns!" she kept repeating.

The celebration wasn't limited to Detroit's Harlem. Cab companies reported that only seven calls were received throughout the city during the progress of the fight. Detroiters listened at their homes, clubs, hotels and then rushed out to buy newspaper extras to read details of the fight. At the Wayne County Jail a group of Negro celebrants who shouted over Louis' victory for several minutes without a let-up, were not restrained by guards.

—*Detroit Free Press* editorial, 4/25/35

Despite everyone else celebrating, Louis was anxious to start his honeymoon with Marva and also to make it back to Detroit for the start of the Tigers/Cubs World Series. He arrived back in Detroit on September 29th, just in time; as it turned out Joe Louis was a Tiger fan!

Joe Louis and his bride were back home today after the most spectacular welcome Detroit's east side has ever seen. For the next few days Mr. and Mrs. Joe will "just rest." In crowded moments of "just-restin'," Joe intends to see at least the first two games of the World Series.

—*Detroit Times* editorial, 9/30/35

The "crowded moments" alluded to by this article references the fact that wherever Joe Louis went at this time the crowds were gathered, similar to the hordes of paparazzi and celeb-chasers of today. The difference between these crowds and the modern paparazzi were the people following Joe Louis were good-natured admirers who simply wanted to catch a glimpse of their hero and perhaps serenade him with a few kind words. An example of one of these moments comes from the Detroit Times as Joe Louis, Marva, and his mother were simply going to church,

Twenty-five hundred Negroes jammed the little church at Clinton Street and Joseph Campau Avenue [Cavalry Church] and its every hall and room until another person could not be squeezed inside. Five thousand more patiently stood outside several hours to get a glimpse of their hero. Thunderous cheers shook the church walls, as Joe Louis and his bride entered, four policemen in a flying wedge clearing a path through the crowd. Joe wore a gray suit of large plaid checks. His shirt was dark brown; so was his tie. He was deadly serious, as usual. Marva, smiling vivaciously, wore a smart black dress, adorned with a corsage of three gardenias. Around her neck was a large silver fox piece and on her hand glittered the four carat diamond engagement ring and diamond studded wedding ring Joe gave her when they were married the night of the Baer fight. With them was Joe's mother, wearing a bright brown dress. Joe's entrance broke up his own party. Photographers' lights started flashing and the crowd got down off the pews they'd been standing on to cheer, and surged forward. Roxborough pleaded in vain for order.

—*Detroit Times* editorial, 9/30/1935

In the process of rising to the top of the boxing world, Joe Louis had become an icon for the black community and a great symbol of hope. That if he could break down barriers, so could others, until the time that no more barriers would remain.

I doubt if any of the heavyweights of the last 25 years could stand up against Joe—and he's just starting. Perhaps his greatest achievement was to do more in six months to break down racial prejudice than any one has ever done.

—City Councilman John W. Smith,
Detroit Times, 9/30/35

As a result of his success inside the ring, Joe Louis was able to become one of the most enduring personalities outside the ring. What stood out was his laid back demeanor and generosity in an era of great human need. At one point in his career he was receiving several thousand letters a week asking for help, prompting him to hire a secretary just to open and respond to his mail. His responses often were accompanied by money and he went out of his way to make personal appearances in order to bring hope to the people who idolized him. There were many examples of his generosity to his friends and family, but he had no peer in his generosity towards the community. He sponsored a softball team called the "Brown Bombers," fought charity fights for different causes including one in World War II that resulted in $100,000 being given to the Army/Navy relief fund. He would identify needs of different communities and buy specifically needed items such as ambulances. He was also constantly giving money to people in different neighborhoods,

Joe isn't very good at making speeches but he had to say something when he presented his gifts—"You want to fill these up and keep 'em filled," Joe said. "That's what I'm trying to do."—To each he handed a small savings bank, with the help of his bride, slipped a little starter, three quarters, into each. Joe understood why those 150 youngsters ran so fast, clutching the banks close, to show the folks at home. It was a big moment down on Chestnut Street.

—Fred Cousins, *The Detroit News*, 12/21/1935

Joe Louis Acclaimed 'Outstanding Athlete of 1935'

By a margin of votes as convincing as any conquest with his fists, Joe Louis stands acclaimed today by the nation's sports experts as the outstanding athlete of 1935, amateur or professional. The 21 year old Negro heavyweight who brought the "million dollar gate" back to pugilism with his knockout punch, tops the individual masculine performers in the fifth annual Associated Press poll. That Louis is not a champion and will not even get a crack at the heavyweight title of James J. Braddock until next September makes his rating as the "athlete of the year" all the more remarkable.

—Associated Press announcement in
The Detroit News, 12/16/35

With Baer out of the picture, the close of the year saw Joe Louis looking at only two more fighters in his way to the heavyweight championship; Max Schmelling and James Braddock. For Louis it had truly been an incredible year. With fourteen fights won (12 by knockout), he had become a massive figure in American sports. He had also become rich as a result. His first bout against Jack Kracken, had netted him $50, only a year and a half later he had taken home $217,337 from the Baer fight. In that span he had won over $350,000 an insane amount of money for the depression years. In the process he had also been named by the Associated Press Outstanding Athlete of 1935. This award was important because it could be won by an athlete from any sport, and the people who voted for it were members of the national media. Which clearly shows the impact he was having nation wide. James Braddock, whose heavyweight championship victory in 1935 was the subject of the recent film "Cinderella Man," only garnered 3 votes to Louis's 182; showing who really captured the hearts and minds of depression era boxing fans in 1935. For all intents and purposes, Braddock was merely a custodian of the belt until Louis had the chance to take it from him. In numerous newspaper articles Joe Louis is referred to as the

"uncrowned champion of boxing." This is why Joe Louis must be considered as a vital part of the City of Champions.

NO ATHLETE enjoys a more popular rank than Joe Louis in Detroit's parade of Champions. He fights Max Schmeling, black brown [Nazi reference] German in June. Then will come the title match with Jimmie Braddock in September. Detroiters believe, as do fans in every other portion of the world, that September will find Joe Louis Barrow looking down from the throne. But so far as 99 per cent of the nation's fans are concerned Joe Louis is the "champion of the world." For the very pertinent reason that he is the greatest fighter in the world today, and quite possibly the greatest of all time.

—Bob Murphy, *Detroit Times*, 4/15/36

After reading about all of Joe Louis' amazing knockouts I began looking at old videos in order to see for myself how good of a fighter he really was. One great resource for viewing these fights was on the site *www.Youtube.com*. I had always considered myself a Mike Tyson fan, but that has definitely changed. The first thing I noticed about Joe Louis was his compact stance and the amazing balance that accompanied his punches. He rarely over swung and never left himself open to counter punches. His precision and punching rhythm overmatched wild punchers. Quick and powerful, his footwork looked distinctly modern compared to the bar room brawler style footwork of the period. His knockout blows were obvious as there was never a question about which shots dropped people like sacks-of-potatoes. His professionalism reminded me of a more modern sports figure, Barry Sanders, for two reasons. The first was that he never took any cheap shots or showed any absurd flamboyance. When the referee got between he and his prey, he quietly turned around and walked back to his corner, much like Barry handing the ball to the ref and trotting back to the sideline. In comparison, many other fighters of this period were constantly trying to reach around the referee and get in a couple of "cheap shots" before clowning around and playing up to the crowd. The other reminder between Joe Louis and Barry Sanders was the quiet confidence. The way that both dominated their sport, making the remarkable seem like "it was just another day at the office," almost like they belonged in a higher league than anyone else. In Louis's case he was akin to a machine, with oppo-

Following his bout with Baer, a Championship fight seemed like a mere formality, as this cartoon demonstrates.
—*Detroit Times* cartoon/Courtesy of *The Detroit News*

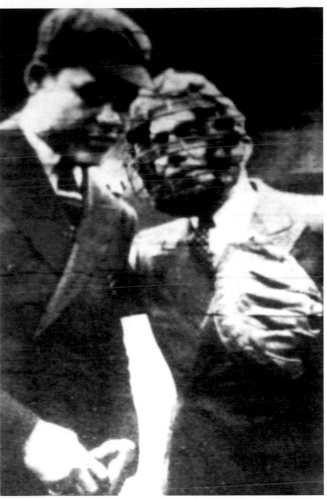

Joe Louis, about to throw out the first pitch on opening day of the 1936 Tiger baseball season.
—*Detroit Times* photo/Courtesy of *The Detroit News*

Joe Louis was "feted," or given a celebratory dinner in his honor. Here he poses with his cake.
—*Detroit Times* photo/Courtesy of *The Detroit News*

A champion in their midst. Joe and Marva stroll down the street as happy onlookers cheer.
—*Detroit Times* photo/Courtesy of *The Detroit News*

nent after opponent sprawled out on the canvas as he simply turned and walked back to his corner. Joe Louis was in fact a dominant, devastatingly powerful fighter and is definitely my new favorite boxer.

To say Joe Louis was important to African Americans in the 1930's would be a tremendous understatement. His rise from obscurity in 1935, allowed black communities to openly celebrate during this City of Champions sports season. His victories would provide a vital link between the three championships and keep the celebrations in the city rolling for literally an entire year. The power of Joe Louis inside the ring would result in him being considered as a "Great Unifier" of the black and white races. In 1938 Joe Louis beat the Nazi, Max Schmelling. This win galvanized an entire country, which was teetering on the brink of World War II. The ex-citement at that time was not because "a black guy" had beaten a Nazi; it was "our guy beat the Nazi." This win was an example of the power Joe Louis possessed in healing social ills because only someone who is ignorant can claim a person is "ours" and still hate him because of the color of his skin.

Throughout the 1935 sports season Joe Louis appeared at many sporting events and in many photographs with white athletes, providing instant visual images of harmony between races. When he threw out the first pitch of the 1936 baseball season, it was another example of him breaking down barriers. The most relevant quote about Joe Louis comes from the New York sportswriter, Jimmy Cannon who said: *"Joe Louis was a credit to his race—the human race."*

This sculpture in Downtown Detroit was commissioned by a $350,000 grant from Sports Illustrated in 1986. It is a 24 foot long arm, suspended by a 24 foot tall pyramid framework. Created by Robert Graham, it represents Joe Louis' power both inside and outside the ring.

—Photo by Kelly Karnesky

Joe Louis was ranked #1 of 100 greatest punchers of all-time in a 2003 edition of Ring Magazine.

—Photo courtesy of *The Detroit News*

In 1982, Joe Louis was given the Congressional Gold Medal (the highest award of the legislative branch). Recognizing him because he; "did so much to bolster the spirit of the American people during one of the most crucial times in American history, and has endured throughout the years as a symbol of strength for the nation."

—Photo courtesy of the *Detroit Free Press*

THE DETROIT TIGERS

The 19th century saw the rise of baseball in America as teams sprang up across the nation. Detroit became a part of this phenomenon in 1881 when its first professional team called simply "the Detroits" played at Recreation Park near the corner of Brady and Brush streets. This early team fielded some of the great players of the era in catcher Charlie Bennett, first baseman Dan Brouthers, and center fielder Ned Hanlon. This early team folded in 1888, but not before winning a "world championship" in 1887 by beating the St. Louis Browns in a fifteen game series. The team resurfaced briefly in 1894, and then again in 1896. The establishment of the modern team that we now know as the Tigers came about when Ban Johnson, who was building a new "American League" of baseball teams accepted the application for a franchise from the city of Detroit. The first owner of this new team was James D. Burns, a wealthy hotel owner and the Sheriff of Wayne County. This resurrected Detroit baseball team began play at its new field, which had been relocated to the middle of the city, and named after the star catcher (and fan favorite) of the early teams, Charlie Bennett.

Picture courtesy of the Detroit Free Press

Bennett Park would be located at the corner of Michigan and Trumbull Ave. and would host its first game in front of 6,000 people on April 25th, 1901. The fans who attended this first game had the privilege of witnessing the spectacular, though at first, the game started out rough for the home team as Milwaukee got off to a 7–0 lead which they extended to 13–4 by the ninth inning. Then the spectacular—Detroit rallied for 10 runs to get the win, capped off with a Frank Dillon double (his fourth of the game).

This auspicious beginning foreshadowed the success of the team in the first decade of the 20th century, but this early team would go through some growing pains as it searched for stability in ownership. After only one year, the team was bought by financier Edward Doyle and then sold to insurance man Samuel F. Angus. In 1904 the team again traded hands when lumber baron William Hoover Yawkey, bought the team for $50,000. One person who was a mainstay throughout this period of ownership instability was Frank Navin, who had been the bookkeeper for Sam Angus. Navin stayed on with the Tigers when Yawkey bought the team and took over the financial operations,

Opening day at Bennett Park. The Tigers were quick to put down roots in the city of Detroit. Here, just visible through the snow, the stands are packed with fans despite the inclement weather.

—Photo courtesy of *The Detroit News*
Obtained through the use of the Alan Feldman Collection

Tiger fans overflow onto the field during a World Series game in 1907 against the Chicago Cubs.

acting as general manager. Navin not only provided a sense of stability in the early few years but eventually became the guiding hand which built the franchise. By 1909 he had earned enough money to buy a majority stake in the team and become its owner. From 1902 until his death in 1935, it was Navin who made the personnel and financial decisions that allowed the team to grow and develop into a stable, rock-solid franchise. Ultimately, Navin's greatest quality was as an astute businessman, and under his guiding influence baseball became an institution in Detroit.

The first few years of the Detroit Tigers existence saw the acquisition of several of the game's early stars including Hall of Fame outfielder "Wahoo" Sam Crawford, third baseman Herman "Germany" Schaefer, shortstop Donnie Bush, catcher "Boss" Schmidt and pitchers "Wild" Bill Donovan, and George Mullin. In 1905 however, Cobb came to town. Tyrus Raymond Cobb had been purchased from the Augusta club of the Sally League (a minor league club affiliated with the Tigers). He was a young, brash, Georgian outfielder, and he was raw talent personified. Cobb would quickly become the game's greatest player and in the process have a profound influence on Detroit Tiger baseball. While his gaudy statistics and charismatic personality enthralled the fans, it was his indomitable will to win which drove the club to a period of American league dominance, unmatched in the team's history even to this day. Cobb was given a free hand by legendary Tiger manager Hughie Jennings to develop his game, as he was such a new breed of talent that he was actually teaching

"Nobody ever approached the game with greater zeal to succeed than Cobb did. He could raise a burning inferno and, at times, the man himself was consumed by its flames."
—Joe Falls

everyone else. The highlight of the Cobb era baseball came in the three American League championships the team won from 1907 to 1909. Though they lost all three World Series' they played in, the Tigers had firmly established their franchise in the city of Detroit.

The increased interest in the Tigers led Bennett Park to be expanded in 1912 from its original capacity of 8,500 seats to 23,000. Then in 1924 the stadium was renamed Navin Field (after Frank Navin) and the capacity increased

"Mickey Cochrane was the second hardest loser I ever saw [Cobb was the first], and the smartest manager. When he managed from the bench, he never made a mistake. Never! And he was tough when he was behind the plate. He'd throw the ball back to Schoolboy Rowe harder than Rowe threw it to him. Schoolie would get a little lazy out there but Cochrane would wake him up every time."

—Charlie Gehringer on Mickey Cochrane
Photo courtesy of the *Detroit Free Press*

idea was to acquire George Herman "Babe" Ruth from the Yankees to be his manager in 1934. At 39 years old the "sultan of swat" was in the twilight of his career but was still the biggest personality in the game. At the very least, fans might come to the games just to watch him take batting practice. Jake Ruppert gave the idea his blessing as Ruth's diminishing skills and increasing demands were becoming a massive burden to the Yankee owner. On contacting Ruth, Navin was more than a bit miffed when the Babe went to Hawaii for a vacation instead of having a meeting to discuss his future with the Tigers. Navin the sharp businessman finally dismissed the idea when the Babe's contract demands were sent to him. His contract would have had to include *"a large salary"* and a percentage of the gate receipts. Navin decided that while the short term prospects of acquiring the Babe would help the Tigers situation, the long term headache would probably not be worth it, and decided to look elsewhere for a solution.

Navin then cast his eye in a different direction. On December 12th, 1933 acting on the advice of Detroit News editor H. G. Salinger; he acquired Gordon Stanley "Mickey" Cochrane from the Philadelphia Athletics in exchange for catcher John Pasek and $100,000 cash. Cochrane had led Philadelphia to three American League Pennants and two World Series titles. He signed a contract with the Tigers for $40,000 a year and agreed to manage the team and also play catcher. To put in perspective how much money Cochrane received it is necessary to look at a source from that time. According to Bob Greene, an avid Tiger fan who went to many games during the mid-thirties, *"seeded rye bread was 9 cents a loaf . . . A seat in the bleachers cost 55 cents, including tax. General grand stand seats were $1.10 and those closer to the playing field were $1.40."* An interesting thing about Cochrane is that his early years in Philadelphia were spent under the guidance of Ty Cobb, [after Cobb left the Tigers he played with the A's for two years] during which the young hitter learned much, *"Cobb freely dispensed batting advice. He taught Cochrane to aim the ball at the pitchers head, resulting in more base hits through the middle."* Any young ballplayer eager to learn, would have benefited from a master of the craft like Cobb. Teaching him some of his tricks indirectly led to a Detroit championship, which Cobb himself never got to experience. This connection and contribution by Cobb is often overlooked. Cochrane

to 30,000 seats. In 1920 Cobb became player/manager of the Tigers when Hughie Jennings was released. Cobb's teams would not repeat the dominance of the previous two decades, only finishing close in the pennant race one time (1924), when a last week collapse kept them from the pennant. 1926 saw the end of an era, when Ty Cobb left the Tigers to play his final three years with Connie Mack's Philadelphia Athletics.

Without Cobb, the Tigers declined in the standings and by 1933, Frank Navin had become concerned. Attendance had dropped to only 4,197 fans a game through the combination of poor play and the financial crunch of the Great Depression. He realized that he had to do something to attract the fans back to the stadium. His first

Depression. It meant the blank stares of broken men. It meant bread lines. The NRA. 'Buy an apple, mister.' Detroit was a city on its knees when Mickey Cochrane arrived from Philadelphia in the autumn of 1933. They saw in him a fighter. They saw in him a self-made man. They saw in him a winner. But mostly, they saw in him hope. A hope that tomorrow would be better. Connie Mack must have sorely needed $100,000 to part with a man of such mettle."

—Joe Falls on Mickey Cochrane
Associated Press Photo

would become the anchor and unquestioned leader of the Tigers, settling for nothing less than victory. Intense in the extreme, he was called "Black Mike" by his teammates for his dark brows which furled into scowls of anger when he was mad. He was an outstanding offensive and defensive catcher and was recognized as such with a Hall of Fame induction in 1947.

It is important to understand the setting in which Cochrane arrived in Detroit. When he arrived in 1933, the Tigers had not won an American League Championship since 1909 and the city of Detroit had been hit hard by the Great Depression. In 1933 the city had no professional football team (the Lions would arrive in 1934), and professional hockey was just catching on (Red Wings hockey arrived in 1932). Detroit needed something to get excited about, and fans of the Tigers hoped that this expensive acquisition would pay off.

Charlie [Gehringer] had a habit of taking the first pitch. We roomed together some when I was with the Tigers and I asked him once why he did it. "So the pitcher can start off even with me," he said.

—Rudy York, *Sport* 1953
Associated Press Photo

Though the Tigers had not played well the previous few years they were not devoid of talent. In fact, a new young core of players was emerging, led by two of the greatest athletes ever to don the Olde English "D," Charlie Gehringer, and Henry Benjamin Greenberg.

Gehringer was an instant success with the Tigers when in 1923 the Fowlerville, Michigan, native was trying out for the team, "*after watching me hit and field at second base, he (Ty Cobb) climbed up to Mr. Navin's office—this with his uniform and spikes on and got Mr. Navin down to watch me . . . they signed me right up.*" In his first three years as a Tiger, Gehringer had been managed by Ty Cobb who took the young player under his wing, "*he spent considerable time with his second baseman on train rides and inside hotel lobbies.*" The soft spoken Gehringer let his play speak for him as he was an outstanding offensive and defensive player, in 1935; Cobb said of him, "*aside from Eddie Collins, the finest second baseman I ever saw,*" Babe Ruth was quoted as saying, "*he's the best player around.*" His manager Mickey Cochrane also had high praise for him:

Charlie Gehringer, "the Fowlerville Flash." One of the greatest offensive and defensive players in baseball history seen sliding into third during a game in the 1933 season.

—Photo courtesy of the *Detroit Free Press*

"His fine intelligence, independence of thought, courage and his driving ambition have won him the respect and admiration of his teammates, baseball writers, and the fans at large. He feels and acknowledges his responsibility as a representative of the Jews in the field of a great national sport and the Jewish people could have no finer representative."

—Bud Shaver on Hank Greenberg
Detroit Times photo/Courtesy of *The Detroit News*

"Gehringer has no equal as a second baseman in either league. He has a fine pair of hands, covers a tremendous amount of ground in either direction and throws fast and accurately from any position. There is no infielder who can go as far and as surely as he can for pop flies." Gehringer was known as the "Mechanical Man," because *"you wind him up in the spring and he goes all summer, hits .330 or .340 or whatever, and then you shut him off in the fall."* He definitely lived up to this "Mechanical Man" nickname as he had a lifetime batting average of .320 while only striking out between 16–42 times every year over the course of sixteen years. He was the M.V.P. in 1937 with a .371 average, and led the American league in fielding percentage nine times. Charlie Gehringer was elected to the Hall of Fame in 1949.*

Henry Benjamin Greenberg or "Hammering" Hank Greenberg, as he would be affectionately known, arrived in Detroit in 1930. A first baseman from New York, it was fortunate for the Tigers that all three New York teams had steady first basemen, because it forced Greenberg to look for opportunities elsewhere. In the era before the amateur draft, players were free to sign with any team they wanted. Hank Greenberg would write the team record books in terms of power hitting despite four years service in World War II. He led the league in homeruns four times, (1935, 1938, 1940, and 1946); runs-batted-in four times (1935, 1937, 1940, and 1946), finished with a lifetime batting average of .319 and two American League M.V.P. trophies (1935, 1940). The true inspiration of Hank Greenberg was his character, which is the subject of several books and a movie. During his career Hank was the target of fans and opposing players alike; due to his ethnicity (Jewish). His ability to thrive despite being the target of racial epithets is legendary, and he stood as a major inspiration for the Jewish community, especially in Detroit. Greenberg represents an important aspect of why the "City of Champions" was so special; the fact that he overcame the adversity of stereotypes and hate to inspire people of all ethnicities. He was one of the early pioneers

· · · · · · ·

*Author's note: The generally accepted statistics for an above average season are; .300 batting average, 25 homeruns, and 100 R.B.I.'s (runs-batted-in).

"Hank was a great team player. But he also used to make me laugh. I'd hit ahead of him and he'd always be saying to me, 'Get 'em around to third.' I finally got the gist of what he was trying to say to me. He wanted the RBI's. He loved those RBI's.

—Charlie Gehringer on Hank Greenberg
Associated Press Photo

Leon Allen Goslin was a steady veteran hitter when the Tigers acquired him from the Washington Senators. His nickname "Goose" was derived from his prominent nose and family name.
—Photo courtesy of the
Detroit Free Press

in breaking down racial barriers. A fan of Hank Greenberg was Bob Greene who said about "Hammering Hank," *"It would be hard for those not alive in those days to appreciate how much of a cult figure Hank Greenberg was."* He was the first professional baseball player to join the armed forces during World War II, elected to the Hall of Fame in 1956 and had his jersey number 5 retired by the Tigers on the same day as Charlie Gehringer's number 2 (June 12, 1983).**

Another key player added to the Tigers in time for the 1934 season was Leon "Goose" Goslin. Coming over from the Washington Senators in exchange for outfielder John Stone, this thirty-three year old future Hall-of-Famer had four excellent years for Detroit. His steady defense in left field combined with his steady offensive performance (hitting 20 homeruns and driving in 100 R.B.I.'S each year) made the trade for him seem like an outright steal.

1935 SEASON

"Baseball during the Depression years provided a rough and tumble sport. Players spit tobacco juice into gaping wounds, and harping fans kept on the players. Pitchers scuffed dirt on the ball to make it do strange things on the way to the plate. The league embraced tough and scrappy players."

—Patricia Zacharias, *The Detroit News*

In Spring Training, 1935 (Lakeland, Florida) Mickey Cochrane told sportswriters, *"we'll win the pennant by 5 games."* He had good reason to be optimistic because his team had won the 1934 American League pennant by 7 games before losing a hard fought World Series against the St. Louis Cardinals' famous "Gashouse Gang." He had other reasons as well. His formidable rotation of pitchers was returning. Led by three of the games' most promising young arms: Lynwood "Schoolboy" Rowe (24 WINS), Tommy Bridges (22 WINS), and Elden Auker (15 WINS); the rotation also featured the veteran Alvin "General" Crowder (9 WINS). Cochrane's team was also returning

....

**Author's note: Retiring a player's jersey is the highest honor a team can bestow on a player. By doing so a team permanently removes the honored players' jersey number from circulation, and no future player for that team can ever wear that number again. Usually the number and name of the player are displayed at the sports venue for all to see in perpetuity.

—Photo courtesy of the *Detroit Free Press*

The famous Medwick incident in Game 7 of the 1934 World Series occurred after Joe Medwick had "spiked" Marv Owen at third base, drawing the fury of the Tiger fans in the bleachers. Medwick was removed from the game by Commissioner Landis after it was deemed impossible to control the enraged bleacherites that are shown here showering the field with debris. This is still the only time in baseball history that a player was removed on account of the opposing fans.

—Associated Press Photo

Babe Ruth shakes hands with the Cardinals and Tigers before the start of the 1934 World Series (from left to right) Dizzy Dean, ace pitcher of the Cardinals, Frankie Frisch, Manager of the Cardinals, Ruth, Mickey Cochrane, and Lynwood "Schoolboy" Rowe, ace pitcher of the Tigers.

—Associated Press Photo

Elden Auker. The "third best" pitcher on the Tigers' staff in 1935. This says more about the quality of the staff than it does about Auker who was a tremendously valuable member of the Tigers, and won 18 games in 1935.

—Photo courtesy of the *Detroit Free Press*

Ervin "Pete" Fox. An excellent all-around outfielder, Fox could run, hit, and play defense as well as anyone in the league. His .385 average in the 1935 World Series would lead all hitters.

—Photo courtesy of the *Detroit Free Press*

Denny A. "Doc" Carroll. The Tigers' trainer, was a master of his craft. He had been specifically chosen by Frank Navin in 1931 when he was looking for someone to restore the strength of Charlie Gehringer's tired arm. His expertise was in arm trouble, and he helped the Tiger players (including Gehringer) regain and stay in their top physical form.

—Photo courtesy of the *Detroit Free Press*

Alvin "General" Crowder. This sturdy veteran pitcher could always be counted on when the Tigers needed him, accounting for 16 wins and 16 complete games in 1935.

—*Detroit Times* photo/Courtesy of *The Detroit News*

Thomas Davis "Tommy" Bridges. The 5 foot 10 inch Bridges paired with Schoolboy Rowe to give the Tigers two aces. Though different in size, Bridges was equally as devastating to opposing hitters. Bridges had "one of the best curve balls baseball has ever known, and the heart of a Lion."

—Photo and quote, courtesy of the *Detroit Free Press*

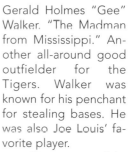

Gerald Holmes "Gee" Walker. "The Madman from Mississippi." Another all-around good outfielder for the Tigers. Walker was known for his penchant for stealing bases. He was also Joe Louis' favorite player.

—Photo courtesy of the *Detroit Free Press*

Delmar David "Del" Baker. Baker was a coach of the Tigers in 1935 but he had come up through the Tigers' minor league system along with Hank Greenberg, Pete Fox, School-boy Rowe, Jo-Jo White and Flea Clifton. It was as head coach of the Beaumont team of the Texas League that these players had been under his tutelage. Many Tiger players would later credit Baker as being the best teacher of the game that they ever had.
—Photo courtesy of the
Detroit Free Press

Herman "Flea" Clifton. A utility infielder known primarily for his glove, he could play first, second, third and short with equal effectiveness. The nickname "Flea" was given to him by Del Baker early in his career because of "his size and his ability to hop around."
—Photo courtesy of the
Detroit Free Press

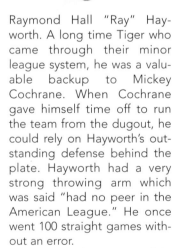

Raymond Hall "Ray" Hayworth. A long time Tiger who came through their minor league system, he was a valuable backup to Mickey Cochrane. When Cochrane gave himself time off to run the team from the dugout, he could rely on Hayworth's outstanding defense behind the plate. Hayworth had a very strong throwing arm which was said "had no peer in the American League." He once went 100 straight games without an error.
—Photo courtesy of the
Detroit Free Press

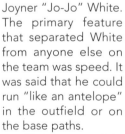

Ralph F. "Cy" Perkins. The story of Tiger coach Cy Perkins dates back to the early days of Mickey Cochrane's career. Perkins was the starting catcher for Connie Mack's Philadelphia Athletics and helped to teach Cochrane the fine arts of being a big league catcher. He did such a good job that the young Mickey replaced him shortly after. The two became very good friends in Philadelphia and Perkins came with Cochrane to coach the Tigers.
—Photo courtesy of the
Detroit Free Press

Joyner "Jo-Jo" White. The primary feature that separated White from anyone else on the team was speed. It was said that he could run "like an antelope" in the outfield or on the base paths.
—Photo courtesy of the
Detroit Free Press

Lynwood Thomas "Schoolboy" Rowe (left). One of the most revered pitchers in Detroit Tiger history, "Schoolie" as he was affectionately known, was an amazingly dominant and durable pitcher, who stood at an intimidating 6 foot 4-1/2 inches tall. There were several stories about how he had acquired the nickname "Schoolboy." One story said that he had been pitching against older competition at a Sunday school picnic and one of these opponents yelled to the hitter: "Come on, don't let that schoolboy strike you out!" However it happened, the name stuck with him for life.

—Photo and quote, courtesy of the *Detroit Free Press*

Elon Chester "Chief" Hogsett. American Indian ballplayers of this time were often given the nickname of "chief," and Hogsett was no exception. This lefty was a valuable relief pitcher for the Tigers, and was said to be so calm on the mounds that people referred to him as "the human icicle."

—Photo courtesy of the *Detroit Free Press*

Marvin James "Marv" Owen. An exceptional hitter and fielder, Owen played six years for the Tigers during which he was a constant at third base. Often overshadowed by his more famous teammates, Owen was a valuable contributor to an infield that would set records for defense, and offensive production.

—Photo courtesy of the *Detroit Free Press*

William George "Bill" Rogell. Rogell, was an outstanding shortstop and teamed with Charlie Gehringer to make one of the best "double-play tandems" in baseball history. He led the American league in fielding from 1935–1937. According to Joe Falls: "Rogell contributed more to the Tigers with his glove than with his bat, and more with his spirit than with both. He was known as a bit of a sparkplug, and he made up for the quietness of Gehringer at second. As he would later say, 'Sure, I made some noise on the field. I was the holler guy. Owen never said a lot, Greenberg never said anything, and Gehringer-he never said a damned thing. So I had to make all the noise. I'd say, 'Come on, you SOB's, let's get going.'" Rogell later became a Detroit City Coucilman, and at 94 years of age, threw out the first pitch in the final game at Tiger Stadium; Sept. 27th 1999.

—Photo courtesy of the *Detroit Free Press*

every member of his lineup that had led all of baseball in hitting (.300 TEAM BATTING AVERAGE) and had led the American League in fielding (.974 FIELDING PERCENTAGE). Despite the early optimism, the Tigers of 1935 started out slowly. So slowly in fact that they had dropped to last place in April and were still in sixth place on May 28th. However, the Tigers began to regroup and move quickly up the standings. That this team could rebound as they did was due to the performance of their players.

Demonstrating amazing durability, Tommy Bridges would pace the pitching staff with 23 complete games and 21 wins, leading all of baseball with 163 strikeouts. "Schoolboy" Rowe, with 21 complete games and 19 wins was second in strikeouts only to Bridges with 140. Rowe also contributed with his bat (the American League had no designated hitter at this time). Always an outstanding hitter, in 1935 he batted .312 (34 HITS IN 109 AT-BATS), highlighted by a game on August 14th when he went 5 for 5. Submariner (called this because of his unusual underarm pitching motion) Elden Auker won 18 (13 COMPLETE GAMES) and led all pitchers in fielding percentage, cleanly fielding 49 attempts without an error. Veteran "General" Crowder won 16 and also had 16 complete games.

The Tiger lineup had a fine year as well, leading all of the major leagues in most offensive categories including: highest batting average (.290), most runs scored (919), runs per game (6.05), slugging percentage (.435), and walks (627). This effort was led by Hank Greenberg who would be named M.V.P. of the season with a .328 batting average, 36 homeruns, and 170 runs-batted-in. Charlie Gehringer came through with his quietly outstanding numbers of .330 BA., 19 HR, and 108 RBI's. Greenberg and Gehringer would be called the "G men" of Detroit, because Gehringer would get on base and Greenberg would drive him in, Gehringer scoring 123 times in 1935. Mickey Cochrane batted .319, right fielder Pete Fox hit .321, and outfielder Gerald "Gee" Walker hit .301. "Goose" Goslin narrowly missed out on hitting .300 with his .292 average but was the third most productive player on the team with 172 hits and 109 RBI's. Shortstop Billy Rogell was also a major contributor with a .275 BA., 154 hits and 71 RBI's.

The Tigers again finished the year with the best fielding percentage (.979) in all of baseball. Gehringer led all second basemen (.985) and Billy Rogell led all shortstops (.971). The Tiger stars had a fine year indeed, but they also relied on other players as well. Players such as

young pitcher Joe Sullivan (3.51 ERA, 125 INNINGS PITCHED)* who had several important early victories, "Chief" Elon Hogsett (3.54 ERA, 96 IP), Vic Sorrell (4.03 ERA, 51.1 IP), and Roxie Lawson (1.58 ERA, 40 IP) all logged in appearances that helped relieve the Tiger starters throughout the season. Marv Owen anchored the hot corner (3rd base), Jo-Jo White platooned (split time) in the outfield, Ray Hayworth backed up Cochrane at catcher, and "Flea" Clifton was the utility player who saw time at 3rd, 2nd and shortstop.

The Tiger efforts in 1935 were also helped by the one million fans who attended the games (151 total games, 30,000 seats; 1,034,929 tickets sold). In fact, the team drew almost double the amount of paying customers than the next closest teams (Cubs, Yankees), a statistical testament to the support showed by the fans, especially during the economic crunch of the Depression. It also shows that the fans supported the team throughout the course of the whole season, when the team struggled early *and* when they rallied. And rally they did. By mid July the Tigers had taken over first place from the New York Yankees, building a nine game lead, before winning the American League Pennant by a margin of 3 games, two short of Mickey Cochrane's preseason prediction.

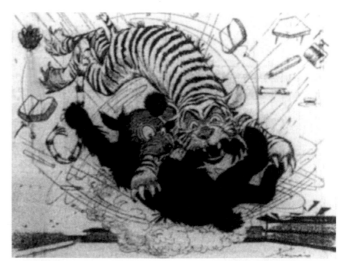

An unknown artist drew this cartoon on the eve of the 1935 World Series.

—*Detroit Times* cartoon/Courtesy of *The Detroit News*

• • • • • • •

* Author's note: ERA stands for earned run average and describes the average amount of runs per nine innings that the pitcher has given up. For example, if a pitcher gives up one run in one inning, his ERA is 9.00, if he pitches nine innings and gives up one run his ERA is 1.00. The lower the number the better, and generally, above average is below 3.00.

The Cubs outfield (left to right) Augie Galan, Freddie Lindstrom, Frank Demaree and Chuck Klein.
—*Detroit Times* photo/Courtesy of *The Detroit News*

The Cubs starting pitchers (left to right) Larry French, Charlie Root, "Big" Bill Lee and Lon Warneke pose for this picture before the start of the World Series.
—*Detroit Times* photo/Courtesy of *The Detroit News*

1935 WORLD SERIES

By finishing first in the American League, and winning the Pennant, the Tigers automatically qualified to play in the World Series (the playoff system would not be initiated until 1969). The Tigers would face the National League champion and World Series nemesis Chicago Cubs. The Tigers' history of playing the Cubs in the World Series was terrible, for it had been the Cubs who had beaten them in 1907 and 1908. Though the players from that time had long since retired, the Cubs were a formidable opponent. A stable of pitchers who had all posted great years was led by 20 game winners Lon Warneke (3.06 ERA), and "Big" Bill Lee (2.96 ERA). The pitching staff also included: Larry French (17 wins, 2.96 ERA), Charlie Root (15 WINS, 3.08 ERA), Roy Hen-

Billy Herman, Cubs second baseman.
—*Detroit Times* photo/Courtesy of *The Detroit News*

Stan Hack, Cubs third baseman.
—*Detroit Times* photo/Courtesy of *The Detroit News*

shaw (13 WINS, 3.28 ERA) and Tex Carleton (11 WINS, 3.89 ERA). The Cubs offense had led the National League in hitting (.288 TEAM AVERAGE) and included several stars. Catcher Gabby Hartnett (.344 BA), third baseman Stan Hack (.311 BA) and second baseman Bill Herman (.341 BA, 57 DOUBLES) were called the Cubs "*big three.*" The offense was also fueled by outfielder Frank Demaree (.325 BA), and emerging outfield star Augie Galan (.314 BA). The Cubs in 1935 had won 21 straight games in the final month to blow past the fading New York Giants and St. Louis Cardinals; winning the National League Pennant by four games. It was because of this win streak that the Cubs were considered the hottest team in baseball going into the best-of-seven World Series.

"The Howling Hordes. Baseball-mad Detroit fans jam their way into bunting-draped Navin Field to see the Tigers battle the Chicago Cubs for the Championship of the World."

—Photo courtesy of the *Detroit Free Press*
—Obtained through the use of the Alan Feldman Collection

GAME 1–NAVIN FIELD
OCTOBER 1ST 1935

In the days before mass media brought sites and sounds to our living rooms, it was important for newspapers to report on the tiniest detail of sporting events for the readers who could not be there in person. It is to our benefit then, that such detailed reporting took place. Reading the following passage, the true nostalgic Tiger fan can share the sights and sounds of the old stadium at Michigan and Trumbull on opening day of that 1935 World Series;

The weather was cool and slightly overcast. The bleacher faithful for this Fall sporting classic had begun to gather, many of them as early as sundown yesterday, sleeping on their feet outside the gates. The first rush of bleacher fans stormed into Navin Field promptly at 9 AM. An hour later more than half the 19,500 bleacher seats were occupied. The early arrivals had opportunity of looking out on an immaculate ball field. Neil Conway's

ground crew had burnished and tidied it to perfection. The outfield smooth and emerald green despite the bleaching Autumn suns, looked as trim as the lawn of some private park. Not a single foot mark marred the surface of the infield paths. Brand new bags had been installed on the bases. They were white as a dress shirt early in the evening. The pitcher's rubber also had been given a coat of fresh white and foul lines and batter's box were newly outlined in white. A thirty piece band entertained the bleacher enthusiasts. It was conducted by that distinguished maestro, Al Schacht, resplendent in baseball pants, a dress coat and his battered silk topper. His repertoire comprised such sturdy favorites as "My Hero," "Take me out to the Ball Game" and "The Man on the Flying Trapeze." Conductor Schacht added verve to his directing by falling flat on his face at the conclusion of each piece. Schacht and the band and a cornetist, who was a pretty good jug-

Aerial view of Navin Field for the World Series.
—Associated Press Photo

gler with two small bats and an indoor baseball, performed in the outfield for the bleacher mob from about 10 o'clock until nearly noon, until the Tigers came out for practice, in fact and that was 11:50 AM. By noon the bleachers were filled except for a few scattered patches in the extreme upper corners.

By noon too the pavilions in right and left field were beginning to fill and a few prudent patrons were trickling into the grandstands. The grandstand parapets and the fronts of the field boxes were festooned in red, white and blue bunting. In the bleachers nearly 25 percent of the fans were girls and women. From home plate the bleachers had a sort of pepper-and-salt brownish gray appearance, studded here and there by the white uniforms of peanut and pop vendors. Then Al Schacht, baseball's official clown, put on a brief burlesque, pitching first to a big Cub and then to a big Tiger (both phoney). Before he was finished Schacht had stripped to the waist. The fans howled and clapped when the Tiger and the Cub ganged up and chased Schacht to the showers.

Half an hour before game time all of the stands were crowded almost to capacity. Only a few box holders and grandstand patrons were sufficiently self-contained to postpone their appearance till the last minute. These few tardy ones were in their seats before play started. The 50,000 broke into a rending, high-pitched roar, almost frightening in its volume, as the Tigers raced out for their final warm-up at 1 o'clock. At this junc-

Managers Charlie Grimm and Mickey Cochrane embrace before the opening game of the 1935 World Series.

—Photo courtesy of The Detroit News

Four members of the Detroit Lions are spotted in the crowd. (From left to right) J. Regis Monahan, George Christensen, Miss R.M. Willis, Mrs. Tom Hupke, Jack Johnson, and Sam Knox.

—*Detroit Times* photo/Courtesy of *The Detroit News*

These two aces squared off for the opening game. Lon Warneke, and Lynwood "Schoolboy" Rowe, two of baseball's greatest pitchers in the 1930's.

—Associated Press Photo

Joe Louis; fresh off his fight with Max Baer, and his honey-moon with Marva-found his way to the World Series.
—*Detroit Times* photo/Courtesy of *The Detroit News*

These "Newsies," were lucky in finding peep holes in this Navin Field gate.
—Photo courtesy of the *Detroit Free Press*
Obtained through the use of the Alan Feldman Collection

ture it was announced via loud speaker Commissioner Landis had ruled any box holder or other first row patron who leaned out and caught or tried to catch a ball in play would be ejected from the park. At 1:10 PM the Tigers returned to their dugout while groundskeepers re-raked and rolled the base paths. The band played "The Victors" with a flourish and moved from the field to their seats in the stand. A few moments later, while Schoolboy Rowe and Lon Warneke put the finishing touches on their pitching practice, the photographers and newsreelmen were chased from the field. The four umpires emerged from their room at 1:25 PM. They held the usual home plate conference with Mickey Cochrane and Charlie Grimm, who shook hands and smiled bleak smiles. The loud speaker blared for opposing lineups. A roar went up as Rowe was announced as the pitcher for Detroit. It was a roar of pleasure; although everybody had

known [for] three days [that] Rowe would pitch, barring death. Fifty thousand people stood uncovered as the band played the Star Spangled Banner at 1:35 PM. Two minutes later the Tigers took the field, running. Umpire Moriarty took out his little brush and dusted off home plate. A Chicago batter, Galan, stepped to the plate. Another cheer burst like drumfire across the field. The game was on. It started at 1:38, eight minutes late.

—John C. Manning, *Detroit Times,* 10/2/35

The picturesque morning of this first World Series game faded into a darker evening, as the hometown club ended up losing the game. The Cubs opened the scoring in the first inning by scoring two runs, due to an error by the pitcher, Schoolboy Rowe, and to a timely piece of hitting by the Cubs catcher, Gabby Hartnett, who drove Herman in with a single. The Cubs opening pitcher Lon Warneke allowed only four hits, pitching a complete game for the win. The Tigers' Rowe was not his usual dominant self, though he also pitched a complete game, scattering seven hits over nine innings. A homerun in the ninth by Frank Demaree was merely icing on the cake for the Cubs as they went on to win 3–0.

GAME 2–NAVIN FIELD
OCTOBER 2ND 1935

The second game of the World Series again saw an over-capacity crowd of 45,000. To accommodate these increasingly larger crowds Navin had opened up a "standing room only" section along the edge of the field. These fans had to be alert to what was going on in the game because if they interfered with the ball in play they were still subject to ejection by Commissioner Landis. Those who were in attendance were die-hards as they braved the elements with the same up-beat fortitude that has become a hallmark of Detroit fans.

The early arrivals were rewarded for their game-ness by an interesting feature, not on the schedule. It was about 10a.m when the storm of rain and wind was at its height. The big tarpaulin, nearly an acre in extent, had been laid snug and neat over the infield last night. A sudden riffle of the gale caught a corner of it and in a twinkle the entire, tremendous covering had been whipped up off the ground. It ballooned out like a vast black sail torn loose from a fantastic, huge pirate vessel. It writhed and crackled and swept half of the diamond and over the first base boxes before the ground crew could get it under control. About 20 men wrestled with it and finally tugged and yanked it back into place. The crowd yelled hearty approval of this incident.

At 1p.m. it was announced in the press box that the official temperature was 48 degrees. Everybody wanted to know if that meant below or above zero. At 1:15 Tommy Bridges and Charlie Root, finishing their warm-up pitches, a work gang came out and sprinkled the base paths to lay the dust that was being swirled around by the wind. Double sweaters and blankets were bundled around both pitchers directly after they had concluded their practicing. Al Schacht put on his fa-

mous burlesque boxing match against himself the last thing before the field was cleared. The entire Cub team crowded around to watch this act. Being National Leaguers, they don't get much opportunity of catching Schacht's acts. They howled with glee. The Tigers were more restrained and remained in their dugout. A high-throated, whistling roar shattered against the walls as the Tigers took

"It was a little different than it is today. Everybody dressed like they were going to the theater or maybe to church. Nobody wore jackets or jeans. We played in the afternoons, and the lawyers would come out from their offices and they would be all spiffed up. The women in the box seats looked just beautiful. You'd think they were there for a garden party."
—Charlie Gehringer quoted in Joe Falls

Fans overflow onto the field as more tickets are sold than seats available.

their places on the field at 1:34 PM. The band played "The Star spangled Banner" and retired. The umpires went to position. Little Augie Galan with Red "51" on his Cub shirt back stepped to the plate and faced Tommy Bridges. The plate umpire raised his hand. The second game was under way.

—John C. Manning, Detroit Times, 10/3/35

This second game saw joy for the home team as the Tigers slashed the Cubs pitching for eight runs. Four of the runs came in the first inning on a one-run double by Cochrane, a run scoring single by Gehringer and a two-run homer by Hank Greenberg. That the Tigers just seemed to be circling the base paths on hit after hit caused the Cubs manager Charlie Grimm to remove his pitcher Charlie Root in the first inning, replacing him with Roy Henshaw. This pitching change barely slowed down the Tiger offense as they scored three more runs in the fourth, one on a wild pitch by Henshaw and two more on a Gehringer single. The final Tiger run came in the seventh as Pete Fox slapped a single into right field to score Gehringer from third base. All of this scoring added to the excitement of the fans;

Those on hand made a lot more noise than on the opening day. Constant waves of yelling and cheering rocketed back and forth across the field. The gallant bleacherites, half of whom had sat all morning through the rain, weren't silent a minute. They cheered long drives. They cheered the hot

dog vendors and the ball boys and the policemen. They cheered everything on the theory, no doubt, that if they cheered loudly enough they would forget that cold and piercing wind. Indeed the noisiest and most sustained burst of cheering to be heard yet during the series came from the bleacher throng three hours before play was called. That happened when the rain finally ceased and the sun-wah but the sun-came out. They cheered the sun as enthusiastically as though it were some strange, new phenomenon they had discovered for the first time in history.

—John C. Manning, *Detroit Times*, 10/3/35

The Tigers' pitcher Tommy Bridges had played very well, pitching all nine innings and allowing only three runs on

Tiger Program for the 1935 World Series.
—Photo by permission of the Baseball Hall of Fame

Hank Greenberg scoring on his 2-run homer into the left field bleachers in the first inning.
— *Detroit Times* photo/Courtesy of *The Detroit News*

Al Schact, the "Clown Prince of Comedy" entertained at 25 World Series in his career with his unusual brand of comedy. He's shown here performing one of his acts with Chuck Klein and Phil Cavaretta of the Cubs before the start of Game 2.
—*Detroit Times* photo/Courtesy of *The Detroit News*

The Cubs Charlie Root (22) tosses the ball to Roy Henshaw as he is removed from the game in the first inning.
—*Detroit Times* photo/Courtesy of *The Detroit News*

six hits to the potent Cubs offense. Unfortunately for the Tigers however, this win would come at a price. In the 7th inning their M.V.P. Hank Greenberg had severely fractured his wrist sliding into home plate and would be lost for the rest of the series (and half of the next season as well). Final Score: Tigers 8, Cubs 3.

Babe Ruth looked in fine form when he caught this ball up in the press box during the fourth inning, to the delight of the fans around him. He gave the ball to a nearby fireman.
—Photo courtesy of *The Detroit News*

The Detroit News "Magic Eye" catches the moment Hank Greenberg broke his wrist. To the horror of Tiger fans.

"Hank starts slide as Hartnett waits for Herman's throw on Fox's hit."

"Hartnett has Herman's throw, a relay from Demaree and is blocking the plate with his knee."

"The wrist was injured as the two men met in terrific impact."

"Umpire Quigley calls Greenberg out, a decision that Hank protested, saying nothing at all of his wrist."

—*Detroit Times* photo/Courtesy of *The Detroit News*

GAME 3—WRIGLEY FIELD
OCTOBER 4TH 1935

A touching thing happened in the dressing room. Joe Groggin, the bat boy was found in a corner crying as though his heart would break. "My mother bought me a new suit," he said. "And they've posted the list of names going to Chicago. I'm not on it." Goose Goslin overheard and immediately took charge. "You're going," Goose assured him. "Darn right," added Cochrane. "Oke by me," snapped Cy Perkins. "Let's the three of us (Goose, Cochrane and Perkins) split the kid's expense." Thus it was decided. And Joe Groggin, a very happy lad, can show his new suit in Midway.

—Bob Murphy, *Detroit Times*, 10/3/35

The Tigers' bat-boy did in fact travel to Chicago with the team, and it was a good thing that he was there. For Groggin and the Cubs' batboy would be busy on this day, cleaning up all the bats that resulted from twenty-two hits between the teams. This Game would turn out to be a wild, seesaw battle between the two clubs that saw three pitchers used for each team, four ejections, and a controversy that would give plenty of fodder for newspaper writers.

Before the game started, the Tigers had to make a difficult decision. Because of his injury in Game 2, Hank Greenberg was out for the series; this represented a major problem, how do you replace one of the most feared sluggers in the game? Mickey Cochrane held a team meeting and opened up the question for suggestions. Schoolboy Rowe offered to play first base, but Cochrane was uneasy about the pitcher's base running skills and defensive ability at first. Cochrane was leaning towards putting himself at first and bringing in his backup Ray Hayworth to play catcher. It was a tough decision but one in which Frank Navin himself stepped in to make. He insisted that Cochrane stay behind the plate, Marv Owen be moved from third to first and the light hitting Flea Clifton be brought off the bench to play third. Cochrane disagreed with the idea as Clifton was one of the weakest hitters on the team. But Navin was insistent on the move; *"I order it, if we lose the series it will be on my head."*

So it was without their M.V.P. first baseman that the

Aerial view of Wrigley Field prior to the start of World Series Game 3.
—Photo courtesy of *The Detroit News*

Hank Greenberg photographed on the bench. His absence represented a significant hurdle for the Tigers to overcome.
—Photo courtesy of *The Detroit News*

Detroit News "Magic Eye" captured the submarine delivery of Elden Auker.
—Photo courtesy of *The Detroit News*

"Magic Eye" showing the "Mercury footed" Flea Clifton rounding second base on a single by Mickey Cochrane in the third inning.

—*Detroit Times* photo/Courtesy of *The Detroit News*

Tigers entered this third game of the World Series. The 45,532 fans at Wrigley Field that day must have hoped that without the game's greatest slugger, their Cubs would take control of the series. Early in the game it looked as though they would, when the home team scored two runs in the second inning, highlighted by a Frank Demaree home run which was drilled into the right field bleachers. Another run in the fifth for the Cubs increased the lead to 3–0. The Tigers managed to chip away at the lead in the sixth inning when Pete Fox hit a triple that scored Goose Goslin. It was shortly after this play that Fox was picked off third by the Cubs' catcher, Gabby Hartnett. Del Baker, the Tigers third base coach, protested the call and was thrown out of the game by National League umpire Ernie Quigley.

In the Chicago half of the sixth, a close play by Charlie Gehringer led Cubs manager Charlie Grimm to storm the field in a livid protest; resulting in his ejection by American League umpire George Moriarty.

It was in the eighth that things got a little wild and when the controversy really started. The Tigers came up to bat and Jo-Jo White led off with a walk. The Cubs' players and coaches on the bench had been hurling abuses at George Moriarty since his sixth inning ejection of their manager. Apparently Moriarty had enough, because he stopped the game and ejected Elwood "Woody" English, and George Stainback, the two other Cubs' coaches, leaving the team essentially leaderless. The argument had lasted many minutes, during which, the Cubs pitcher Bill Lee stood on the mound in freezing conditions. When order was restored, the Tigers pounded four runs out to first tie the game and then take the lead 5–3. This "Moriarty incident" would be seized on by the media in Chicago and Detroit. The papers in Chicago were quick to complain about the abusive language that the umpire had used and also the fact that Moriarty had played for Detroit back in the Ty Cobb era, being so highly regarded in those years that he had served as the Tigers' captain in 1911. Detroit newspapers scoffed at the Cubs objection to Moriarty's language, "*to anyone who has ever visited a major league dugout, it is more or less laughable to hear ball players objecting to profanity from any source. It is their own chief means of communication.*"

Lost among this whole incident was an outstanding piece of base-running by the Tigers' Billy Rogell and Pete Fox. A series of singles by the Tigers had tied the score

Stanley Hack   Bill Lee   Manager Grimm, Moriarty, & Cavaretta   Goslin
The start of trouble in the 6th inning between the Cubs and Moriarty.

—Photo courtesy of *The Detroit News*

3–3 leaving Rogell at first base and Fox at third. The two players decided to try a double steal in order to "squeeze" Fox home. The theory of the double steal is that the base runner on first attempts to steal second and draws the throw in his direction at the same time as the runner on third steals home. Forcing a mistake by the Cubs, Rogell and Fox executed the steal perfectly to give the Tigers the lead,

> *Bill Rogell pulls off first with the idea of negotiating a double steal with Pete Fox at third, but Gabby Hartnett's throw to Herman traps Rogell between first and second, with Fox penned at third. Herman and Cavarretta begin chucking the ball back and forth between them while Rogell is scooting first this way and then that. Meantime, Fox is sticking to third because the lads are keeping their eyes on him, too. Suddenly Cavarretta, who has hold of the ball at the moment, decides to personally race Rogell. He starts after William full tilt and, sure enough, he outfoots Rogell in a brief sprint, proving to one and all Cavarretta can run. But while he is catching Rogell the wily Fox sneaks home from third before Cavarretta is aware of his purpose. By the time Cavarretta turns to throw to the plate, Fox is there, chuckling to himself.*

—Damon Runyon, *Detroit Times*, 10/5/35

"Get Out Says Moriarty." "Woody" English and George Stainback were ejected in the 8th inning for hurling abuses at Moriarty. This photo was taken at the moment of the event. After the ejection of all three coaches, the Cubs were left leaderless as the game went into extra innings.

—Photo courtesy of *The Detroit News*

The Cubs sent "Big" Bill Lee to the hill to face Elden Auker in this third game.

—Associated Press Photo

Jo-Jo White came through with what would be the game-winning hit for the Tigers. Here he is photographed shortly after connecting for that hit, a single to center field that would turn into a double when Demaree threw the ball home.

—*Detroit Times* photo/Courtesy of *The Detroit News*

"Magic Eye of the double steal which led to the Tigers 4th run in the 8th inning, giving the Tigers a 5–3 lead. Cavaretta chases Rogell tagging him out, but as he looks up, Pete Fox is already on his way home to tie the score–too late for Cavaretta to throw.

—*Detroit Times* photos/Courtesy of *The Detroit News*

The excitement of the Tigers taking the lead was short lived, as the Cubs scored two runs off Schoolboy Rowe in the very next inning, to tie the game and send it into extra innings. Both teams had been wearing out the other's pitching staffs, as Rowe was the third pitcher used by the Tigers while the Cubs' Larry French was the third pitcher used for Chicago. As the game extended into extra innings, tension reigned supreme with both teams fully realizing the importance of the next run. The Cubs best chance at that run came in the very next inning (10th) when Freddie Lindstrom led off with a double. With Gabby Hartnett coming up to the plate, things looked dire as the powerful catcher was the main run producer in the Cubs lineup. At this point the lack of managerial decision making came into play;

Manager Charlie Grimm had been banished by Umpire Moriarty in the last half of the sixth inning. English, Chicago's non-playing captain, had been chased off the bench by Moriarty along with Stainback in the eighth. Joe Corriden and Roy Johnson, the coaches, were on the field, but it is doubtful if either assumed authority. If Hartnett received any orders they probably came from Lindstrom on second. It is not likely that Hartnett himself chose to sacrifice. Hitters like Hartnett like to hit, not bunt. But bunt he did: Rowe was wary. He could not believe Hartnett would bunt even after he attempted it and missed for the first strike. Rowe charged in with every pitch as did Owen, but Clifton played back in case Hartnett crossed Rowe with a swinging cut at the ball. He didn't. Hartnett dragged a beautiful bunt down the first

base line. Were he as fast as any other man in the Cubs' lineup he would have beaten it out, but Hartnett is slow. Cochrane leaped out, chased the rolling bunt down the line and threw Hartnett out as Lindstrom sped into third.

—Bud Shaver, *Detroit Times*, 10/5/35

Though Hartnett's sacrifice bunt was successful in moving Lindstrom over to third, the next two Cubs hitters failed to drive him in. This one play fueled endless speculation, about what would have happened had Hartnett attempted to swing? This is a question that will never be answered.

It was the Tigers turn at bat in their half of the eleventh. A leadoff single by Rogell was neutralized on a terrible bunt by Marv Owen which went to the shortstop, who cut Rogell down at second. But on the very next play a bit of good fortune went the Tigers' way when Freddie Lindstrom bobbled a ground ball that allowed Flea Clifton to reach first, and Owen to advance to second. A strikeout by Rowe left Jo-Jo White in position to be the hero for Detroit. He took advantage of his opportunity by lacing a single into center field which allowed the fleet-footed Owen to score from second. This run would prove to be the winner when Schoolboy Rowe came in and shut down the Cubs in their half of the eleventh. Final score: Tigers 6, Cubs 5.

In winning this game the Tigers had shown that they could overcome the loss of Greenberg, and as a result had changed the complexion of the series. Had the Cubs won they would have taken the series lead and left more people (perhaps even the Tigers themselves) wondering if they could win without Hank. In an article by Babe Ruth, the former slugger emphasized that point,

Cochrane throwing out Hartnett on his controversial bunt in the tenth inning.
—Photo courtesy of *The Detroit News*

The Cubs' Stephenson takes a called third strike as Cochrane, Rowe and the rest of the Tigers begin to run off the field-completing their 6-5 victory.

—*Detroit Times* photos/Courtesy of *The Detroit News*

"That victory of the Tigers over the Cubs in the third game of the World Series is likely to have a marked effect on the outcome. It will add to the confidence of the Tigers and shake the Cubs' belief in themselves. For the American League champions proved they could win with their most dangerous hitter out of the lineup."

—Babe Ruth, *Detroit Times*, 10/5/35

GAME 4–WRIGLEY FIELD OCTOBER 5TH 1935

They don't take their baseball quite as seriously here as they do in Detroit; that is, they don't ordinarily, but today all Chicago is talking nothing but baseball. In hotel lobbies, on street cars and buses, on street corners is one universal topic of conversation. Mr. and Mrs. Chicagos are chattering just one thing. The talk goes something like this; "Hold that Tiger. Stop that Tiger." That is the wistful chant you hear all the way from the swarming, central Michigan boulevard section to this north side district where, in this big, neat ballpark, [the] Chicago Cubs are preparing right now, pretty grimly, to engage our American League representatives in this fourth game of the 1935 World Series.

—John C. Manning, *Detroit Evening Times*, 10/5/35

Entering this game, both teams had practically worn out their best pitchers. Rowe, Bridges, and Auker had pitched the majority of innings for the Tigers; while Warneke, Lee

and French had all been exhausted by the Cubs. In order to make any of these players available to pitch again in the series, both teams would have to let them rest for at least one game. As a result, both teams were forced to rely on their next-best pitchers in this game four duel. On paper the matchup favored the Tigers, who were sending veteran Alvin "General" Crowder to the hill against "Tex" Carleton, a pitcher they had battered when he played for the Cardinals in the 1934 World Series. Though both pitchers had similar statistics in 1935, this day would witness the General's finest hour.

Crowder had won 16 games during the course of this season but none were prettier or more important than his game four performance. Pitching all nine innings he allowed only one run, while striking out five and walking two.

He gave up only five hits through the nine innings, one of those a home-run by Gabby Hartnett in the second. As if to show that the home run was a fluke, Crowder struck out the next three batters in that second inning.

Not content to merely pitch his team to victory, the General helped to account for both Tiger runs. The first, he scored in the third inning after hitting a single to get on base. He advanced to third via single by Jo-Jo White, before scoring on a Gehringer double. The second, and game winning run, came in the sixth. With Flea Clifton on second, Crowder hit a ball to third base which Bill Jurges couldn't handle, resulting in an error for the Cubs and Clifton scoring for the Tigers.

Although the final score of this game was only 2–1, it was not nearly as close as the score might indicate. While Crowder had pitched great, the Cubs' Tex Carleton had pitched terribly. He was behind in the count to almost every Tiger hitter who came to the plate; walked seven in seven innings and allowed 17 batters to reach first. Over the course of his seven innings, he had loaded the bases twice and three times had two runners on. The Tigers had been threatening all game; they just couldn't drive in any runs. The Detroit News article of the game said, *"The Tigers might have scored eight or nine runs—they had the chances needed for clusters of tallies, but something always happened."* An example of one of the *somethings* that happened was the "fake catch" by Augie Galan. In the second inning with Goose Goslin on first, Pete Fox hit a double into left field but the left fielder (Galan) drifted back casually as though it was a lazy pop fly. Goslin, mo-

Interior view of Wrigley Field during the 1935 World Series.
—Associated Press Photo

Alvin "General" Crowder warming up. His performance in Game 4 was one for the ages.
—Associated Press Photo

Gabby Hartnett hits this pitch into the right field bleachers in the 2nd inning. Accounting for the lone Cubs run on the day.
—*Detroit Times* photo/Courtesy of *The Detroit News*

Another wasted opportunity. Cochrane is forced out at the plate on this play in the third inning. The Tigers had runners in scoring position all day but failed to score repeatedly.

Crowder scoring on Charlie Gehringer's double in the third inning. The General not only pitched the game of his life, he was involved with both Tiger runs in what turned out to be a close 2–1 Detroit victory.

—*Detroit Times* photos/Courtesy of *The Detroit News*

mentarily thrown off by this, ran only partly toward second before the ball dropped and he realized it was a hit. The center fielder, Freddie Lindstrom was able to cut the ball off and have it back to the infield before Goslin could get around third and score. Two batters later, the inning was over with the Goose still on third, Galan and his unconventional tactic had in fact saved a run. Besides this "fake catch," the Cubs made outstanding plays all day, time after time denying the Tigers of big innings. An especially outstanding play was made by Bill Jurges, who made a sensational leaping stab of a line drive. His play was made especially relevant in that it ended an inning in which the Tigers had loaded the bases.

Despite a threatening ninth inning, the Cubs bounced into a double play to end the game, leaving General Crowder and the Tigers winners of Game Four and possessing a 3–1 Series lead. Though it was apparent that the Tigers were missing their main run producer in Hank Greenberg, they had won again and were a single win away from their first World Series Championship.

GAME 5—WRIGLEY FIELD
OCTOBER 6TH 1935*

The weather today was unseasonably cold for baseball, as it has been throughout this battle of the lake cities for the world's title, but after a night of light rains and a morning of heavy rains and a morning of heavy fogs the skies cleared, and a brilliant sun shone down on Wrigley Field as the crowd which in paid attendance totaled 49,237 and contributed $213–$483 to the series fund, descended upon the arena.

It was a gathering that appeared to be hoping for the best, but fearing the worst. It was getting its last view of the series and there was a feeling none could hide that this might also be the last time the 1935 classic would be put on view anywhere.

—John Drebinger, *New York Times*, 10/7/35

. . . .

*Author's note: It is important to note that information on this Game 5 was very difficult to obtain, and pictures of the event even more so. An error in record keeping from this time leaves a small gap in our collective understanding of this game. It is urged that any private collector with original newspapers concerning Game 5 contact the author or other historical society and attempt to fill in this gap, for the sake of posterity.

Interior view of Wrigley Field during the 1935 World Series.
—Photo courtesy of *The Detroit News*

With only one more win needed to take home their first World Series Championship, the Tigers sent Schoolboy Rowe to the mound to face the Cubs' Lon Warneke. The two aces had both pitched in two games already, with Warneke having thrown 11 innings, and Rowe 12. Both had pitched at the end of game 3, which meant that they were pitching on only one full day of rest, an example of durability that is almost unheard of in the modern game.

Besides the two pitchers, the difference-maker in this game would come from a very unlikely source. Chuck Klein, a Cubs outfielder had once been an outstanding hitter, but had faded into near irrelevance over the course of the year. That he was in the lineup for this game at all was due to an injury to Freddie Lindstrom at the end of game four. In the third inning of this game he sent a pitch from Rowe over the fence in right for a two run homer and an early Chicago lead. The two runs seemed like they would be enough as Lon Warneke demonstrated the same mastery over the Tigers that he had shown in his past two outings. The score stayed at 2–0 as Warneke cruised through the fourth, fifth, and sixth innings. It was in the seventh that things got interesting for the Tigers as Charlie Grimm removed his ace from the game, to the shock of all the Cubs' fans in attendance,

Manager Charlie Grimm of the Cubs made one of the grandest and most dramatic gambles in baseball history yesterday when he risked final World Series defeat to save pitcher Lon Warneke's arm. In a truly heroic gesture, Grimm placed the welfare and career of the young man above the glories of a world championship victory and the thousands of dollars that goes to the winning team. Nearly 50,000 fans were stunned when the raucous voice of the loudspeaker swept across Wrigley Field at the beginning of the seventh inning. "Attention please! Attention please!" Boomed Announcer Pat Piper's voice. "Lee is now pitching for Chicago!" A second silence. Then like a rising wind, gasps and ejaculations of amazement surged through the stands and bleachers—wave upon wave. Rookie Bill Lee, who was knocked out of the box in the Series' third game, was going in suddenly—and for no apparent reason—to replace the mighty Warneke. Lee was going in when the Cubs enjoyed only a 2–0 lead of the Tigers—a meager advantage indeed over a club that might go on a batting spree at any minute and tag the Chicagoans with their fourth and final defeat of the series. "What the H___? Has Charlie Grimm gone crazy?" The fans wanted to know. Several minutes later the loud speaker announced that Warneke had injured his shoulder. A massed "Oh___!" of sympathy greeted this explanation.

Warneke could have pitched out the game, the lean, sandy faced Arkansas right hander admitted in the noisy Cubs' dressing room after the game. "In fact I wanted to stay in there throwing, but Grimm wouldn't let me," Warneke said. "I was mighty sore when he took me out. It was one game I wanted to last through. So much was at stake." But Grimm never hesitated, despite the tremendous stakes involved. "As soon as catcher Gabby Hartnett told me, at the end of the sixth, that Lonnie had pulled a muscle in his shoulder, I

"Magic Eye" of Schoolboy Rowe. This Detroit star pitched great the entire series but was foiled by the Cubs' Warneke twice. Schoolie pitched 21 innings all told, completing two full games, striking out 14 while walking only 1 batter and a series E.R.A. of 2.57.

—Photo courtesy of *The Detroit News*
Obtained through the use of the Alan Feldman Collection

Two owners shaking hands. P.K. Wrigley (left), shakes hands with Frank Navin as Mrs. Navin looks on.
—*Detroit Times* photo/courtesy of *The Detroit News*

Detroit Manager Mickey Cochrane (in street clothes) watches the Cubs take batting practice before an unidentified World Series game.
—*Detroit Times* photo/courtesy of *The Detroit News*

Cubs 1935 World Series Program
—By permission of the Baseball Hall of Fame

"Magic Eye" of Lon Warneke. Warneke proved to be the most dominating pitcher in this World Series, pitching 16.2 innings and allowing only 1 run for a microscopic 0.54 E.R.A. In this game 5 he would face Schoolboy Rowe for the second time in the series.

—Photo courtesy of *The Detroit Times*

yanked him right out of the game. Listen—the arm and the future of that pitcher mean a lot more to me than any world championship. After all, we're human beings in baseball, and it's the man that counts in the game—not the won or lost percentages or the gate receipts."

—Jack Cuddy, *The Detroit News*, 10/7/35

Removing the dominant Warneke and bringing in the shaky Bill Lee immediately changed the complexion of the game. Warneke had only given up three hits in six innings without walking a single batter. In his three innings of work Lee gave up four hits while walking two; and in the process gave up a run on a Pete Fox single. But after three nerve racked innings Lee had held the Tigers at bay. The Cubs offense had even helped him out with another run when Bill Herman tripled in Augie Galan.

The Cubs had won 3–1 despite a fine performance by Rowe who pitched his second complete game of the Series. The Schoolboy again the victim of poor Tiger run support. If anything else positive could be taken from this game, it was that the Tigers were leaving Chicago with a 3–2 lead in the series and they could now win the Championship at home.

GAME 6—NAVIN FIELD
OCTOBER 7TH 1935

There was the merry howl of the mob. Cow bells jingled. Leather lungs must have vibrated under the pressure being applied. Possibly there has never been a more crazy crowd at an American sporting event than the one at Navin Field today. The sun was playing hide and seek during most of the game. There was still a chill in the air, but not nearly so much as in other games. It was the best baseball day of the series. The crowd was by far the most colorful of the series. They came "loaded for bear," or maybe "loaded for Cubs." Noisy happy and carefree, they were set for "the kill."

—Bob Murphy, *Detroit Evening Times*, 10/7/35

Game 6 would be the closest, hardest fought and most dramatic game of the entire World Series. Tommy Bridges started for the Tigers and Larry French took the hill for the Cubs. This game would be a back and forth contest with both teams combining for 24 hits. The surprising thing was that despite all the hits it was a fairly low scoring affair, and both pitchers had complete games. The Tigers began the scoring in the first inning with a Pete Fox double scoring Mickey Cochrane. The Cubs tied it in the third

Photo of bleacherites in left-field during the World Series. Then as now, a special bunch: "And of course there were the bleacherites seated in left-field and making a racket from start to finish at every game. They were a rowdy lot and were there to let off steam."

—Charlie Gehringer
—*Associated Press* photo

"Magic Eye" of Tommy Bridges. Starting pitcher for the Tigers in Game 6.
—*Detroit Times* photo/courtesy of *The Detroit News*

when Bill Herman hit a single to score Bill Jurges from second. A sacrifice by Bridges in the fourth gave the Tigers a temporary lead that lasted until the fifth, when Herman lined a two-run homer into the leftfield bleachers to give the Cubs the lead 3–2. In the sixth Marv Owen's first and only hit of the series scored Billy Rogell to tie the game and set up one of the most amazing finishes in the history of the World Series. With both teams tied going into the ninth inning the Cubs came up first. The Cubs third baseman, Stan Hack, hit a leadoff triple and the entire Tiger faithful let out a collective gasp. With the winning run

ninety feet away their hopes now rested on the arm of Tommy Bridges and the gutsy ace of the Tigers responded. First he struck Jurges out, and then induced French into a weak grounder back to the mound. The final out came with a loud ovation when Augie Galan hit a weak pop fly to Goose Goslin in left field. Could the Tigers win it in the ninth? Indeed they could! The leadoff batter Flea Clifton struck out, but Cochrane beat out an infield single to Herman. Gehringer hit a grounder to the first baseman Cavaretta, who touched first but couldn't get the throw to second in time to get Cochrane. Now

Stan Hack's leadoff triple in the ninth over Gee Walker's head set the stage for one of the greatest clutch pitching performances of any World Series. In this picture, Walker and Fox are in pursuit of the ball which lies in the deepest corner of the park. (Inset) Tommy Bridges pitching the ninth.

—*Detroit Times* photo/courtesy of *The Detroit News*

Two perspectives of the same dramatic finish. (Above) Goose Goslin's base hit with two outs in the ninth, scores Mickey Cochrane from second as Pete Fox gives him the "all clear" sign. The $60,000 (bottom left), refers to the amount of money earned by the Tigers for winning the World Series, a tremendous amount in the depression era.

—*Detroit Times* photos/courtesy of *The Detroit News*

—Photo Courtesy of *The Detroit News*

Cochrane advancing on a single by Gehringer in the first inning. Cochrane would advance on a very similar play later in the game to set up one of the greatest finishes in World Series history.

—*Detroit Times* photo/courtesy of *The Detroit News*

"Dejected but scrappy." Cubs walking off the field at the end of Game 6.

—*Detroit Times* photo/courtesy of *The Detroit News*

Goslin; man on second, two outs, bottom of the ninth-laced the base hit over the second baseman's head, giving Cochrane just enough time to speed home from second, and sending the city of Detroit into delirium!

Goslin's hit to drive in Mickey Cochrane was a moment in the history of the Tigers (and the city) that, despite the passing of more than 70 years, should be etched in the minds of every fan;

> *It was something to see—Mickey Cochrane stabbing his spikes into the plate with the winning run and his [team's] first world's championship, and then going mad, like a young colt, leaping and cavorting about, shaking his bare, dark head. He ran all the way back to the screen then whirled in a dance of victory, hurling himself into the arms of his players, punching and thumping them, reeling to the utmost of his buoyant, exuberant Irish nature in the victory for which he had fought so hard. When Cochrane stood on second, a lone figure in white, I have never seen such will and energy from a single person. He **had** to come home. He **willed** to come home. I believe if Goslin hadn't hit he would have stolen home from second base.*

> —Paul Gallico, in Joe Falls,
> *Baseball's Great Teams*

It's hard to imagine why such a dramatic ending to a World Series is not ranked up in the top endings of all time. Especially since it was the first in the history of this proud franchise. Every year around World Series time, one media outlet or another will rank the top five or ten dramatic wins of all-time and this ending is never even considered. The combination of "Goose" Goslin's game winning hit and the game saving stop by Tommy Bridges should easily be considered for *the best* combination of offensive and defensive clutch performances of all-time. Further consideration should also be given to the fact that the Tiger's lost the M.V.P. of baseball in the second game. His replacement (Flea Clifton) went hitless for the entire series and yet they still won. The performance by the Tigers in overcoming this loss should definitely be considered as one of the savviest examples of team play in World Series' history. One other important thing to note is that despite Clifton going hitless, he still received cheers during the last game, a testament to the character of the fans. One thing that can never be overlooked was the celebration that ensued after this win, a celebration the likes of which the city of Detroit had never witnessed before.

SCENES OF CELEBRATION FOR A WORLD SERIES CHAMPION

Immediately after Cochrane crossed the plate and the team had started celebrating, the fans began their celebration. For a Depression-weary people they took full advantage of this opportunity.

> *Fans streamed out of the stands and Tiger bleachers, blotting out the field and front of the dugout. Police had to block them off or they would have streamed into the dugout and clubhouse.*

> —Bud Shaver, *Detroit Evening Times*, 10/7/35

> *Let Time's ancient bough shed decaying worlds as the rattle of machine guns echoes along Ethiopian trails. This makes no difference at all in the city that waited and won at last—from a dynasty of Hughie Jennings, Ty Cobb, Sam Crawford, and Wild Bill Donovan to that title winning punch that Goose Goslin fired in the ninth as Mickey Cochrane delivered the big run in person. After a brief sporting span of some 25 years, that jungle-throated roar from 48,000 human throats as Goslin singled and Cochrane scored is one of the reverberations I won't forget. It was the pent-up vocal outbreak of nearly 50 years and it exploded with the suppressed power of nitroglycerine when the big moment came.*

> —Grantland Rice, in Joe Falls,
> *Baseball's Great Teams*

> *Before 6 PM every downtown street was jammed with scores of thousands of milling, shouting, singing celebrants. By 7:30 o'clock it had become about impossible to move traffic. The streets were lined from curb to curb with motor cars, all with horns going constantly. The motor traffic was so blocked and snarled that cars moved less than a*

The Tigers rush into the dugout as fans pour onto the field.
—Photo courtesy of *The Detroit News*

Moments after the Tigers' first World Series Championship, the field was mobbed by these fans.
—*Detroit Times* photo/Courtesy of *The Detroit News*

—*Detroit Times* photo/Courtesy of *The Detroit News*

Radiating from the scene of victory, the celebrations carried out into the streets and allowed people to forget about the depression. The following pictures speak for themselves.
—Photo courtesy of *The Detroit News*

—*Detroit Times* photo/Courtesy of *The Detroit News*

—Photos courtesy of *The Detroit News*

Three heroes hug following their World Series victory. (Left to right) Mickey Cochrane, Goose Goslin, and Tommy Bridges.
—Photo courtesy of *The Detroit News*

block in an hour. Street cars and buses were in the same condition. Hundreds of impatient fans actually abandoned their automobiles as near a curb as they could, and joined the mobs afoot. These abandoned cars—some of them in the center of streets—added, of course, to the indescribable confusion. It was a good-natured confusion though. Ticker tape, torn telephone books, confetti and odd papers of all descriptions were ankle deep on downtown streets a few minutes after Cochrane scored the winning run. Police reserves were called out. Sirens screamed. Horns started honking, not to cease until daylight. Thousands began to invade the loop district.

On Griswold Street, Detroit's Wall Street, paper in the air appeared as snow. On Washington Boulevard, especially near the Book-Cadillac Hotel, baseball-mad fans congregated. Cars packed the streets. It would have been possible to cross Woodward Avenue by walking from car to car without stepping into the street. The noise increased. Horns honked incessantly. One young fellow parked his car in an alley off State Street, between Washington Boulevard and Griswold Street, inserted a pin at the side of the horn button, and let it go. High-schoolish young men roared around and around the popular corners blasting the exhausts of their cars with banging crashes. Merchants sold out of their Halloween stock of horns and other orange and black noise

makers. Tin pans, rattles, squawkers, whistles, and all other types of din producers were put into play. Bar rooms were packed. Downtown hotels turned their main dining rooms into cocktail-lounges.

—*Detroit Evening Times* editorial, 10/8/35

Even the City Hall clock went haywire. It had been sounding regularly for 15 years, ringing every hour on the hour. Now it was clanging every sixty seconds. An exuberant fan had climbed into the tower and changed the timer.

Then the inhabitants of this great city of more than a million began to boil. The street scenes that night were never matched before in a World Series. No city ever went as mad over baseball as Detroit. There was a rush to the central part of the city. Pedestrians blew tin horns and motorists honked those on the cars as they snailed through the downtown streets almost hopelessly clogged with the product that has earned Detroit world-wide fame. Facades of buildings were draped with ticker tape, the streets cushioned with confetti. Toward midnight the din increased instead of abating. The discharge of firecrackers and bombs, the staccato barks of backfiring cars and shrieks of sirens and blasts of horns kept on in continuous roar to early morning. Guests in downtown hotels could not sleep until three hours after midnight. Even machine guns were rigged up in office windows to add to the noise. Natives of Detroit admitted that the noise and clamor were greater than on Armistice night [after WWI]. When merrymakers through sheer exhaustion finally decided it was time for bed, the city looked as if a cyclone had hit it. All the next day, the whitewings were employed cleaning up the litter.

—*Reach Official American League
Base Ball Guide*, 1936

The streets downtown became rivers of confetti. Out of the windows of tall and seemingly sedate buildings came streams of this and that. Telephone books, ticker tape and blue prints went flying to the highways. Credit papers and the last wills and testaments of distinguished landholders *were trampled underfoot. Traffic became a hopeless mess. Back-firing was the order of the evening. A snake dance was held in Capitol Park right after Cochrane scored and the hugest Laocoon group in history got itself terribly involved. Reserve police were called out. Goose Goslin couldn't get to the Book-Cadillac Hotel where he lives and where he wanted to enjoy a quiet cup of coffee for his nerves. The City Hall clock started to strike some hour or other and found it couldn't stop. It got to be 1935 o'clock. World Series time.*

—George Stark, *The Detroit News,* 10/8/35

From these many different sources it is easy to see the excitement that resulted from the Tigers winning their first World Series. The fact that there was a celebration of this magnitude taking place in the midst of the Depression is also amazing but these eye witness accounts definitely show how much joy was brought to the city because of the Tigers.

Detroit Tiger Testimonial

The day following the World Series Championship, the city of Detroit held a testimonial dinner for the Tigers at the Book-Cadillac Hotel. The dinner was open to the public and the 800 people who attended (tickets were $5.00 a head), witnessed a unique setup. The main tables were arranged in the shape of a diamond. Cochrane was placed at the head of the diamond or "home plate," the rest of the Tigers were seated around the diamond by position. Hank Greenberg at "first plate," Charlie Gehringer at "second plate," and so on. The rest of the attendees were seated around the diamond or on the "bench." It was an event for the fan or at least the fans that could get out of bed after the night before! It was designed to be a fun laid-back event where the *"captains of industry sat down at the same table with Detroit's barbers and bakers."* According to the Detroit Times who covered the event, it was a night of much *"howling and merry-making,"* where all the players had a chance to speak (if they wanted). Harvey Campbell acted as toast-master of the ceremony along with Mickey Cochrane, who introduced the players and tried to goad each one of them into saying at least a few

(Left to right) Tommy Bridges, General Crowder and Goose Goslin talk during the Detroit Tiger Testimonial dinner.
—*Detroit Times* photo/Courtesy of *The Detroit News*

words. Campbell's best line of the night captured the idea of how sports could help heal the city's financial woes; *"Let's all of Detroit get the 'Mickey Cochrane' spirit. We'll be as unbeatable in the business and financial world as the Tigers are on the field of battle."* Each of the players took turns saluting the city and the fans for all of their support. Even the batboy Joe Roggin got a chance to speak and he told the jovial crowd how he *"was the luckiest and happiest boy in the world."* Cochrane came through with a rather amusing anecdote when he joked that he was going to Wyoming to look for bigger game than the Cubs, *"probably grizzly bears,"* said the laughing manager. Even umpire George Moriarty was at the dinner, and his controversial part in the World Series being well known, was the subject of much humor. Of the suitcases he received as a gift he said; *"If this had been given to me by another team I could mention, I would figure to open it and find a one-way ticket to Siberia."*

The Tiger players were presented with many different types of gifts from different Detroit businesses including: radios, dressing gowns, pen sets, rawhide bags and boxes of candy for their wives. While Frank Navin received the most interesting gift, as People's Outfitting Company presented him with a Tiger skin rug for his office.

It was at this dinner that Frank Navin made the announcement that over the winter Navin Field would be expanded by 12,000 seats at a cost of $500,000. The resulting expansion of the stadium would keep hundreds of men employed during the winter and would provide another example of how invested the Tigers were in the

Umpire and former Tiger George Moriarty was present at the dinner and was the subject of much humor for his role in helping bring the Tigers their first World Series Championship.

—*Detroit Times* photo/Courtesy of *The Detroit News*

Mickey Cochrane posing next to a rug given to Frank Navin by the People's Outfitting Company. The rug was 10.5 by 15 feet, with a 42 inch Tiger in the middle. The company thought it appropriate that "the head Tiger of them all have a rug for his lair."

—*Detroit Times* photo/Courtesy of *The Detroit News*

Mickey Cochrane and Frank Navin at the Testimonial Dinner.

—*Detroit Times* photo/Courtesy of *The Detroit News*

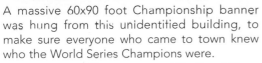

A massive 60x90 foot Championship banner was hung from this unidentified building, to make sure everyone who came to town knew who the World Series Champions were.

—Photos courtesy of *The Detroit Newss*

1935 World Series Champions, The Detroit Tigers.
—Photo Courtesy of the Detroit Tigers

community. It was said of the dinner that night, "*It was a championship climax to a championship season and not a single Tiger missed anything that came over the "plate.*"

FUTURE GENERATIONS WILL NEVER FORGET . . .

In the years to come, when the myriad fans assembled there, are in their easy chairs before the fire they will tell this story to their children. They will tell the story not only of the galloping Goose, who fired the shot, but they will sing the saga of Tommy Bridges. Tommy who took a leaf out of good old General Crowder's manual of arms and pitched with a courage the amazed spectators never believed could reside in so frail a frame . . . And we graybeards of the years to come will be telling our children and our children's children how poetic justice once descended on Navin Field as the long October shadow fell softly across its broad green carpet, how it fell over the slender shoulders of Tommy Bridges like a mantle and how it draped it-

self about the broad proportions of the Goose and Mickey Cochrane, two battle-scarred heroes of many a World Series contest whose combined talents produced the run that brought the World Championship to Detroit. We will be telling too about Flea Clifton and Marv Owen; Owen who made but one hit in the whole series, but who made it when it counted most, when it had to be done to keep the Tigers in the ball game.

We were telling you about the wounded Greenberg and the crippled infield that battled its way to glory, about Gehringer and Rogell and Fox and Walker and all the others. Because there is today glory enough for all. The story of this final thrilling game is in the records now. But the greybeards of the years to come will never lose its pulsing drama and they will be the historians who will tell future generations the glamorous background that will make the World Series of 1935 live as long as baseball lives.

Such exploits as this World Series produced need retrospect to be truly appreciated they gather sanctity with the years. But this is today and today

"Mickey Cochrane had a way of reaching men's minds, bodies and souls. He was the right guy, in the right place at the right time. Detroit badly needed a man like him to lead the Tigers. He was more than a man catching for a ball club. He was more than a man managing a ball club. He was a symbol-as strained as that may sound-a symbol of hope for a city down on its luck. If Black Mike could do it, well, the rest of us could do it. That's what people say it was like in Detroit in the 1930's."

—Joe Falls in Baseball's Greatest Teams, Detroit Tigers
Photo courtesy of *The Detroit News*

The Tigers were given Championship rings to commemorate their World Series Championship, this particular example comes from the baseball Hall-of-Fame.
—*Photo by permission of the Baseball Hall-of-Fame.*

we tell the world. Monday night we told the world and today we have a slight headache. But the headache doesn't crowd out the memory of Monday night.

—George Stark, *The Detroit News*, 10/8/35

This article by George Stark of The Detroit News leaves little doubt how important this first World Series title was to Tiger fans of this era. It also captures the importance of 'why' we should take a fresh look at this. To the people of this time there was no doubt that it would live on in the memory of every Detroit fan simply because the grandfathers and fathers would pass it down through stories. The question remains as to why it has faded from our collective memories so badly? The answer I believe, is that many of the people who lived at this time are now gone. The very people who George Stark assumed "would tell this story to their children"

lived through a depression and fought in a World War. Many people may have recounted the importance of this story to their children, but still many others didn't. Seventy-three years have passed since this time, long enough to cloud the memory of even the most diehard Tiger fans, leaving the charge of recounting these events to a new generation. It would be to the eternal shame of every Tiger fan, if this story would continue to sit on the shelf and gather dust until it disappeared completely from our memory.

This first World Series championship was very important for the Tiger franchise. In beating the Cubs, they were able to shake the monkey off their backs that had existed since the first two Series' losses in 1907 and 1908. No longer would this rival city be able to brag about a clean sweep of the Tigers. It also removed the monkey of a fact that Detroit had not won a championship in the modern era (the title won in 1887 came before the first World Series in 1903). By winning their first championship, a precedent was established that allowed the city to look forward to its next title. Little did the people of Detroit know they wouldn't have to wait a year to celebrate that next title, in fact they wouldn't even have to wait two months. The new professional football franchise that had arrived in town only the year before, was putting a season together that would continue the parade of championships; and give the city of Detroit an early Christmas gift.

THE DETROIT LIONS

ORIGINS

Football is an institution in Detroit, with sellout crowds coming to watch the Lions win or lose every Sunday. The Thanksgiving game every year has become as much a part of the holiday as the turkey. But football in Detroit has not always been. In fact the early history of pro-football in the city was marred by failure upon failure of teams trying to put down roots. In the early part of the twentieth-century it was college football that reigned supreme. The University of Michigan had already asserted its dominance in the new sport, but football was still viewed mainly as a collegiate game. However, as personalities and stars emerged from these amateur ranks, interest began to generate for professional gridiron games.

The first attempt at establishing a football team in the city was in 1920 with the Detroit Heralds. They were charter members of the American Professional Football Association, the organization that would morph over the next few years into the league we now know as the National Foot-

ball League. The Heralds were a sad sack team who underwhelmed fans with a first-year record of 1(WIN)–3(LOSS). The following year fared no better for the team as they won only one out of seven games 1(WIN)–5(LOSS)–1(TIE). The poor play and lack of interest resulted in the team folding after only two years. The next team to appear was the Detroit Panthers in 1925. This team fared better in the standings with an 8–2–2 (2ND PLACE) record its first year, but slipped below mediocrity in 1926 with a 4–6–2 (12th PLACE) record. This team also folded after only two years. Seeking to draw a little good fortune from the name of the successful university team, the Detroit Wolverines emerged in 1928. The team was built around several older players from the city and one of the game's early superstars, Benny Friedman. Friedman had been the star player for the University of Michigan and his skills of running, and especially throwing the football, guided the Detroit squad to a successful seven win inaugural season (7–2–1 3RD PLACE). Considered the first great passer in pro-football history, his 20 touchdown passes in

1932 photo of the Portsmouth Spartans playing the Greenbay Packers.
—Photo courtesy of the Detroit Lions

The First Lions team, 1934.
—Photo courtesy of the Detroit Lions

1929 would set the record until 1942. Unfortunately for the city, his 20 touchdown season came with the New York Giants, as the team had been purchased by Giants owner Tim Mara. The owner had in fact purchased the whole Detroit Wolverine team for the purpose of acquiring Friedman. Several years would pass before Detroit would get its next Pro Football team. But little did anyone know that the groundwork for that team was being laid at that moment in the town of Portsmouth, Ohio.

The Portsmouth Spartans officially became a team for the 1930 NFL season. Their first season was subpar with a 5–6–3 record, but the second year was much more successful as they ended up in second place with an 11–3 record. That the team was much improved in 1931 was due to its acquisitions of three new players. The first was Earl "Dutch" Clark, an All-American quarterback at Colorado College. He won the NFL's rookie-of-the-year award in 1931 and would go on to be a perennial All-Pro throughout the course of his Hall-of-Fame career. Grover "Ox" Emerson, a stalwart offensive guard from the University of Texas, was a rookie in 1931 and quickly became a force in the league. The other rookie was George "Tarzan" Christensen from the University of Oregon. Christensen was considered *"one of the most highly respected linemen"* in the league. As a two way player (offense and defense), he consistently received All-Pro recognition, and along with Dutch Clark and Ox Emerson was named to the NFL All Decade team for the 1930's.

In 1932, the team finished with a record worse (6–1–4) than in 1931 but they managed to finish tied with

the Chicago Bears for 1st place. At the time, there was no championship contest so a special game had to be created to decide who would take the league title. Chicago ended up winning the game and the title by the close score of 9–0. The popularity of the championship game led the league to split itself into two divisions, Eastern and Western, in order to have a title matchup every year.

1933 was the final year for the Portsmouth Spartans. Despite their success, the financial pinch of the Great Depression had been playing havoc on the team. One of the first casualties of the poor state of the teams' finances came when the team's best player Dutch Clark retired and took a job as the athletic director of the Colorado School of Mines. The Depression realities for this small town team were further evident in the revenue drawn from fan attendance. The team would regularly draw 5,000 people to watch the free practices but only 2,000 paying customers for the games. The crunch was getting so bad that players were receiving shares of stock in the team to subsidize their salaries. After a 6–5 season, the team began negotiations for a move to a new city.

The effort to bring the Spartans to Detroit was led by George Richards, the owner of the WJR radio station. The NFL had longed to see a team in Detroit, as it was a large city with a dense population, and it was viewed as an attractive and untapped market. On April 9th at a luncheon at the Hotel Statler, Richards and a group of investors were granted permission to move the franchise to Detroit. The new owners had to settle the teams' debt, which was $7,952.08, before purchasing the team outright for

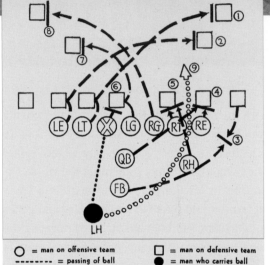

Diagram (right) and the demonstration of the same play (above) shows the effectiveness of the "single-wing" offense at focusing power to a weak point of the defense. Using this offense the 1936 Lions set the NFL single season rushing record with 2,885 yards. A record that stood until the 1972 Dolphins broke it with the help of an extra two games. (The league had just added two games to the schedule).

○ = man on offensive team   ☐ = man on defensive team
‑ ‑ ‑ ‑ = passing of ball   ● = man who carries ball
▄ ▄ ▄ = course of players other than ball carrier
○ ○ ○ ○ = course of man with ball

the sum of $15,000. This amount could not have seemed too much for the group of investors who would become the first owners of the Lions; as there were 23 prominent members of the syndicate. Of the 23 members, six were high-ranking Detroit businessmen in different auto companies, prompting a joke from newspaper writer William F. Fox Jr., "*Potsy [Clark] (coach of the Spartans/Lions) will sure have a tough time deciding what kind of car he should own after a few meetings of the board.*"

Because of the previous failures, moving a team into the city was seen as a gamble. Especially at this time (1934) when the Tigers were having a great season and the city was going "baseball crazy." Rather than compete against the baseball team, Richards wanted to associate his team *with* them, to improve the odds of success. It was for this reason that he kept with the jungle theme of the Tigers when he renamed the team the "Detroit Lions." In an interview by Jerry Green with the NFL's oldest player, it was Glenn Presnell (former Spartan and Lion tailback) and his wife who chose the jersey colors which are still the same to this day, "*He (George Richards) showed us several jerseys on a table, my wife and I picked the Honolulu Blue and Silver.*" Richards's next step was to give his coach Potsy Clark enough money to lure Dutch Clark (no relation) out of retirement. With Dutch back in the fold, the team was ready for its inaugural year in Detroit.

The team that played that first season in 1934 had the same roster as the team which had been so competitive

in Portsmouth. Alongside Dutch Clark, Ox Emerson and George Christensen the team fielded an excellent lineup: Jack Johnson (tackle), Maury Bodenger (guard), and Clare Randolph (center), Regis Monaghan, Tom Hupke, and "Long" John Schneller rounded out the offensive line. The skill positions consisted of Leroy "Ace" Gutowsky (fullback), Ernie Caddel (wing back), Roy "Father" Lumpkin (blocking back) and Glenn Presnell (tailback, quarterback). Harry Ebding and Ed Klewicki were the "ends," or wide receivers as they're known in today's game.

Photo of Potsy Clark "the little Colonel", coach of the Portsmouth Spartans and first coach of the Detroit Lions.

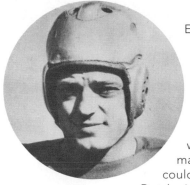

Earl "Dutch" Clark, Quarterback. The Lions' first "superstar," Clark was a supremely talented runner and was always near the top of the league in rushing. According to his teammates though it wasn't raw talent that made him great: "No one could follow a block like Dutch. He wasn't the fastest or biggest back, but he was very smart and a true field general." Clark was the first Lion elected to the Hall-of-Fame, a charter member of the first class of 17-inducted in 1963.

—Photo courtesy of *The Detroit News*
Obtained through the use of the Alan Feldman Collection

Ernie Caddel, Left halfback. Always an outstanding runner and receiver, Caddel led the lions in both categories in 1935, rushing 87 times for 450 yards and catching 10 passes for 171 yards. An interview by Bob Murphy (Detroit Times) with Potsy Clark, explained the value of Caddel to the Lions: "He's the greatest man running to his left I've ever seen," said Potsy. "A fine defensive back, one of the greatest pass receivers in the business, does the kicking off for us, and a few other little odds and ends. Did you know that Caddel completed four of the six passes he attempted? Well, he did, and all four went for touchdowns."

—Photo courtesy of *The Detroit News*
Obtained through the use of the Alan Feldman Collection

William "Bill" McKalip, End. Talented defensive end for the early Lions teams, he played his college ball at Oregon St.

—Photo courtesy of *The Detroit News* Obtained through the use of the Alan Feldman Collection

Clare Randolph, Center. Linemen, then as now were never given the same publicity as the "skill positions," prompting Bob Murphy (Detroit Times) to say: "every team has their unsung heroes, and Randolph is number one of the "unsungers" in my book."

—Photo courtesy of *The Detroit News* Obtained through the use of the Alan Feldman Collection

Glen Presnell, Quarterback. Oftentimes overshadowed by the famous Dutch Clark, Presnell was one of the best ever. He was a better passer and kicker than Clark, and when he retired he held the Lions record for the longest field goal in club history. His record 54 yard field goal was the only score in a 1934 game, beating the Packers and was not broken until 1995, when Jason Hanson kicked a 57 yarder.

Roy "Father" Lumpkin. Though Lumpkin only played for the Lions in 1934, his services with the organization dated back into their days as the Portsmouth Spartans. A tough half back, he was a key man for the Lions defense that didn't give up a point until the eighth game of the season. The Lions of 1934 fielded one of the greatest defenses ever, giving up (on average) less than a touchdown a game.

Leroy "Ace" Gutowsky, Fullback. Another member of the Lions' talented backfield, Glen Presnell said of him: "Ace was a wonderful fullback, he had the fastest start of any in the game. We had a lot of spinner plays and he could spin and hit back into the line as fast as anybody I've ever seen."
—(Quote from an interview of Presnell by Richard Wittingham in *What a Game They Played*)

Chuck Bernard, Center. Bernard was an All-American from the University of Michigan and was a valuable member of the interior line.

Tom Hupke, Guard. Though small by today's standards, Hupke used every bit of his 5 foot 10-1/2 inch frame to open holes for the Lions backs.

Grover "Ox" Emerson, Offensive and defensive Guard. One of the key linemen for the Lions. He was a stalwart two way contributor out of the University of Texas.

Jack Johnson, Left tackle. One of the largest men of the early Detroit Lions teams, Johnson stood at 6 foot 4 and was a valuable contributor, especially on the offensive side of the ball.

Harry Ebding, Right End. A St. Mary's College product who enjoyed a solid four-year Lions career. He was the team's receiving leader in 1934, with 9 receptions for 257 yards.

Grid and Iron, the Lions first mascots. They were donated by John Millen of the Detroit Zoo.
—Photo courtesy of the Detroit Lions

THE DETROIT LIONS

Frank Christensen, Fullback. Another member of the Lions talented backfield, Christensen was the best punter on the team. Here he is shown practicing his craft.

George "Tarzan" Christensen. Captain, Offensive/Defensive tackle and the most physically feared player on the Lions.

The reason the team had so many backs was because the Lions (just like most teams at this time) played in an offensive formation called "the single wing." This type of offense is not used in professional football any longer although it is still used in several high schools and colleges across the nation. Though there are many variations of the "single wing," the principal remains the same. With three or four backs in the backfield, the center would snap the ball directly to any one of them. Usually the snap would go to the quarterback/tailback who was considered the lynchpin of the offense, because it was he who had to be a triple threat (run/pass/kick). This offense used deception and misdirection in order to focus power towards a defensive weakness. Defenses at the time predominantly played in a "5–3" formation (5 defensive linemen, 3 linebackers) with many of the offensive players also playing on the defense. This "iron

man" football, where players play both offense and defense is brutal, especially over the course of a 12–13 game season, and still inspires a sense of awe from modern-day players and fans.

Before the Lions even played a game in Detroit, a tremendous amount of effort went into marketing the team to potential fans. A radio show on WJR had Potsy Clark as a frequent guest, while the team made appearances in three different newsreels that appeared in 100 theatres. They also advertised in countless periodicals and newspapers. The team held youth training camps to try and bond with the community, and leading up to the first game sent out invitations to many prominent Detroit celebrities and civic leaders. A final addition to the team was provided by John Millen of the Detroit Zoo, who gave the Lions their first mascots. Two lion cubs named "Grid and Iron," would provide a physical reminder for fan and foe alike that there were new cats in Detroit and they were about to grow into kings of the pro-football jungle!

1934 Season and 1st Thanksgiving game

The Lions first game was played on September 23, 1934, at the University of Detroit Stadium and resulted in a 9–0 victory over the New York Giants. Besides being the first win ever for the team, it was also the first shutout of a string of seven consecutive shutouts in their inaugural season. To put it mildly, the Lions came out and dominated in 1934, winning their first ten games in a row. Along with the string of wins came the fan support. The first game of the season the team drew 12,000 paying fans, while the twelfth game they drew 26,000.

There was also a little extra significance to this twelfth game of the season. The Lions record was 10–1 (the Green Bay Packers having broken their win streak the week before; 3–0) and they were very much in championship contention as they faced the 11–0 Bears. Also, this would be the first Thanksgiving game hosted by the Lions. The game was made even more relevant by the fact that it would be the first football game broadcast on the radio, coast-to-coast. George Richards had thought up the idea hoping to get more exposure for the league. He used his connections at WJR; and along with NBC president Deke Aylesworth, set up a ninety-four station broadcasting network that would allow everyone from New York to California to listen to this important "clash of the titans" live matchup.

By the grace of Jack Manders' mighty toe and the clicking of two scintillating forward passes [the]

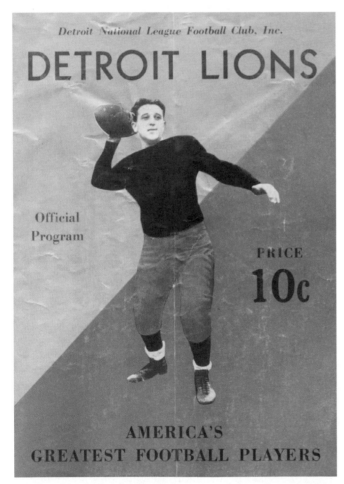

Program cover for the first Lions game-September 23, 1934. Pictured on the cover is Harry Newman of the New York Giants, another of the game's first stars. The Lions won that first game, beating the Giants 9–0.

1935 advertisement for WJR. The owner of this radio station, George (Dick) Richards, was responsible for bringing the Lions to Detroit. The increasing demands for radio entertainment, helped push the capabilities of the radio which in turn improved communication throughout the country.

—*Detroit Times* photo/Courtesy of *The Detroit News*

Chicago Bears today rule all that is great in the West in professional football.

Manders millionaire toe from Minnesota yesterday in University of Detroit Stadium was the steel-bladed weapon that spelled the difference in points between two super-football machines, paving the way to a tremendous victory over the Detroit Lions, 19–16, in a thrill-saturated pigskin tussle—a tussle the like of which has been rare, if equaled on the gridirons of a football minded nation.

Twenty-six thousand persons witnessed the spectacle—26,000 minor characters in gridiron drama, a crowd enthralled and pitched to fever heat as act upon act of football at its finest was paraded before their eyes.

—Leo Macdonell, *Detroit Times,* 11/30/34

The game was a back-and-forth struggle which captivated listeners. Though it ended in a 19–16 loss for the Lions, a precedent for live coast-to-coast games had been established and more games would be transmitted. The significance of this radio broadcast should not be overlooked, as it was innovations like these that increased the communication capabilities of the entire country. The radio industry in the 1930's was beginning to take off and one of the things that listeners wanted was sports. By giving listeners what they wanted, the networks made money for themselves and drove them to create more networks in order to reach more people, tying the country more closely together. That the country could communicate so rapidly over the radio would prove to be especially important when World War II came about in 1941.

The loss to the Bears on Thanksgiving, coupled with a loss to the same Chicago club the following week (10–7) left the Lions in second place despite a very successful 10–3 inaugural season.

1935 SEASON

The Lions entered the 1935 season full of optimism. Much like the Tigers; the Lions had come very close to championship glory in 1934. Also, like the Tigers, the Lions were returning their core of players from the previous season. In fact, with the exception of "Father" Lumpkin, the entire Lions roster was returning. The Lions started out the season on September 20th with a very encouraging 35–0 mauling of the Philadelphia Eagles, but this season would be much more competitive than the last.

Photo from the 1935 Thanksgiving game shows an unidentified Lions back grinding his way through the Bears line.

—Photo courtesy of the Detroit Lions.

same Packer team (20–10) that had already beaten them twice.

A game ten tie to the Chicago Bears (10–10) gave them that ever precious gift going into their second Thanksgiving game, hope. They would have to face the same Chicago Bears for the second week in a row, in a game that would have extra importance for several reasons. The Lions, (even when they were the Portsmouth Spartans), had not beaten the Bears in the last eight attempts dating back to the 1931 season. The prestige factor was also very high, as this game was going to be broadcast coast-to-coast, another loss to the Bears would have been embarrassing. The final most important reason for the Lions to win this game, was that all of their hopes for a try at the championship would be gone with one more loss. 18,000 fans at the University of Detroit Stadium and a nation of radio listeners, were witnesses to the Bears' loss by the score of 14–2.

You're only as good as your competition? Well the Lions had plenty of it. Chicago's Bronko Nagurski (right), was the most difficult man in football to tackle, and Curly Lambeau (above) of the Packers, were two of the early legends of Professional Football.
—Associated Press Photo

Game 2 at home against the Chicago Cardinals was a 10–10 tie. The Lions next three games were on the road and began with a loss (10–12) to the Brooklyn Dodgers, followed by a win over the Boston Redskins (17–7) before losing the third game in Green Bay to the Packers (9–13). The Lions' record improved to 4–2–1, after home victories over the Boston Redskins (14–0), and Chicago Cardinals (7–6). This season was turning out to be a brutal stretch of games for all the teams in the Western Division as no clear favorite emerged and the different clubs battled for first place. The Lions lost their eighth game of the season in Green Bay (7–31) and dropped to last place with only four games remaining in the season. Despite their position in the standings, the Lions knew it was a close race between the four teams in the Western Division, and if they could get some wins they would still be in the championship picture. The very next week they responded by beating the

A crowd of approximately 18,000 cut down by the inclement weather, saw Dutch Clark, Detroit's brilliant captain, again rise to supreme heights to score both of Detroit's touchdowns in a grueling game that was bitterly fought. To win, the Lions played smartly, combining a ground and air attack that for the exception of a brief time in the final period dominated the game.

—Leo Macdonell, *Detroit Times*, 11/29/35

The Bears knew what they were up against early. They started from their 29-yard line, made 27 yards in six plays, putting the ball on the Lions' 44-yard line. The Bears set up their pet play. Nagurski went banging up against the line. Then Molesworth started a buck the same way and tossed a bullet pass over center, in-

Standings

1935 Western Division Final Standings

	Win	Loss	Tie	Win/Loss%	PF	PA
Detroit Lions	7	3	2	.700	191	111
Green Bay Packers	8	4	0	.667	181	96
Chicago Cardinals	6	4	2	.600	99	97
Chicago Bears	6	4	2	.600	192	106

1935 Eastern Division Final Standings

	Win	Loss	Tie	Win/Loss%	PF	PA
New York Giants	9	3	0	.750	180	96
Brooklyn Dodgers	5	6	1	.455	90	141
Pittsburgh Pirates	4	8	0	.333	100	209
Boston Redskins	2	8	1	.200	65	123
Philadelphia Eagles	2	9	0	.182	60	179

A look at the final standings in the western conference shows how close the finish really was

tended to get Nagurski loose beyond the line of scrimmage.

It is the Bears favorite play, but it didn't work. Randoph, who followed Nagurski like a shadow all day, knocked it down. When Nagurski tried hitting the line again, Randolph almost wrenched his head off for a yard loss.

And there was always Clark, ready to run, pass or receive. The Bears never figured him out all day and before it was over tried to get rid of him by breaking him in two.

The Lions had a line, too, with big George Christensen ripping up things like a wild bull. It didn't make much difference who was in there yesterday, whether it was Sam Knox and Ox Emerson at guards, or Regis Monahan and Tom Hupke. Whether Big Chris and Jack Johnson were at tackle or Red Stacy and Jim Steen; Ed Klewicki and Long John Schneller at ends or Butch Morse and crippled Harry Ebding.

That was the kind of a team the Lions were yesterday. They were ready for anything and

stopped one of the most feared running attacks in football and smothered the Bears' passes as well.

The Lions didn't stop at bottling up the other fellows. They went to town themselves, using every weapon in the bag, plucked out with rare judgment by Dutch Clark. Not even when a quick kick was downed on the 1-yard line did the Lions seem worried. They knew their strength, gave the Bears a safety with virtually a contemptuous gesture, a little later after intercepting a pass on the 1-yard line.

By that time there wasn't any doubt about the outcome.

–Bud Shaver, *Detroit Times*, 11/29/35

The result of this game was huge for the Lions, they had eliminated the Bears from title contention and they had given themselves a legitimate shot at going to the championship. The Bears however, would still have a role in deciding who would play in that game. Going into the final game of the season, the Lions needed to beat the Brooklyn Dodgers, and they needed the Bears to beat their cross-town rival Chicago Cardinals. The Lions would get their win with a 28–0 shutout. The following week, the Bears beat the Cardinals 13–0, giving the Lions the Western Division crown. This 1935 season had proved to be a very close race indeed. Only one win separated first and last place. The Cardinals had dropped from first to last place in one week. The Lions' winning percentage was only .33 ahead of the second place Green Bay. Curly Lambeau's Packers had beaten Detroit twice that year and had one more win than the Lions. Because tie games didn't count for or against a team and the Lions had tied twice, the Packers (who had lost one more game) had a lower winning percentage than Detroit. Out of all of this confusion, one thing was certain—the Lions were headed to the Championship game.

NFL CHAMPIONSHIP GAME

On December 15, 1935, at the University of Detroit Stadium, 15,000 fans braved the snow and sleet to watch the NFL Championship game between the hometown Lions and the visiting New York Giants. While the Lions in 1935 had to fight, claw, and battle their way through the Western Division, the Giants had romped their way

The 1935 NFL Championship game was played at the University of Detroit Stadium, first home of the Lions.

to a second consecutive Eastern Conference title. The Giants were coached by one of the game's early innovators (future Hall-of-Famer) Steve Owen, and were looking for their second consecutive NFL championship. The Giants could boast of having one of the best passing offenses in the game to go along with a tough defense that had tied the Packers for giving up the fewest points. Along with their coach, the Giants team included two future Hall-of-Famers in center/linebacker Mel Hein, and triple-threat halfback, Ken Strong. It was the Lions, however, who would demonstrate offensive and defensive prowess on this day.

The rain and sleet would play a major factor in this game as the weather got worse as the game wore on. Generally, when a field gets muddy and slippery, a teams' passing attack is greatly diminished and that was the case for this game. The Lions completed only two passes the whole game, but they came when they needed them. In the opening series, Glen Presnell threw the first, a completion to Frank Christensen. The second, thrown by Ace Gutowsky was caught by Ed Klewicki. These two plays were part of a 61 yard scoring drive that was capped by an Ace Gutowsky touchdown.

The Lions started about their own 39 yard line and Glen Presnell whipped a pass down to Frank Christensen which sent the Lions bounding down the veldt. Then Ace Gutowsky shot one down the center of the field and Ed Klewicki grabbed it as it bounded off a Giants finger tips.

I was glad I was in my seat by that time, because I had a chance to see one of the most astounding pieces of offensive line work that ever occurred on a football field. The ball was somewhere near the 10-yard line and Ace Gutowsky took it on a spinner and went over the goal line for a touchdown without a Giant player so much as pinching the calf of his leg. A spinner, mind you! And not a hand laid on him! When did you ever see a line put on such offensive line charging and blocking as that! And when will you ever see it again?

—Bud Shaver, *Detroit Times*, 12/16/35

The Giants looked as though they would respond in kind, as they drove down the field on their next possession. This drive ended at the Lions 26 yard line when Frank Christensen intercepted Ed Danowski's pass and returned it 28 yards. The following drive lasted only two plays and when it was over the Lions would have their second touchdown,

It was a typical Dutch Clark run and one of the best of the season. Nobody makes that kind of a run but Clark. It is his patented special and yesterday it worked like a charm. He knifed through tackle as he usually does and when he was into the secondary he didn't seem to be running at all, just stepping on air. Giant arms reached for him, but he was gone, a wisp of smoke that curled al-

These three New York Giants played massive roles in getting their team to this Championship game, (left to right) quarterback "big" Ed Danowski, Coach Steve Owen, and halfback Ken Strong.

—*Detroit Times* photo/Courtesy of *The Detroit News*

most lazily down the field. Suddenly there sprung up a wall of men, who were not smoke, but sturdy blockers. They were strung out diagonally across the field, and racing toward him was a gang of red shirted tacklers. Suddenly Clark swerved, raced straight toward the sidelines until he was on the right side of that diagonal wall of blockers. The Giants were in hot pursuit, but they were all on the wrong side of the field. With that graceful pivot in the mud and swinging stride Clark had turned the picture over. A moment before he was hemmed in with tacklers. The next second, he had escaped and was speeding down behind a wall of blockers. The wall ended a little short of the goal line, but Dutch doesn't need any help for the last 10 yards if only two men are in his way. He flipped his hips away from one, changed direction and glided like an eel through the empty arms of another for a touchdown. No muddy football field ever blossomed a prettier run than that.

—Bud Shaver, *Detroit Times*, 12/16/35

The Giants would regroup in the second quarter, scoring on a 42 yard touchdown pass from Danowski to Ken Strong, cutting Detroit's lead to 13–7, but it would prove to be the last points of the afternoon for the New Yorkers.

In the second half, the Lions blocked a punt and recovered the ball at the Giants' 26 yard line. Five plays later Ernie Caddel scored on a reverse, making the score 20–7.

And then Ernie Caddel went scooting around the ends, his muddy road was lined with red shirts in the mire.

—Bud Shaver, *Detroit Times*, 12/16/35

The score that finally put the game out of reach came after Raymond "Buddy" Parker (future coach of the Lions' 1950's teams) intercepted a pass and returned it to the 10 yard line. He finished what he started a couple of plays later when he scored from the 4 yard line. Final score: Lions 26, Giants 7.

The result of the game was attributed to the Lions offensive and defensive linemen, who thoroughly dominated the line of scrimmage.

The Lion line went right on breaking holes in the Giant wall. The Giants are big but they didn't have the speed and finesse of Potsy's front wall. Presnell, Dutch Clark, Gutowsky and Shepherd pounded through rifts at the tackles through which you could have charged the Fourteenth Cavalry without harming a hair of a horse.

The Lions would rely heavily in this game on their talented trio of backs (from left to right), Frank Christensen, Ace Gutowsky, and Dutch Clark.
—Obtained through the use of the Alan Feldman Collection

Ed Klewicki catches an Ace Gutowsky pass and is wrestled down in the first quarter of action.
—*Detroit Times* photo/Courtesy of *The Detroit News*

Detroit's ends and tackles were smashing in and the pounding New York's tackles took was something to behold. That was no soft line the Giants had either. Del Isola and Mel Hein caused plenty of trouble after the Giants got their backs humped up in the second half, but two such linemen as they couldn't halt the unified, crashing assault of the whole Lion front wall. The Lions kept beating 'em across the line and that told the story.

—Bud Shaver, *Detroit Times,* 12/16/35

The muddy, freezing conditions also played havoc on the Giants passing offense. The aerial attack of New York was further hampered when they lost Tom Goodwin; their outstanding receiver had broken two ribs early in the game. The Lions were also bolstered by the support of their 15,000 fans, despite the horrendous weather conditions.

Following the game, the newspapers were filled with descriptions of excited fans, and scenes of happy, muddy heroes:

If you permitted snow and slush to tie you to the fireside instead of depositing you upon the cold, damp benches at University of Detroit Stadium yesterday, you sacrificed a great thrill for common comfort. The Lions didn't let the snow and slush stop them. They arose from the icy ooze as clean and bright a bunch of champions as ever scuffed the good earth. The good earth was still clinging to them when they charged into the field house, singing and shouting as only victors can. They were caked from head to foot with black muck, but the clean light of victory blazed from their mud-rimmed eyes. In a slithery, muddy field the Lions outcharged; outfought and outgeneraled the New York Giants, the best pro football team in the east, and until they met the Lions, the champions of the world.

—Bud Shaver, *Detroit Times,* 12/16/35

The mud blackened champions; the shouts and the jostling; owner Dick Richards, apoplectic with pride; John W. Smith, president of the council, punching hairy chests and slapping bare backs. Coach Potsy Clark in his battered hat and mud-stained pants; Long John Schneller shouting for his first gold football 'as big as a toy balloon,' Ed Klewicki's battered grin of triumph.

—Bud Shaver, *Detroit Times,* 12/16/35

Most of the Lions had their portion of the slop and slime, but if there had been some way to ship the dirt on Ox Emerson's face to his native Texas, then the farmers of that section never would be worried over fertilizer.

Jack Johnson, one of the line heroes, gets recognition as letting out the loudest yells. Jack's vocal works would have done credit to a whole tribe of warring Indians.

Fans were pouring through the door in droves. There was back-slapping, handshaking and cheek kissing. Yep, no kidding, plenty of cheek kissing. Dutch Clark, exhausted from the well-meant plau-

dits, finally walked over and asked some one to guard the door. His wish was obeyed but just about the time Dutch issued this request owner Dick Richards arrived with a gang of friends. They stormed in like so many wolves on the prowl. 'Great stuff, boys! Yelled Richards. Great stuff, boys!'

—Bob Murphy, *Detroit Times*, 12/16/35

The story of the Lions' championship was not reserved only for the people of Detroit. An article by Earl Hilligan was written and sent out across the State of Michigan via the Detroit wire service and doesn't exactly give the feeling of journalistic impartiality,

DETROIT LIONS CRUSH NEW YORK 26–7 FOR PRO TITLE

Detroit Lions ruled as King of the professional jungle after grinding the defending title holders into the mud of the University of Detroit's Stadium Sunday afternoon . . . A snowstorm and sodden field

were unable to halt the relentless march of the Lions as they hurled two deft aerial thrusts in the early moments of the game and then unleashed a devastating ground attack…The great play of the Detroit line was one of the prime factors in the lion's victory. The hard charging forward wall opened yawning holes for the backs to run through for consistent gains, and vicious tackling checked the Giants attack every time it became dangerous.

—Earl Hilligan, (Detroit Wire Service)
in Kalamazoo Gazette, 10/16/35

The tone of this article reads much like an adventure story, making the Lions' seem rather heroic. At the very least they sound dominating, which is what someone looking to support a team would be looking for. Because the Lions were new to Detroit, they were also new to the State of Michigan as well. People in Detroit were quickly becoming Lions fans, but they were within the 'radial city.' The true mark of creating a solid fan base is to 'cast a wide net' and try to grab fans from the entire state. The description of the game leaves the reader almost sorry

Ace Gutowsky rammed through the Giants line on this play in the first quarter to score the Lions' first touchdown.
—*Detroit Times* photo/Courtesy of *The Detroit News*

Ernie Caddel sweeping around the left end with a convoy of blockers for the Lions third touchdown.

—*Detroit Times* photo/Courtesy of *The Detroit News*

that he (she) was not there; combined with the idea of the Lions as a heroic/unstoppable team equates to a recipe for the creation of new fans. That the Lions are today an important part of the sporting culture across Michigan has its roots in this first championship.

CELEBRATING THE LIONS CHAMPIONSHIP

Detroit would celebrate the Lions victory, and as a result, new fans were born. People are always looking for a reason to celebrate especially in rough times (i.e. Depression) and this would be no exception, though they wouldn't party wildly in the streets as it was the dead of winter. The Lions, like the Tigers, were given a testimonial dinner. The Lions testimonial was held at the Detroit Athletic Club two days after they won their championship. This was a very important event in the history of the team because it represented an official introduction to the citizens and society of Detroit. By receiving the same treatment as the Tigers they were now seen to be on the same level, as champions in their own right,

The Lions were tamed last evening at the Detroit Athletic Club in a manner that suits all Lions—including the domestic and jungle types. They were tamed and soothed by sparkling, inspiring speeches. The best chefs of the city tossed meat in their jaws, and these same ferocious beasts of the

gridiron found themselves dined, wined, and feted in a manner becoming champions of the world in any sport, be it ping pong or shooting one-eyed muskrats. Officers and directors of the Lions Club pitched the party-and they pitched it with the same skill and finesse that Tommy Bridges employed in the ninth inning of the 1935 World Series. I mean to stand here and tell you the world champion Lions last evening were on the receiving end of one of the finest and most heart-felt banquets any city ever accorded conquering heroes.

—Bob Murphy, *Detroit Times*, 12/18/35

The speech given by mayor Frank Couzens captured the importance of the occasion to the franchise,

I salute you in behalf of Detroit's sportsminded thousands. You Lions have become a vital and everlasting part of our scheme of things.

—Bob Murphy, *Detroit Times*, 12/18/35

Among several other speeches about the city and fans was a speech by Dutch Clark who chose this moment to talk about his favorite aspect of what makes a Detroit fan so special,

In behalf of the team, let me thank you for sticking with us during those dark moments before we fi-

Owner Dick Richards congratulating his players in the locker room after the Lions won their first championship.
—*Detroit Times* photo/Courtesy of *The Detroit News*

nally struck our championship stride. A team doesn't need encouragement when it's on top. But a team, such as ours, certainly needed help from somewhere when we seemed headed for the bottom. You gave it to us, and, you got a championship in return. A town like Detroit will keep on getting champions and producing championship teams as long as you offer inspiration such as we received.

—Bob Murphy, *Detroit Times*, 12/18/35

At the banquet the Lions were given blue flannel blankets and parkas that George Richards had promised them at the start of the season. It was a gift the Lions needed due to the weather and locations they played in. The gift of the parkas is a testament to a more innocent age of sports, when items like matching parkas were considered a luxury and not an expected accessory. The team was also promised a trip to Hawaii for winning the championship. Honolulu was specifically chosen in reference to their (Honolulu blue and silver) jersey colors. There was a catch to this trip however, the team would have to play their way out there, through a series of exhibitions across the country. On this 12,000 mile road trip they first beat the "National League All-Stars" in Denver (33–0), then the "Pacific Coast champi-

Two Scenes from the Lions Testimonial Dinner at the Detroit Athletic Club

(Left to right) George Christensen, Glen Presnell, and Ox Emerson present Hugh Dean of Chevrolet with a ball used in the championship game.
—*Detroit Times* photo/Courtesy of *The Detroit News*

(Left to Right) Potsy Clark, Charles F. Navin (secretary-treasurer of the Detroit Tigers), Mirt L. Briggs (a Lions director), and George Richards look at a program from the championship game.
—*Detroit Times* photo/Courtesy of *The Detroit News*

"The American Football Player." One of the most famous Pro-football pictures ever taken. It is of the Lions first Hall-of-famer Earl "Dutch" Clark, and was taken by legendary Detroit News' photographer, William A. Kuenzel.

—Photo courtesy of *The Detroit News*

ons "(67–14), followed by the League All-Stars (42–7) and then an exhibition win against the Green Bay Packers (10–3). When they actually arrived in Hawaii they beat Pop Warner's All-Stars (30–6) before starting a nice, long, and well-earned vacation.

The most important aspect of the Lions winning the championship in 1935 was that they won it in the same year as the Tigers. The failure of the previous teams in putting down roots shows that the success of the Lions franchise was far from guaranteed, especially since the previous attempts had come during more prosperous times for the city of Detroit. It must be emphasized that in order for a team to be successful, it must have the support of the community. By first associating the unstable Lions with the rock-solid franchise of the Tigers, a common bond was created. When they became champions in the same year, the elation of the fans spilled over from the Tigers to the Lions and tied them together to a much larger degree. The Lions did not end up winning another championship until 1952. These questions arise: Would the fans have turned up? Would the franchise have been around long enough for the team to reach its "Golden Age"

in the 1950's, if the Lions had failed to win over the course of its first 18 years in Detroit? If this team had not won in 1935 and established itself as quickly as it did, there is a very realistic possibility that the Lions would have folded long ago, and the state of football in Detroit would have had an entirely different outcome, if any at all.

However, this parade of champions had not yet reached its conclusion, for at this very moment the Detroit Red Wings were fighting their way through the 1935–1936 season. In a little less than four months from the Lions winning their title, the Red Wings would add the Stanley Cup to complete the sweep of major professional sports championships.

"Mud-blackened Champions," celebrating. (Left to right) Dutch Clark, Ernie Caddel, and Ed Klewicki.

—*Detroit Times* photo/Courtesy of *The Detroit News*

Mickey Cochrane, Joe Louis, and Potsy Clark pose for this picture shortly after the Lions had won their first NFL Championship.
—Photo courtesy of *The Detroit News*

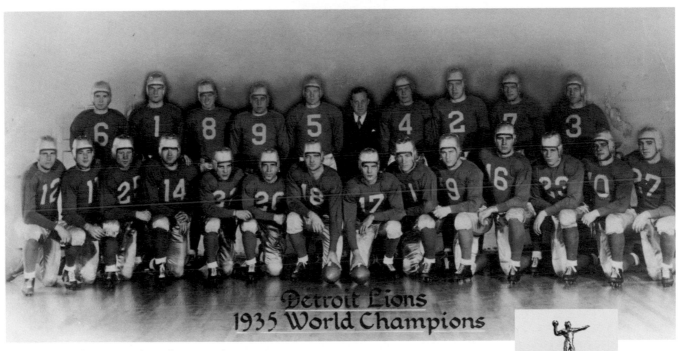

Team photo of the Lions first Championship team.
—Photo courtesy of the Detroit Lions

The Ed Thorpe Memorial Trophy, given annually to the NFL Champions in the years before the Super Bowl. This one was awarded to the Lions in 1935.
—Photo courtesy of the Detroit Lions

4

DETROIT RED WINGS

Any discussion about the origins of professional hockey in Detroit must begin with the story of a man named Charlie Hughes. Hughes was born in Grand Ledge, Michigan, in 1881. Graduating from the University of Michigan in 1902, he became a sportswriter for the Detroit Tribune. That he was gaining in notoriety and influence became obvious in 1915 as Hughes had gained enough influence to help create the Detroit Athletic Club, one of the most important institutions in the city of Detroit. He then became the club's first manager. Under management of the D.A.C. he published a magazine for the club and was able to draw in an array of new and influential members. In 1926 Hughes was able to demonstrate the merit of bringing a professional hockey club to Detroit to several members of the D.A.C. Hughes' main argument was that an up and coming city needed to have several sports teams in order to compete in the growing phenomena of American professional sport. On May 15, 1926, the idea was officially adopted and the group led by Charlie Hughes paid the $100,000 franchise fee to the National Hockey League. The first players were added on October 5, 1926, when the Detroit Hockey Club purchased the rights of fifteen members of the Victoria (British Colombia) Cougars Hockey Club. The Victoria club had been good, competing for the Stanley Cup the previous year but their team struggled financially. Of those fifteen players purchased from Victoria, nine of them were signed to contracts. The name "Cougars" was kept in order to associate the team with the big cat theme of the well established Tigers.

The Detroit Cougars first year in the league was something of a disappointment. The team had finished with a record of 12(WINS)–28(LOSSES)–4(TIES), and had lost $84,000 in the process. Hughes decided that what the team needed was a change in management, and so he

—Photo courtesy of The Detroit News

hired Jack Adams; a player who had just retired after a productive 7 year playing career that included two Stanley Cup championships. The hiring of Adams as General Manager and coach would turn out to be one of the most important moments in the Detroit club's history.

Adams would turn out to be a very good coach, but it was his skills as General Manager which really guided the franchise. He was an outstanding judge of talent and he would be the only GM, Detroit Hockey would know until 1962. Adams immediately went to work, overhauling three-fourths of the roster through trades and acquisitions. The new GM's first year in Detroit was also the first year the Detroit club played in the city. The team had been playing across the river in Windsor while their new stadium was being built. Olympia Stadium had finally been completed, and on November 22, 1927, the first game was played at the stadium that would be the team's home until 1979. This stadium was nicknamed "the big red barn," and was designed by C. Howard Crane, the outstanding architect who had designed several other buildings in Detroit, including the Fox Theatre and Detroit Opera House. Designed to a similar plan as Madison Square Garden, which had just opened in New York the year before, opening night at Olympia left an impression on all who were there.

Detroit got its first real taste of big league hockey and liked it. More than 14,000 wildly enthusiastic fans saw one of the most rapid exhibitions in the Olympia last night that it has been their pleasure to witness. The hockey morsel pleased their palates and they yelled themselves hoarse.

It didn't seem to matter a bit that the Detroit Cougars lost to the Ottawa Senators by the nar-

row score of 2 to 1. It was the spectacle it-self that charmed the populace.

It is true that local fans who like the ice game have had opportunities to view it across the river, but never before has it been brought right home to them in a big way. Hockey, they discovered, is foot-ball set to lightning.

The athletes flashed around the big expanse of ice like shooting stars, but every electric movement meant something. They squirmed, dodged, ducked, danced, and pirouetted on their flashing blades with such rapid-ity that at times the eye could not quite follow the maneuvers.

The University of Michigan band played airs that are patri-otic on both sides of the border. "America," the "Star Spangled Banner" and the "Maple Leaf For-ever" were received enthusiastically. The specta-tors stood while the Canadian anthem was being played and the Canadians uncovered when the American anthem was given, making it a happy party all around.

Before the game started, Mayor Smith went to the center of the ice and on behalf of his admirers presented Coach Jack Adams of the Cougars with a huge floral piece. Members of both teams stood around in appreciative attitudes.

In addition to the game itself, there was enter-tainment in the shape of graceful skating by Gladys Lamb and Norval Baptie, regarded as the best pair of fancy skaters in the world. Gladys looked warm while doing her toe dances and other clever stunts on skates despite the fact that she was dressed as if for a ballet on a steam heated stage, instead of on a large expanse of ice.

—Bert Walker, *Detroit Times*, 11/23/27

The first few years in Olympia were a rough time for the Detroit Club as a majority of the fans who attended the games were from Windsor and attended the games for the primary purpose of heckling and booing the new club.

Jack Adams, the man who would guide the Detroit Hockey Franchise from its' infancy to its' Golden age of the 1950's. He is the only man to have his name engraved on the Stanley Cup as a player, coach, and General Manager.
—Photo courtesy of *The Detroit News*
Obtained through the use of the
Alan Feldman Collection

These fans were an especially rowdy bunch and came over in large numbers when-ever the Cougars were playing a Cana-dian team. As Jack Adams would later say, "*I've never seen a place like this in my whole life, there just can't be another city in the world where the home team isn't popular. Even when we win, which I admit isn't too often, we get booed. Things just have to change around here.*"

This rough time also included the beginning of the Depression and the tough financial situation that inevitably followed. Atten-dance at games dropped so signifi-cantly, that Jack Adams was seen canvassing the city, door-to-door trying to sell discounted tickets. At one point Adams started exchang-ing goods such as potatoes for entry to games; anything to put people in the seats. A quote by Jack Adams re-membering this time puts his plight into perspective, "*if the greatest star in the game was available to us for $1.98 we couldn't have afforded him.*"

In 1930, the team tried a publicity stunt in order to draw attention to the club. A newspaper competition gave the public a chance to write in and vote for a new team name. Several names received votes, including the "Trojans", "Magnetos", and "Wanderers," but the name "Fal-cons" won the contest. True to their word the team name was changed, and for the 1930–1931 season, the Detroit Falcons played at Olympia. The jerseys were also changed to incorporate gold lettering, the only time in the history of this hockey club that red and white were not the featured colors.

This change in name and jerseys did not help the club. The 1930–1931 Falcons finished with the worst record in the league. The following year saw the team's record improve but not their finances as the team was nearly bankrupt. This period of time may have been hard for the Detroit hockey club, but it turned out to be insur-mountable to other franchises as many of the teams in the league were forced to fold or relocate to other cities. It was at this point, when the fate of the club was so uncertain, that a savior arrived.

The first home of Detroit hockey, Olympia Stadium.
—Photo courtesy of Ilitch Holdings.

Ebbie Goodfellow in 1931 wearing a Falcons jersey. Detroit's first superstar, Jack Adams said about Ebbie: "He was Gordie Howe before there was a Gordie Howe."
—Associated Press Photo

The men who changed hockey in Detroit forever. James Norris Jr. (left), and Norris Sr. (right) watching a game.
—*Detroit Times* photo/Courtesy of *The Detroit News*

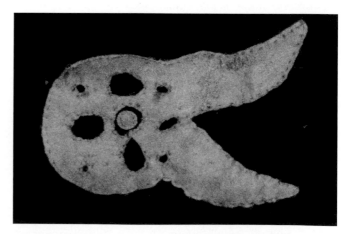

An original Montreal "Winged Wheelers" patch. This was the inspiration behind the iconic Red Wings logo.
—Courtesy of the Hockey Hall of Fame.

James Norris was a 53 year old Chicago millionaire with a deep desire to own a professional hockey club. Unable to buy the Chicago Blackhawks, he cast his eye to Detroit. At the cost of $100,000, Norris bought the entire franchise, including Olympia Stadium and the club's minor league team, the Detroit Olympics. As a young man, Norris had played hockey for an amateur team called the Montreal "Winged Wheelers." Figuring that a picture of a winged wheel would fit in well with the city's fame as the Motor City, in 1932 he changed the logo and renamed the team the Detroit "Red Wings."

Arriving with James Norris was his son James D. Norris Jr. who also worked with the team. To differentiate between the two, Norris Sr. was known as "Pops" and he immediately went to work stabilizing the finances of the team, and opening up his pocketbook to acquire players. The elder Norris also worked with the other owners to curtail rising salaries by initiating the first "salary cap," of $7,500 per player. This move definitely raised the ire of several players, but at a time when a factory worker was making 40 cents an hour, the complaints fell on deaf ears. Norris also tore up Jack Adams previous contract, retaining the coach on a season by season "probation," which ended up lasting 15 years.

While the bank account of the team had been nearly empty before the arrival of Norris, their cupboard of talented players was full. A core of emerging stars had been steadily acquired by Adams since he had arrived in 1927, all of whom would become Red Wings' legends. Larry Aurie, a firebrand at right-wing, was among Adams' first acquisitions. Looking back later in his life, Jack Adams would call Aurie his "*all-time*" favorite player because of his hard work and tough play, despite his small stature. Herbie Lewis, a flashy playmaker at left-wing, was acquired in 1928, and was elected to the Hockey Hall-of-Fame in 1989. Adams would call Lewis and Aurie, "*as great a pair of wingmen as ever flashed across the ice.*" In 1929, one of the most revered names in the history of Detroit hockey arrived, Ebbie Goodfellow. His Hall-of-Fame career spanned fourteen years with Detroit; first as a center and then a defenseman; he captained the team for five years. Goodfellow was a star amongst stars, and Adams' greatest quote of these early players was reserved for him, "*Introducing Ebbie Goodfellow, Need I say more? The mere mention of his name is enough.*" John Sorrell arrived in 1930; he was a solid, consistent left-wing who played for nearly a decade. Doug Young, a hard checking defenseman arrived in 1931 and captained the Red Wings from 1935–1938. It was with this core group that Detroit went to the Stanley Cup playoffs, first in the season that spanned from 1932–1933 (losing to the New York Americans in the semi-finals), then in 1933–1934 (losing to the Chicago Blackhawks in the finals).

Before the 1934–1935 season, Adams overhauled a part of his roster with another group of players who would play significant roles in this story. Syd Howe, a Hall-of-Fame center/left-wing played for twelve years with the Red Wings. He was always near the top of the league in scoring, and when he retired in 1946 he was the all-time leading scorer in NHL history. Normie Smith arrived to replace the outstanding goalie John Ross Roach. Smith would enjoy the best years of his career while playing with the Red Wings in the mid-thirties, and would set an amazing precedent for playoff goaltending. Ralph "Scotty" Bowman (unrelated to the future coach), Bucko McDonald, Gord Pettinger, and Wally "the pest" Kilrea were all added to give younger depth.

The result of 1934–1935 was disappointment in the win column as the new players meshed with the core group and the team finished well out of the playoff chase. Never one to accept failure in any form, Jack Adams continued adding and subtracting players, bringing in wingers Pete Kelly, Modere "Mud" Bruneteau, and Hec Kilrea (brother

"Ready for Anything." (Left to right) Ebbie Goodfellow, Bucko "the socko" McDonald, John Sorrell and Larry Aurie await their next shift on the ice.

—Photo courtesy of *The Detroit News*
Obtained through the use of the Alan Feldman Collection

"Just Before the Battle." (Left to Right) Hec Kilrea, Modere "Mud" Bruneteau, Pete Kelly, and Marty Barry suit up for action before a game.
—Photo courtesy of *The Detroit News*
Obtained through the use of the Alan Feldman Collection

(Top) The first "Howe" to lace up for the Red Wings. Syd Howe was an incredible offensive talent.
—*Detroit Times* photo/Courtesy of *The Detroit News*

(Right) Lack of helmets often resulted in head and facial injuries. Here Herbie Lewis is getting his broken nose taped.
—Photo courtesy of *The Detroit News*
Obtained through the use of the Alan Feldman Collection

Normie Smith. This young Red Wings Goalie would put on one of the most amazing displays of playoff goaltending in hockey history.
—Photo courtesy of *The Detroit News*
Obtained through the use of the Alan Feldman Collection

of Wally Kilrea). His biggest acquisition however was via trade with the Boston Bruins, that sent All-Star Cooney Weiland to the Boston Bruins for an up-and-coming center named Marty Barry. This trade would prove to be one of the greatest that Adams ever made, as the future Hall-of-Famer became an outstanding scorer for the Wings, leading the team in points his first year. Of Barry, Jack Adams had high praise, calling him; *"the greatest center in the business and the key man of the greatest line in hockey."*

Coming off their disappointing fourth place season, the Red Wings of 1935–1936 had much to prove to themselves and to the rest of the league, as the naysayers had been calling them overachievers for their success in 1932–1934.

As it turned out, the Red Wings would prove these naysayers wrong with an outstanding season during which they remained in first place the entire season, except for one day. It would have been much less nerve-racking if the one day they dropped out of first had come earlier in the season, instead of a seven game winless streak at the end, nearly tarnishing their place in the standings. However, this brief slide turned out to be only a minor worry as a key win on the second to last day of the season ensured that they would finish in first place.

Hockey during the Depression was in fact different than it is today. The most noticeable difference to a modern fan was the equipment, or lack of it. Players did not wear helmets, and goalies did not wear masks. However, some did wear leather head straps for slight protection or wool caps to keep their heads warm, and it was considered good gamesmanship to try and knock them off an opponent. There were many cases of goalies and players suffering terrible head and facial injuries but the tough, rugged players of this age tended to scoff at helmets of any kind. There were also less games at this time (48 compared to 82), as there were far fewer teams in the league. Teams' rosters were also fewer during the depression, oftentimes limited to only 15 players. The smaller rosters resulted in more ice time for players which were only grouped into two or maybe three lines and it was not rare for a player to be on the ice for an entire game. There were no zamboni machines to refresh the ice, so the chopped up slush that resulted from skate blades was merely swept away with a broom. By the end of games, many rinks would look like an icy-morass that slowed the up-and-down pace of the game, as players slipped and tried to avoid breaking their legs in the chunked out divots. Fights and hard checking were as much a part of the game as they are today.

In 1935–1936 there were eight teams in the NHL, separated into two divisions, American and Canadian. The playoff format at this time was called "intersectional" and called for the first place teams of both divisions to play each other and the second place teams to play each other. This system seems very strange to us today, and it was irritating to people back then as well. The concern was that the two first place teams would pound on each other, increasing the chance of injury and fatigue, and the second place winner could simply cruise into the Stanley Cup finals with a better shot at an upset. Concluding the 1935–1936 season, three teams in the American Conference (Boston Bruins, New York Americans, and Chicago Blackhawks) had tied for second. As a result the three teams plus the second place team from the Canadian

Pete Kelly, the sturdy Detroit Winger. Notice the sweaters that hockey players wore at this time were different than the jerseys worn today.

—Photo courtesy of *The Detroit News*
Obtained through the use of the Alan Feldman Collection

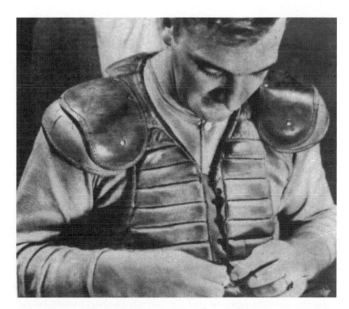

Hec Kilrea shows off the pads worn by hockey players of this era.

—Photo courtesy of *The Detroit News*
Obtained through the use of the Alan Feldman Collection

Members of the Detroit Red Wings get their skates sharpened by equipment manager Bill Collett. (From left to right) Herbie Lewis, Collett, Marty Barry, and Larry Aurie.
—*Detroit Times* photo/Courtesy of *The Detroit News*

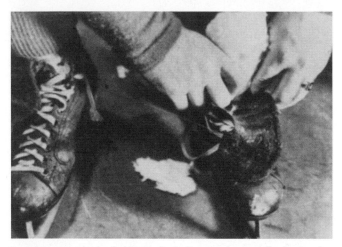

Ice skates typical of this period. Cotton was stuffed into the tongues to keep the laces tight.
-Photo courtesy of *The Detroit News*
Obtained through the use of the Alan Feldman Collection

1935 STANLEY CUP SEMI-FINALS

Game 1:
Detroit Red Wings vs. Montreal Maroons:
Montreal Forum, 3/24/36

The confident Thomas Patrick Gorman today proclaimed to the world that his Montreal Maroons will eliminate the Red Wings and go on to win another Stanley Cup championship. "If we hurdle Detroit—I mean when we hurdle Detroit we will have eliminated our strongest opposition. The Maroons this season are the best all-around collection of hockey players of all the teams I have had in the playoffs."

—Leo Macdonell, *Detroit Times*, 3/24/36

The Red Wings traveled to the Montreal forum for the opening game and by the end of it they would feel like they had been there for a week. This was the "marathon game," a six-hour contest that would become one of the most famous in the history of the NHL. For the first three periods of the March 24th game, the two teams fired shot after shot on each others' goals with no success.

As the third period became the fourth, fifth, sixth, seventh, eighth, and then ninth; both players and the 10,000 fans wondered if the game would literally *ever* end!

"Up and down they move—down and up. The pace kept slackening. They were fighting with their heads and hearts, two great, game hockey teams. A great save robbed Ward. Another brilliant save robbed Barry—a grim, bitter struggle.

—Leo Macdonell, *Detroit Times*, 3/25/36

Three tons of ice was removed by the sweepers who struggled in vain to keep the rink clean. In between periods the teams were given various concoctions of brandy, coffee and sugar to keep their blood pumping. Every time one team or another looked as though they were about to score, camera flashbulbs exploded in a cacophony of light. Photographers went through a weeks worth of film in a single night as each tried to capture the winning goal. Finally, as the clock was running out in the fifth overtime, a rarely used Red Wing rookie by the name of

division (Toronto Maple Leafs) went to the playoffs initiating the first quarter-final round in NHL playoff history. The Red Wings meanwhile had to face the powerful Montreal Maroons in the first round. The Maroons were a well balanced and dynamic club that had won the previous year's Stanley Cup. Featuring several outstanding players of the day in captain Hooley Smith, Lionel Conacher, and Dave Trottier, the Maroons had not lost a game in over a month. The winners of the Canadian Division were heavy favorites to win the Cup, as bookies had the "smart money" on them at 8–5. The bookies placed the Wings odds at 3–1.

Normie Smith's 75 goal shutout of the Maroons made him the defensive hero of the game and etched him permanently into the lore of early Red Wings' history.
—*Detroit Times* photo/Courtesy of *The Detroit News*

Modere "Mud" Bruneteau cleanly handled a pass from Hec Kilrea and buried the goal to end the game, becoming a legend in his own time.

> *"All I know is this," said Bruneteau. "Hec had the puck and he was skating like the devil. He broke through the last two men and cut to his left. I swung down the right, turning toward the net. Just as I got there, Chabot lunged toward Hec, who passed to me. I had plenty of space to shoot through, and the puck grazed his arm. I happened to be there and that's all, Hec Kilrea deserves the real credit. He's the one who made the play. I just batted it into the net."*

—Leo Macdonell, *Detroit Times*, 3/25/36

But as much credit as Bruneteau got for his goal, it was the two goalies who had truly played their hearts out. Montreal goalie Lorne Chabot had only given up the single goal after stopping 80 shots, while Normie Smith had shutout the Maroons and saved 75!* The fans had really received their money's worth of hockey as the record-setting total time was 176:30; three and a half minutes shy of three full games.

• • • • • • •

*Author's note: The generally accepted view of a better than average game for a goalie is saving 30–35 shots and "shutting a team out," meaning he doesn't allow a goal.

"Make it Another." Potsy Clark of the Lions stops by Olympia to wish captain Doug Young and Jack Adams well, as they prepare for their quest of the Stanley Cup.
—*Detroit Times* photo/Courtesy of *The Detroit News*

The stories in the newspapers following this game told of the extraordinary happenings that had taken place in its duration. One such story was the speech that Herbie Lewis gave before the final overtime period. Apparently the Wings were silent at that point, just trying to catch enough breath to return to the ice when Lewis provided them with a moment to laugh,

> *"The fellows were down on the floor, dead tired," said Jack [Adams]. "No one was saying anything. No one had that much energy. [All] of a sudden, Herbie leaped to his feet, smiled and yelled to the gang. 'Say fellows,' said Herbie, who was trying to appear as fresh as a daisy. 'Isn't this a joke on Charlie Jacobs, the Olympia concession man. He's waited all his life for a hockey game that would go this long. He'd make a thousand dollars if this game had been played in Detroit.' "Do you know?" asked Adams, that Lewis pulled the team right back into good spirits. He made them forget they were tired. It was a great psychological move by one of the game's greatest. Our fellows went out*

and ended the game in the next period. I give this little wisecracker part of the credit."

—Bob Murphy, *Detroit Times*, 3/26/36

Other stories of the extraordinary discussed the play of an emerging defenseman named Bucko "the Socko" McDonald, who had a breakout performance in this first game,

"I've been watching hockey for 43 years," declared Jim Norris Sr. "That's too long to admit. But let me say here and now that I've never seen a greater exhibition of body checking than Bucko McDonald gave tonight." Adams slammed his fist against the trunk and chimed in: "I tell you it is unbeliev-

able that a kid could check them so clean and yet so effectively."

—Bob Murphy, *Detroit Times*, 3/26/36

It would be hard to overestimate the importance of this game for the Red Wings. When they travelled to Montreal for the first two games of this best of five series, they were hoping to leave with one win. Not only had they gotten that win in the first game, but they had stood toe-to-toe with arguably the best team in hockey, and emerged victorious. The result was a tremendous boost of confidence that would only increase as the playoffs wore on.

Stanley Cup Semi-Finals Game 2: Montreal Forum, 3/26/36

Victory for the Red Wings tonight would give the Adams men a tremendous advantage, as the teams shift to Detroit for the third game of the series Sunday. [The] Maroons have reason to remember Bucko McDonald's terrific body checking, as well as Normie Smith's brilliance in the nets and Mud Bruneteau's sterling goal. "Smith played fine hockey," Gorman declared. "But he was lucky too. We'll beat him tonight."

—Leo Macdonell, *Detroit Times*, 3/26/36

Fans attending the next game might have thought that it, too, would be a "Marathon game," as it remained scoreless after two and a half periods. Tensions mounted as first the Maroons coach directed his anger at one of the referees, and then the crowd physically demonstrated their unhappiness,

Between the first and second periods Tommy Gorman grabbed Bill Stewart going to the dressing room and a hot argument took place. And Bill offered to take the Maroons' boss out into one or two alleys.

Angered by a decision which sent Ward to the penalty box, the crowd poured debris on the ice and there was a brief delay while attendants cleared the ice.

—Leo Macdonell, *Detroit Times*, 3/27/36

As both teams rushed up and down the ice it was the Red Wings who finally broke it open mid-way through the

The offensive heroes for the Red Wings in the "Marathon Game." Hec Kilrea (right) made the pass that set up Modere "Mud" Bruneteau (above) for the game winning goal in the ninth period.
—*Detroit Times* photo/Courtesy of *The Detroit News*

Though Johnny Sorrell (10) was stopped on this shot by Montreal goalie Lorne Chabot; the Red Wings would score three times en route to a 3–0 game two win.

—*Detroit Times* photo/Courtesy of *The Detroit News*

third period with a flurry of goals by Syd Howe, Herbie Lewis, and Larry Aurie.

This time the power play worked. Howe, starting a sensational rush from his own zone, carried over the blue line and squeezing between Evans and Wentworth rifled the puck high in the corner at Chabot's right, a beautiful achievement that claimed the admiration of disappointed Montreal fans.

The goal by Lewis was a solo and even more spectacular. With Maroons trapped in the Detroit zone, Larry Aurie and Lewis broke away all alone. Just after they had crossed the blue line Aurie fell to the ice, leaving Lewis to go on alone, which he did in a dramatic manner. As the charging Lewis neared Chabot, the Maroon goalie, with a great lunge, dived out to block the shot. As he came Lewis stopped suddenly, still clinging to the puck, whirled around and came back a second time to punch home the rubber with the big Montreal goaltender far out and leaving behind a yawning net. It was one of the coolest bits of play that old timers here remember.

Then with less than a minute to go, Aurie scored with the assistance of Marty Barry and Lewis. While not so theatrical as the others, the play was effective. Chabot got a piece of the rubber but it dropped to the line and bounced inside.

—Leo Macdonell, *Detroit Times*, 3/27/36

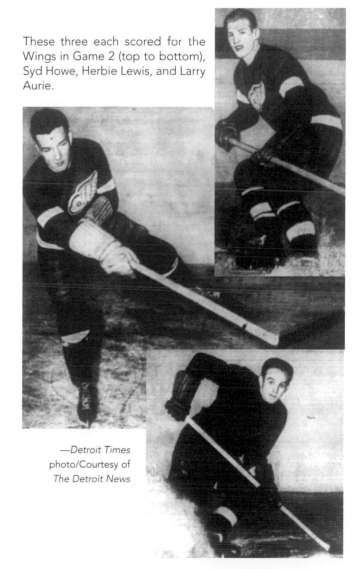

These three each scored for the Wings in Game 2 (top to bottom), Syd Howe, Herbie Lewis, and Larry Aurie.

—*Detroit Times* photo/Courtesy of *The Detroit News*

Another outstanding performance by Normie Smith left the Maroons scoreless, and as the final bell sounded, the Wings were now two games up and headed back home to try and wrap the series up at Olympia.

Stanley Cup Semi-Finals Game 3: Olympia Stadium, 3/29/36

Detroit's high-flying Red Wings, Stanley Cup bound, came home this afternoon to be greeted by a rip-roaring reception and an impromptu downtown parade. Hundreds of fans crowded the Brush street station to pay tribute to Jack Adams' men who took both games from the Montreal Maroons on the latter's home ice. "Where's Smith," yelled the crowd. "Give us Normie Smith." The gallant little Detroit goalie was one of the last to be sighted by the crowd. He blushingly received the ovation, and then entered a car with Mrs. Smith. Most of the players' wives were on hand to greet them. Cars had been provided for the occasion, and a police escort brought the players from the depot on a tour through part of the downtown district. Signs were painted on all the cars. "Stanley Cup bound," one sign read ... "Hail the conquering heroes," was another ... "City of Champions" was another. Ruddy faced Jack Adams beamed at the reception that carried with it much back-slapping for him. "This is the first time anything ever happened like this so far as hockey is concerned in Detroit," he said. "It'll make the boys fight all the harder."

—Bob Murphy, *Detroit Times*, 3/27/36

With a welcome like the one the Wings received as they returned to Detroit, it was clearly obvious that the fans were behind them. It was also obvious that the city was boiling with Championship fervor. A newfound confidence was radiating from the Red Wings, who just a few days before were being called "underdogs." Captain Doug Young, usually a soft spoken individual now captured the feeling of all the Wings, *"It will be all over after Sunday."*

In the first period of the third game, the Maroons finally scored on Normie Smith. Despite the score, the Wings goalie had set the record for "longest shutout sequence" in NHL history at 248 minutes, 30 seconds. This record of not allowing a goal in the equivalent of 4 straight games still stands today, and will never be bro-

ken. Very quickly after the Maroons goal, Detroit came back with two of their own, the first by Johnny Sorrell, and the game winner by Scotty Bowman. For Bowman the goal was extra sweet as the tough defenseman had been playing with 33 stitches in his face,

Scotty clicked off the goal that did the business. He says 33 stitches in the schnozzle are worth a league championship goal. To make the achievement more dramatic he scored half lying and sitting on the ice, battling home a puck that he had snared from Marty Barry, who had relayed a pass from Larry Aurie.

—Leo Macdonell, *Detroit Times*, 3/30/36

The performance by Smith and the 2–1 win had the fans going wild. Even the Maroons were impressed by the strong play of the Wings and their three game sweep and demonstrated this by clapping and patting the Wings on the back,

As Red Wings skated off the ice winners of their second league championship wild scenes prevailed last night, a deluge of debris flooding the ice. While Maroons rushed here and there on the ice to congratulate their rivals the huge crowd stood in the seats—men roaring and women shrieking their joy. Normie Smith was fairly swamped with Maroons who raced toward the Detroit goal to slap his back and shake his hand. His brilliant work in the nets in the three games was more popular, perhaps, with an opposing team than the victory of any goalie in history.

—Leo Macdonell, *Detroit Times*, 3/30/36

In the midst of all the excitement, another piece of good news reached the celebrants. The Red Wings minor league club (Detroit Olympics) had started their semi-final matchup against the Syracuse Stars on the same night as the parent club had started their series against the Maroons. Now, on the same night as the Red Wings were celebrating their win, so too were the Olympics,

About this time someone broke through the door with news that the Olympics had defeated Syracuse to cinch the International Hockey League championship.

—Bob Murphy, Detroit Times, 3/30/36

The first and only goal allowed by Normie Smith in the series came on this play by former Red Wing Gus Marker (9).

—*Detroit Times* photo/Courtesy of *The Detroit News*

Johnny Sorrell's (10) score on a Wally Kilrea pass, tied the score in the second period. Notice the arrow in the picture pointing to where the puck went in.

—*Detroit Times* photo/Courtesy of *The Detroit News*

Scotty Bowman shoots the puck past Lorne Chabot as he is falling down. The goal proved to be the game winner for the Red Wings. Final score: Montreal Maroons 1-Detroit Red Wings 2.

—*Detroit Times* photo/Courtesy of *The Detroit News*

Good sportsmanship abounded as the Maroons mingled with the Red Wings, offering their congratulations and well-wishes for the finals bound Detroiters.
—*Detroit Times* photo/Courtesy of *The Detroit News*

"Captain Doug Young made Bob Gracie (No.11) hurry his shot and, Smith easily turned the puck aside as it rolled lazily toward the corner of the net."
—*Detroit Times* photo/Courtesy of *The Detroit News*

"Game but beaten Maroons" leaving the ice following their defeat.
—*Detroit Times* photo/Courtesy of *The Detroit News*

"Dave Trottier made Smith leave the net to make a great stop. To the right of Trottier is Hec Kilrea (No.12). No.2 is Doug Young and No.8 is Syd Howe."
—*Detroit Times* photo/Courtesy of *The Detroit News*

"Bob Gracie, Montreal center, skated around the net and tried to poke the disc past Normie Smith into the far corner, but Normie dropped to his knees just in time to prevent a score. It was one of the best plays of the night."
—*Detroit Times* photo/Courtesy of *The Detroit News*

1935–1936
STANLEY CUP FINAL:
DETROIT RED WINGS VS.
TORONTO MAPLE LEAFS

Jack Adams giving his team some words of wisdom in this staged photo.

—*Detroit Times* photo/Courtesy of *The Detroit News*

Due to the four team playoff battle taking place between all of the second place teams, the Red Wings were forced to wait ten days between their last game against the Maroons and their first Stanley Cup game. During this layoff, Jack Adams was determined to keep his players sharp by practicing every day. In addition to the practices, he set up an exhibition with the Olympics, as they too were waiting on their opponent for the Teddy Oke Championship series (IHL equivalent of the Stanley Cup). One thousand people watched an interesting display of hockey as the Olympics were beaten by their parent club despite Normie Smith, Marty Barry, Larry Aurie, and Herbie Lewis having all suited up for the minor leaguers. Although Jack Adams had told all of his players to be careful during this exhibition, he was more concerned with the ten day layoff than he was about the risks of injury.

> *"A week's layoff is a long stretch,"* Adams explained, *"and we needed scrimmaging of that kind, if only to keep eyes sharpened in passing and timing. A layoff often is worse than too much work. It takes a game or two to get back on edge and we can't afford to give away any games in a short championship series."*

—Leo Macdonell, *Detroit Times*, 4/4/36

These three Red Wings (left to right) Larry Aurie, Marty Barry, and Herbie Lewis suited up for the Olympics for an exhibition against their own club. Adams (far right) wanted both teams to stay sharp as they awaited their championship matchups.

—*Detroit Times* photo/Courtesy of *The Detroit News*

The Red Wings take time during a practice session to pose for this photo before the start of the Stanley Cup Finals.
(Left to right) Manager Jack Adams, Scotty Bowman, Mud Bruneteau, Syd Howe, Bucko McDonald, Gordon Pettinger, Herbie Lewis, Larry Aurie, Red Kelley, Johnny Sorrell, Wally Kilrea, Doug Young, Ebbie Goodfellow, Hec Kilrea, Marty Barry, and Normie Smith.

—*Detroit Times* photo/Courtesy of *The Detroit News*

On April 3rd 1936, the championship matchups were decided when the Windsor Bull Dogs beat the Buffalo Bisons, and the Toronto Maple Leafs won their series against the New York Americans. The Olympics would now face the Bull Dogs for the Teddy Oke trophy, at the same time as the Red Wings were playing the Maple Leafs for the most prized possession in professional hockey—the Stanley Cup.

The Toronto Maple Leafs had always been a major rival to Detroit, because of the proximity to each other in distance and talent. Toronto had won the Stanley Cup as recently as 1931–1932, and the team that played in this series was just as talented. Featuring many of the early stars in hockey history the Leafs' roster fielded seven future Hall-of-Famers including: King Clancy, Charlie Conacher, Hap Day, George Hainsworth, Red Horner, Buscher Jackson, and Joe Primeau. Of these players, it was Conacher who led the flashy—high scoring attack of the Leafs. He had led the NHL in goals with 23 and everyone knew that his production would be the key in deciding Toronto's fate. Along with these seven Hall-of-Fame players was the owner of the Leaf's, Conn Smythe. This hockey legend was optimistic about his teams' chances and promised the Wings, *"a tough battle."*

Stanley Cup Finals Game 1:
Olympia Stadium, 4/5/36

Striking early and with lightning effect, [the] Red Wings at Olympia last night swept to a smashing triumph over [the] Toronto Maple Leafs, 3 to 1, thereby drawing first blood in the Stanley Cup finals—world series of hockey.

—Leo Macdonell, *Detroit Times*, 4/6/36

The standing room only crowd of 12,763 fans witnessed the opening game shellacking of the Maple Leafs. Normie Smith kept up his outstanding goal tending, while Bucko McDonald, Syd Howe, and Wally Kilrea scored for the Wings,

The fascinating McDonald, demon of body-checkers turned into a scoring threat, accounted for his marker in thrilling solo after he had snared the rubber in center ice, raced it into scoring position and fired deadly past the bewildered George Hainsworth, veteran of many championship campaigns. The red light flashed McDonald's goal at 4 minutes and 53 seconds, with customers still being seated, and its blaze was the signal for a tremendous outburst from a hockey mad crowd that came for thrills and got them early.

The roar of the crowd was still resonating through huge Olympia when Howe added the second tally, likewise a theatrical achievement in which Doug Young, captain of the Red Wings, collaborated. Taking Young's pass in center ice, Howe dashed in from right wing and with beautiful stick handling beat the Toronto defense and fired the disc into the net on Hainsworth's short side. It was a beautiful bit of work, Howe not having more than a few inches space between the goalie's pads and the post through which to drill the shot. The red light pitched the already delirious fans into another outburst, only in greater volume, the mammoth congregation as one leaping to its feet with men roaring and women shrieking. The building fairly shook with the demonstration and Howe was all but squeezed to bits by his joyful teammates.

And as the battle flamed with first one team and then the other surging down [the] ice in threats that kept the fans in a whirl came Wally Kilrea with the third Detroit counter which, like the others, was a spectacular deed. And once again the crowd was plunged into hysteria with the flashing of the light. Young Bruneteau, who has played brilliantly in the playoffs and was the hero of the record game in Montreal, aided Kilrea in as smart hockey as has been seen on Olympia ice. Snaring the puck Bruneteau broke down center ice with Johnny Sorrell at his left and Kilrea at his right. As they moved through center ice Bruneteau faked a pass to Sorrell, pushed the rubber over the ice to Kilrea and Wally raced in to click.

—Leo Macdonell, *Detroit Times*, 4/6/36

Even a goal by Toronto's Buzz Boll that came ten seconds after Wally Kilrea's goal did not dampen the enthusiasm of the Wings' faithful. Among these fans was a man who was being sighted more frequently at Detroit sporting contests, Joe Louis,

Scenes of Action from Game 1

—*Detroit Times* photos/Courtesy of *The Detroit News*

"Herbie Lewis circles the net and makes Hainsworth drop to save."   "Lewis pins Day against the net."

"George Hainsworth, Toronto goalie, comes out of his net to stop a rush by Larry Aurie (6) and Marty Barry (7)."

(Left) "Normie Smith, Detroit's sensational goalie stops Shill's drive from right of net.

(Bottom) "Wall Kilrea, the younger of the Detroit Red Wings' two Kilreas, who has gained the nickname of "The Pest" by persistent and effective poke and hack checking in the playoffs, is seen scoring the third Red Wing goal. He finished perfectly to beat goalie Hainsworth after Mud Bruneteau, the Rookie star, on a great play which he started in the Detroit zone, had passed to Wally. Bruneteau intercepted a Toronto pass just across the Detroit blue line. Breaking away from the jam of players, Bruneteau, still off-balance, almost lost the puck near mid-ice, but recovered it in time and, skating into Toronto ice, passed to young Kilrea, who finished the job."

—*Detroit Times* photo/Courtesy of *The Detroit News*

Joe Louis was among the spectators in the crowd to see the opening game of the Stanley Cup Finals.
—*Detroit Times* photo/Courtesy of *The Detroit News*

"Three fledgling Red Wings who bagged the goals." Each of these three young Red Wings scored a goal in the opening game against Toronto to give Detroit a 3–1 victory. Pictured are (from left to right) Syd Howe, Bucko "the socko" McDonald and Wally "the pest" Kilrea.
—*Detroit Times* photo/Courtesy of *The Detroit News*

Joe Louis, another illustrious son of this great city of champions, saw the Wings move closer to the Stanley Cup. Wearing the usual dead pan, the Brown Bomber had little to say. "Toronto reminds me of my pool game," he said to an assembled group at intermission. "They can't get the ball in the pocket."

—Bob Murphy, *Detroit Times*, 4/6/36

It was McDonald's goal in this game, however, that must be emphasized and which Jack Adams would rank among his favorite moments of the playoffs, describing it as: *"one of the prettiest scoring plays I ever saw."* It was this goal which really got Olympia jumping,

But coming while the Wings were a man short—with Larry Aurie in the box-it sent the huge crowd into a state of vocal convulsions that made the ice palace quiver and tremble. It was the mightiest salute ever to beat down the ear drums of the all-conquering Red Wings. The rising crescendo of sound continued for what seemed like minutes. Larry Aurie was beating his stick against the boards of the penalty box. On the ice the Red Wolves showered the giant kid with hugs, backslaps and embraces. Capt. Doug Young slapped his defense mate with a fond fierceness. Normie Smith, back in the nets, was prancing back and forth, tapping his stick

against the ice. But the roar of the crowd continued. Men forgot dignity as they stood waving hats and screaming. And the dear little ladies, God bless them, yip-yapped and tugged at whomever happened to be closest to them. "My, what an ovation," declared Jack Adams in the dressing room long after it was over. "That was the darndest moment of my life," admitted Bucko. "I felt so silly when it was all over. I didn't know whether to laugh or cry. The crowd kept roaring and I felt numb all over. It's a sensation you can't describe." Yes, if the walls of Olympia could talk they probably would tell you that the mightiest ovation it has ever known was experienced last night when Bucko McDonald scored the first goal of the Stanley Cup series.

—Bob Murphy, *Detroit Times*, 4/6/36

A description of this first game would not be complete without some of the more colorful moments that took place throughout its course. These scenes give a glimpse into the personality and character of hockey at this time,

On one mixup around the Detroit goal, Syd Howe crawled in the net and stretched out to help ward off any possible shots. When the scramble was over, Normie Smith rubbed his gloved hand across Syd's head in appreciation.

Red Horner tried to get to Syd Howe to test out

one of his best Sunday punches in the last period after a penalty had been called on him. A. G. Smith, the official, stopped him to quiet the flaming haired giant. After Red emerged from the 'cooler' he dashed about the ice like a mad bull. The crowd gave him a shower of boos that rattled the roof.

One fan went into a rage when Charley Conacher, the great Leaf wingman, sailed into Bucko McDonald from the rear with his stick against McDonald's head. The fan stood for a minute or so, leaning over the boards, and giving Charley a neat verbal going over.

Owner Jim Norris was especially pleased over the way Herbie Lewis handled Chuck Conacher, ace of the Maple Leafs. "It was a master-ful job," said Norris. "I'm pretty proud of it myself," added Herbie.

Connie Smythe, Leaf manager, wore an Easter lily that some Wing fan put in his lapel. "You'll need plenty of lilies at the end of this series," de-clared the fan. Connie took it with a smile.

There [were] two fights among the specta-tors. One was a honey with a pudgy gent taking care of two youthful neighbors behind him.

—Bob Murphy, *Detroit Times*, 4/6/36

Stanley Cup Finals Game 2: Olympia Stadium, 4/7/36

"Just a feeler," Frank (King) Clancy declared. "The real series starts tomorrow night." "We gave the Red Wings a game handicap to even things up."

"[The] Red Wings were hot." Smythe said, "It's our turn to get hot tomorrow night. I still think we can win the cup."

—Leo Macdonell, *Detroit Times*, 4/6/36

These two quotes were published on the eve of the sec-ond game of the series and reflect the feelings of the Maple Leafs. Of course players and owners on a team must project a certain confidence in order to play, but it shows that the Leafs still lacked respect for the Red Wings. In the course of this second game, the Wings would demand that respect, as the byline for the newspa-per following the game makes perfectly clear,

They were still digging Goalie George Hainsworth out of puck-flooded nets as triumphant Red Wings, pluming themselves, early today left for Toronto after crushing the Maple Leafs 9 to 4, to set new scoring records for modern hockey in the worst defeat ever handed a team in the Stanley Cup championship playoffs.

—Leo Macdonell, *Detroit Times*, 4/8/36

This game was never close, even from the very beginning as Wally Kilrea scored after only one minute and thirty seconds. Goals by Marty Barry, Herbie Lewis, and Bucko McDonald arrived over the course of the first period with Toronto only answering with one.

Striking early and cyclonic as they did in the first tussle between the two, Red Wings flooded the Toronto net with three goals inside of 10 minutes and 5 seconds, plunging the throng into a hysteria from which it never recovered as goal after goal was exploded into the nets.

—Leo Macdonell, *Detroit Times*, 4/8/36

Two goals in the second period by Johnny Sorrell and Gord Pettinger extended the lead as Toronto again, could answer with only one. The lead at the end of the second was stretched to 6–2 as the Wings began to exploit the primary weakness of Toronto; the defensemen,

Only a part of the scoring can be charged to Hainsworth. Only a supergoalie could have with-stood those attacks without help other than a pa-pier-mâché front put up by his mates.

—Leo Macdonell, *Detroit Times*, 4/8/36

The massacre continued throughout the third period as Sorrell, Pettinger, and McDonald all scored their second goals of the game, Toronto answering with two. With all of the goals and assists, only four Red Wings failed to register a point. Sorrell leading all scorers, with four points com-ing on his two goals and two assists. Even when Toronto switched their lineup and tried to attack the entire third period with five forwards, the Wings had still dominated,

Blind fury was not enough to stop the smooth and polished red-clad whirling dervishes that made monkeys out of what was once regarded as

Charlie Conacher and Scotty Bowman battle for the puck behind the Red Wing net.

—Detroit Times photo/Courtesy of *The Detroit News*

Normie Smith kicks the puck away from Conacher before he could get his shot off.

—Detroit Times photo/Courtesy of *The Detroit News*

"The End of a Perfect Evening"
Bucko McDonald scores his second goal of the game, and ninth overall for his team. (Notice the puck just about to cross the line)

—Detroit Times photo/Courtesy of *The Detroit News*

"Six Red Wings Who Shot in the 9 Goals That Beat Toronto Maple Leafs."
These six Red Wings are all smiles after the 9-4 romp of the Leafs in Game 2. (From left to right) Johnny Sorrell (2 goals), Wally Kilrea (2 goals), Bucko McDonald (2 goals), Herbie Lewis, Marty Barry, and Gord Pettinger.

—Detroit Times photo/Courtesy of *The Detroit News*

hockey's greatest aggregation. It was dazzling, dizzying hockey that beat down the blue-clads of Toronto to give the puck chasing fans of Detroit their greatest night. The spectacle of young McDonald, two years out of the amateurs, and the scrappy Wally Kilrea and others unknown until this season, pomping over and around the Leafs, provided a treat of treats for those who witnessed the night.

—Leo Macdonell, *Detroit Times*, 4/8/36

Charlie Conacher hadn't scored in the first game, but how long could the Wings keep the "fast-express of the Leafs" at bay?

—*Detroit Times* photo/ Courtesy of The Detroit News

This game was a truly dominant demonstration of the Red Wings in front of their home crowd. Amid all of the goal scoring was a truly exceptional performance by Herbie Lewis, who had kept the dangerous Charlie Conacher bottled up, and goalless. Before the series, people had said that "as went Conacher, so went the Leafs." Conacher had no goals in two games and the Leafs had no wins in two games. With the team rolling on all cylinders, the Wings caught the train out to Toronto full of confidence and looking for the third and final win that would clinch them the Stanley Cup.

Stanley Cup Finals Game 3: Toronto Maple Leaf Gardens, 4/9/36

With the Red Wings arriving in Toronto, the momentum of the series had taken a huge turn in Detroit's favor. The once-confident Maple Leafs were now hoping for a win of any kind and were now reduced to amusing anecdotes about their struggles. One such anecdote comes from Frank Selke, *[Conn] Smythe's right hand man, wants two pucks on the ice for tonight's game. "It isn't fair for the Red Wings to have a puck all alone!"*

The Red Wings were even getting in on the banter. When a reporter asked Bucko McDonald how he had hurt his wrist in game two, he responded by saying, *"from overexercising it in scoring goals."*

In front of 14,000 fans at the Maple Leaf Gardens, the

Red Wings got off to a good start when Scotty Bowman scored midway into the first period,

Taking Pettinger's pass in the Detroit's sector, where Toronto's forwards were trapped, Bowman paved the way for his marker with a sensational dash down the ice after eluding Blair, who came out to meet him. As Bowman swung in from left wing he stickhandled in beautifully feinted Hainsworth out of the cage and drilled the puck in behind the hapless Maple Leaf goalie, a smart piece of work for the Toronto born Detroit player.

—Leo Macdonell, *Detroit Times*, 4/10/36

The game continued to favor the Red Wings when Marty Barry *"humiliated"* Charlie Conacher in the second period. Conacher was skating with the puck and zigzagging his way up the ice—around several Wings and had only Barry to beat for a break away chance on goal. This type of play had been Conacher's trademark, and he looked primed to use it, when Barry skated in and cleanly stole the puck to start a break going in the other direction. The break didn't result in a goal but it did leave everyone impressed, once again by Barry's handling of Conacher.

A goal by Mud Bruneteau in the second kept the momentum of the game firmly in Detroit's favor,

Bruneteau scored Detroit's second goal with a freak shot that must have set some sort of a record for distance in a playoff final. The shot, lifted from center ice, fully 10 feet in front of the Toronto blue line, bounced on its way to the net and as it did Hainsworth stepped out to stop what seemed to be an easy save. The rubber bounced and Hainsworth nicked only a piece of it and the disc was deflected into the net. The crowd was stunned.

—Leo Macdonell, *Detroit Times*, 4/10/36

Mid-way through the third period Syd Howe batted in a third goal for the Wings on a pass from Wally Kilrea and Gord Pettinger. At this point the Stanley Cup was brought out near the ice on a table and Frank Calder, the NHL president, started moving towards it to make the formal presentation. Two minutes later a goal by the Leafs' Joe Primeau brought cheering from the crowd for finally ending Normie Smith's shutout. Two minutes after that, the crowd was really given something to cheer about,

Abandoning all defense [with] five minutes to go. [Regis] Kelly rushed spectacularly down right wing with [Frank] Finnigan's pass to rifle a sizzling shot that found its mark hard in the corner at Smith's right for a Toronto goal. Smith didn't have a chance on the shot.

—Leo Macdonell, *Detroit Times*, 4/10/36

The Wings seemingly insurmountable three goal lead had been cut to one as the minutes ticked away. The Leafs maintained their pure offensive attack hoping to get a goal and tie the game. With forty-two seconds left—they got it,

Forty-two seconds to go—and the roof came off the building as Kelly scored to tie the count. The goal came on a faceoff in which Primeau won the draw and Kelly snared his mate's puck and jammed it inside of Smith at the corner of the net.

—Leo Macdonell, *Detroit Times*, 4/10/36

Normie Smith under tremendous pressure, had allowed the three goals, but he had, in fact, saved 22 shots in this third period alone, many of which were described as *"outstanding."* Incredibly, something happened that would blur the boundaries of sports, logic, nature, and magic. Several people saw it, but even they couldn't believe their eyes, and Bob Murphy of the Detroit Times was the only one bold enough to actually write about it,

A most unusual thing happened just a second or two before Pep Kelly shot the tying goal with 42 seconds left to play in the third period. A young kid threw a rabbit's foot from a place above the Detroit goal. This rabbit's foot landed on the wire just back of Smith. Several newspapermen noticed it. To be sure their eyes were not betraying them; one of the number went on the ice at intermission time and verified the report. It really was a rabbit's foot.

—Bob Murphy, *Detroit Times*, 4/10/36

Going into overtime, it was now anyone's game, but it was the Leafs who had the momentum and fate, or magic, or something was on their side. Barely thirty seconds into the extra period, Buzz Boll scored the game winner,

Five of the Leafs came racing down the ice. Out of a mad scramble; "Mud" Bruneteau regained the puck and lifted it over his own net. The puck was held against the boards. A faceoff followed with Wally Kilrea and Billy Thoms trying to win the draw. Again the puck rolled into the corner where Art Jackson pushed it to "Red" Horner. All of the Leafs were fighting for the puck and "Buzz" Boll was left uncovered in front of the Detroit net. Through the massed players, Horner pushed the disc to Boll, who stalled with his shot until Smith made his move and then picked an open corner perfectly. Only 31 seconds had been played in the overtime when the game ended in a Toronto victory.

—Lloyd Northard, *The Detroit News*, 4/10/36

The scene in the Red Wings' dressing room after the game was initially one of dejection. All of them were stunned, and they knew that newspaper reports were being printed up at that very moment talking about the possibility that the momentum in the series had been lost due to this "miracle game." It was at this point that one of the greatest legends in Red Wings' history, spoke,

The Red Wings dressed in almost complete silence. Doug Young talked to a friend in low tones in one corner of the room. Jack Adams sat on a trunk saying nothing. Normie Smith undressed slowly, looking at the floor. It was Ebbie Goodfellow who first broke the silence. "Say," shouted Ebbie, tucking his shirt in his pants, "what the h___? The pressure is still on those guys, we'll get them Saturday night." Adams came off his trunk with a thump. "We won seven straight games," he shouted. "The law of averages was against us." "We'll take care of them Saturday night," inserted Johnny Sorrell. The Wings then completed dressing and strolled out, one by one, to go to their hotel. "Forget this one," was Owner Jim Norris' advice.

—Bob Murphy, *Detroit Times*, 4/10/36

In this picture Joe Primeau scores the first Toronto goal with 8 minutes and 6 seconds left in the game.
—*Detroit Times* photo/ Courtesy of *The Detroit News*

Syd Howe, shown above, scored the third Red Wings goal, giving his team a 3-0 lead mid-way through the third period of this potential Stanley Cup clinching game.
—*Detroit Times* photo/ Courtesy of *The Detroit News*

Regis "Pep" Kelly (15) scores his second goal in 5 minutes to tie the game. According to Bob Murphy of the Detroit Times, a child in the crowd threw a rabbit's foot which got caught in the back of Normie Smith's net-seconds before this photo was taken.
—*Detroit Times* photo/ Courtesy of *The Detroit News*

Conn Smythe hugs "Buzz" Boll after the latter scored the game winner. Boll's score completed Toronto's "Miracle Win" which saw the Leafs score 4 goals in 8:37 seconds.
—*Detroit Times* photo/ Courtesy of *The Detroit News*

Stanley Cup Finals Game 4:
Toronto Maple Leaf Gardens, 4/11/36

Would being so close, only to collapse, affect the Wings? The players themselves hooted at it. And they are the ones who must give the answer.

— Bob Murphy, *Detroit Times*, 4/10/36

Riding high on the crest of their "miracle win," the Maple Leafs skated into this game a much more balanced and steady team than what they had demonstrated previously. Joe Primeau scored the first goal of the contest, late in the first period; much to the delight of their 14,728 fans.

The Red Wings were up for the game however, and played up and down the ice with an intensity that matched the importance of this game. At one point Ebbie Goodfellow and Charlie Conacher demonstrated this intensity *"as the game flared [and they] mixed with fists."* It was Goodfellow, who scored the Red Wings' first goal-midway through the second period,

He broke fast from his own defense zone and passed to Johnny Sorrell on the left wing, drawing the Leaf defense. The return pass was perfect and so was Goodfellow's delayed shot to tie the score.

— Lloyd Northard, *The Detroit News*, 4/12/36

Goodfellow's first goal of the playoffs was followed almost immediately by a goal from Marty Barry,

In less than a minute the Wings were in the lead. Barry headed the rush and gave Lewis a quick short pass inside the Leaf blue line. Lewis made a perfect pass that allowed Barry time enough to draw George Hainsworth out of position and pitch the puck into a wide open net.

— Lloyd Northard, *The Detroit News*, 4/12/36

Detroit knew that a one goal lead was tenuous at best, especially after their experience in the previous game. They continued their attack into the third period and were rewarded with a goal from Pete Kelly, his first of the series,

Kelly took Aurie's pass on the line with Barry and Lewis, and the change had hardly been made when Kelly scored from in front of the net with Lewis' pass. The goal was very apparent but the

These three Red Wings (from left to right) Johnny Sorrell, Herbie Lewis and Ebbie Goodfellow look relaxed as they prepare to try again for their first Stanley Cup Championship. Goodfellow would score his first goal of the series mid-way through the second period.
— *Detroit Times* photo/ Courtesy of *The Detroit News*

Pete Kelly (15) beating George Hainsworth to the top corner with the Red Wings' third goal of the game. This score gave the Wings a two goal lead, but after their experience in the previous game, the Detroiters knew that no lead was safe.
— *Detroit Times* photo/ Courtesy of *The Detroit News*

The Leafs' frantic rush netted one goal, but the Wings were able to keep their lead until the final whistle sounded. Shown here is a moment from the last three minutes. Notice the body check Bucko McDonald is laying on Charlie Conacher behind the goal!

—*Detroit Times* photo/ Courtesy of *The Detroit News*

light did not flash. Stewart didn't miss it and goal was counted over the protests of the Leafs.

—Leo Macdonell, *Detroit Times*, 4/12/36

The two-goal cushion didn't last long for the Wings as only one minute later the Maple Leafs' Bill Thoms scored a goal on Smith from 15 feet out. With time running out the crowd was rejuvenated by this goal, as Toronto attempted to comeback as they had the night before,

Sensing another finish like that in the first game here the crowd was in an uproar. Frantically the Leafs fought to come level with the Wings. They fought viciously, with each rush fiercer than the one before. There was a temporary lull as the lines were changed. Six minutes to go.

Primeau drove Smith to his knees. Young broke away with Barry's pass and was in on Hainsworth all alone only to lift the rubber over the top of the net. Barry too, swept away and missed a nice chance with nobody around him, Hainsworth coming far out of the net to save. Five minutes to go.

Kelly missed the net with Art Jackson's pass. Young golfed the puck out of danger, McDonald tumbled Conacher in a vicious check. Three minutes to go.

Howe rushed a shot and almost scored on a rebound. Hainsworth made two grand stops on Kelly, and Wally Kilrea. Two minutes to go.

Lines changed. Goodfellow iced the puck into Toronto territory. One minute to go.

Toronto again changed players and renewed the attack. They batted in center ice. Two seconds to go.

They faced off.

THE BELL!

—Leo Macdonell, *Detroit Times*, 4/12/36

Though the Red Wings had not won their championship at home, there were plenty of Detroit fans on hand to help the team celebrate. The scenes of celebration immediately afterward were well documented and quite vivid,

As soon as the whistle sounded the death knell of the Leafs' hope of overtaking the rampaging Wings, the Red Wing rooting section became a section reserved for lunatics. Derbies, programs, jewelry and money shot on the ice. So did Goldie Smith, Red Wing scout. You never saw a he-man kiss another one as Goldie did his namesake Normie. But Goodfellow had beaten Smith to that honor. As Smith cracked his stick on the ice as the whistle sounded, Goodfellow had him.

Johnny Sorrell, and Marty Barry, always the gentlemen, rushed for George Hainsworth, the Maple Leaf goalie, and shook his hand. Little George, a gentleman too, shook hands quickly and ran for Normie Smith. The two clasped hands and the crowd cheered. It was a wild moment. Jack Adams, the most emotional man in hockey next to Connie Smythe, surprised everyone. He didn't do anything. He just sat there with sort of a stunned smile, a frozen one. Then suddenly Jack

(Left to right) Pete Kelly, Ebbie Goodfellow, and Marty Barry; all goal scorers on the evening-show their happiness as a photographer captures this image of them in the showers.

Jack Adams leads his team in cheering for his first Stanley Cup in Detroit.

—*Detroit Times* photo/ Courtesy of *The Detroit News*

Adams realized he had gained the ambition of his life—the Stanley Cup for Detroit. He jumped up, grabbed Mr. Norris' hand and the hands of every one of the players. Back to the dressing room the victory parade started. The Toronto crowd, the most fanatical throng that ever cursed a referee and hated a rival team, showed their sportsmanship. They gave the Wings a wild cheer as they started to march to the exits. Back in the dressing room the first person to greet Adams was Connie Smythe, the losing manager. "You've got one of the best hockey clubs of all time, Jack." Smythe said. Then Edward W. Bickle, executive member of the Maple Leaf Gardens, showed his sportsmanship by shaking hands with Adams and throwing his arms around him. He was almost in tears at the Toronto loss, however.

—*Detroit Free Press* editorial, 4/12/36

Following the on-ice celebrations, NHL President Frank Calder informed James Norris that the Stanley Cup presentation would not be at the arena but at the Royal York Hotel, where a large suite had been set up. Norris agreed with the plan but threw in one condition, *"providing I can fill it (Stanley Cup) with champagne and give all of my players a drink!"* His one condition was granted and the celebration in the Royal York Hotel in Toronto commenced,

One of the first things Adams did after returning to the Royal York Hotel Saturday night was to call his father and mother in Fort William, Ontario, on the long distance telephone. "This is the happiest moment in my life," said Jack. "The Stanley Cup is sitting on the table right here in front of me. I wish you could be here to see it." There were plenty of other people to see it. The room was packed with Red Wings and well wishers. The Stanley Cup was filled with champagne and emptied time and again. Ed Oulette, of Windsor liquor control commissioner of Ontario, suspended all regulations so that the supply would be unlimited. The Red Wings burst out into song. They serenaded Owner Norris, his son, Jim, Adams and sundry others. The singing was a trifle off key. If the hockey playing had been as bad, there would have been no singing.

—Lloyd Northard, *The Detroit News*, 4/13/36

Mr. James D. Norris and son Jim, entertained in Toronto Saturday night and Sunday morning. Those present were members of the Detroit Red Wings and anybody else in Toronto who found it possible to squeeze up to the champagne table in the Norris suite. It really was a celebration. The players gulped champagne and Mr. Jack Adams, the man who fines the boys $50 for reading a beer ad, just smiled and shouted: "Go to it boys, It's our night." And did "our boys" go to it! One might have suspected they had trained on champagne since the cradle. Only one man refused to drink champagne and that was Mr. Adams himself. A dozen times he put his lips up to the Stanley Cup and sipped, but it was just a gesture.

The tenor of the entire celebration was joyous.

(From left to right) James Norris Jr., Herbie Lewis holding the Stanley Cup and James Norris Sr. after the game at the Royal York Hotel.

—Photo courtesy of the Hockey Hall of Fame.

Captain Doug Young shows his joy at the Red Wings winning their first Stanley Cup.

—*Detroit Times* photo/ Courtesy of *The Detroit News*

The Red Wings all chipped in to buy "Smitty" the train porter a leather Red Wings jacket, for all of his help on their travels to Canada. (Counter clockwise from Smitty) Ebbie Goodfellow, John Sorrell, Syd Howe, Herbie Lewis, Larry Aurie, Doug Young, and Bucko McDonald.

—*Detroit Times* photo/ Courtesy of *The Detroit News*

Jack Adams and the Red Wings arrive in Detroit with the city's first Stanley Cup.

—Photo courtesy of the *Detroit Free Press*

Adams had his hand twisted several thousand times. So did Norris and his son Jim. In fact it was Norris who was the center of the party. Norris might deny it, but never in his entire life has any accomplishment so pleased him as to bring the Stanley Cup to Detroit. At least 50 strange women kissed him.

—Doc Holst, *Detroit Free Press*, 4/13/36

The party continued on the train ride back from Toronto to Detroit. Most of the players had not slept since 10 a.m. the day before, and would not sleep for quite awhile. As the train stopped briefly in Windsor, several crowds congregated around the train area. But this was only a hint about what awaited them in Detroit,

A throng that jammed the lobby of the Michigan Central Station Sunday afternoon and overflowed into the streets, paid its tribute to Jack Adams and his Red Wings for bringing to Detroit its first Stanley Cup. Jack Adams, [holding] the Cup as though it were a baby, marched triumphantly through the lane provided by police. Beside him was Capt. Doug Young. On the other side was roly-poly Normie Smith, the outstanding hero of the 1936 playoffs. Following Adams, Capt. Young, and Normie, came the rest of the team, all of them marching quite well, considering that none had been to bed since they arose Saturday morning at 10 AM. Some of them would

have gone to bed but from the rink in Toronto to the Olympia nobody would let them. Anyway, they didn't want to go to sleep. Stanley Cups don't come out of slot machines.

At Windsor the boys began to be nervous as they saw crowds of Canadians gathered around the station. It was an indication of what was to follow at the Michigan Central Station.

James D. Norris, the man whose money made the Stanley Cup possible for Detroit, hung in the background like an embarrassed boy. Mrs. Adams had to drag him into the victory march from the train through the lane of hockey enthusiasts. At first he pretended not to hear Mrs. Adams and her earnest pleas that he should share in the greatest hockey honor any city could have. Even after a dozen persons pulled his coat, he merely nodded and then when everybody started to march, Norris dodged into the background. "I didn't win the Cup," he told reporters. "I'm just glad I could be of some assistance. It was my one ambition of my life to have a Stanley Cup for Detroit. My ambition was realized through those fellows and that man carrying the Cup." That man carrying the cup was Jack Adams. "Jack gave me the most harmonious hockey club the game ever has known." Norris continued. "He's a wonder, Jack is. There's none better."

As the victorious hockey stars reached the center of the station corridor, the crowd forgot to make a lane and pushed around them for autographs and souvenirs.

—Doc Holst, *Detroit Free Press*, 4/13/36

When we got back to Detroit after the game, the town had gone wild. There seemed to be thousands of people at the railway station and we were driven in a procession to Olympia where another celebration took place.

—Ebbie Goodfellow in Stan Fischler,
"Those Were the Days"

If the Red Wings had thought that they would be sleeping anytime soon, they were mistaken. On the day they returned, a few managed naps, but all went to watch the final IHL championship game between the Olympics and Bulldogs. The Olympics did in fact win the championship, and in dominating fashion. They had won all six games in the playoffs, sweeping both Syracuse and Windsor to win the Teddy Oke Trophy. There was a certain bond between the Red Wings and Olympics at this time. Many of the Red Wings players had come from the ranks of the Olympics, and many times throughout the course of the year injuries had forced the Wings to "call-up" players from their minor league club. As the two teams were in the playoffs together, they attended each others' games to show support, and in the final game all of the Wings were present in the stands and in the dressing room to help them celebrate the win.

All of the Red Wings rushed to the dressing room after the game to offer congratulations to Hughes and his men. Owner Jim Norris, Jim Norris Jr. and others were there.

—Bob Murphy, *Detroit Times*, 4/13/36

The Red Wings' motorcade heads to Olympia to watch the Olympics last game for the Teddy Oke (IHL Championship).
—*Detroit Times* photo/ Courtesy of *The Detroit News*

Another view of the Wings' motorcade and the streets crowded with fans, trying to get a glimpse of the first Stanley Cup in Detroit.
—Photo courtesy of the *Detroit Free Press*

RED WINGS AND OLYMPICS TESTIMONIAL BANQUET

There was much hilarious hey-hey and hey-nonny-nonny, to say nothing of considerable emotional stuttering and sputtering, at last night's banquet at Hotel Statler in honor of Detroit's two hockey champions—Red Wings and Olympics. It was one of the grandest affairs of its kind you ever attended, but, even at that, it was only infield practice for the big doings ahead, Saturday night, at Masonic Temple, when all of this town's champions will be housed under one roof as the crazed sporting clan pays tribute.

—Bob Murphy, *Detroit Times,* 4/16/36

Like the Tigers and Lions before them, the Red Wings (and Olympics) were given a congratulatory dinner in honor of their championship. It was very important that the Red Wings be given this testimonial by the city as they were being recognized on the same level as the Tigers and Lions. It was also important because it was an official welcome by the city of Detroit to the *Red Wings*; never again would the name be changed.

The toastmaster for the banquet would be Harvey Campbell who had served in the same capacity for the Tigers and Lions, and he first introduced Jim Norris Sr. as *"the greatest guy Detroit ever allowed to live in Chicago."* Norris' speech was very poignant as he alleviated a concern of many people in the room with what he had to say,

A second or so later Mr. Norris, sportsman, scholar and gentleman—above all, gentleman—came back with a public promise that never would he become interested or attempt to purchase any other club in the National Hockey League. "I'll stick with Detroit all the way," said Norris, thus vetoing all rumors that he has designs on gaining control of other clubs—notably the [New York] Americans. "We may buy another minor league club at some time or other, but it will be only to assure the Wings of more reserve strength."

—Bob Murphy, *Detroit Times,* 4/16/36

Many other scenes followed the speech by Norris, as the landmark dinner carried on into the night,

"The Pest" (Wally Kilrea), Ebbie Goodfellow and Herbie Lewis took top honors for Red Wing oratory. Adams explained how Donnie Hughes (Olympics Coach) thought Wally Kilrea the greatest player in the world, and that Donnie probably wouldn't trade Wally for either Marty Barry or Charlie Conacher. "Well Jack," said Wally, after being introduced "I'd trade you for Donnie!" Which caused the guys and gals to chuckle no little. And then Brother Hec Kilrea, oldest player in point of hockey service on the team, remembered that he and Adams played together on the old Ottawa Stanley Cup winner in 1926–27. "I think Jack's a sissy because he still isn't playing," said Hec.

Doug Young made his maiden speech and drew down an ovation. Dr. Boze Bordeau, O's trainer, had a little side battle with a waiter over the chances of getting a little pickled herring, but in the main things moved along remarkably smooth. K.T. Keller of the Chrysler organization and one of the town's red hot fans, suggested that Detroit assemble all its cups and place them downtown so that visitors to the city might be inspired. Mayor Frank Couzens slipped in a line that drew a chorus of hee-haws. "Saw a game the other night," said the mayor. "The woman in front of me apparently didn't realize what a fast game hockey really is. She finally declared herself: 'Why don't they quit changing lines and give the boys a chance?'" Mud Bruneteau pulled a novel act. Jack Adams told the Wings that failure to respond with

(From left to right) Normie Smith (No.1), Wally Kilrea (No.9), Bucko McDonald (No.3) and Larry Aurie (No.6) pose with their jerseys for this picture; to leave no doubt about what year it was when the Red Wings won their first Stanley Cup.
—*Detroit Times* photo/ Courtesy of *The Detroit News*

1935–1936 Stanley Cup Champion Detroit Red Wings
—Photo courtesy of the Detroit Red Wings

1935–1936 IHL Champion Detroit Olympics

Teddy Oke trophy. Symbol of IHL supremacy, won by the Detroit Olympics in 1935–1936.
—Photo courtesy of the Hockey Hall of Fame

The two trophy's won by the Red Wings in 1935–1936, left is the Prince of Wales trophy, and on the right is of course the original Lord Stanley's Cup.
—Photo courtesy of the Hockey Hall of Fame

some kind of speech would cost $50. Bruneteau took care of this by making his short talk in French as the crowd howled. It really was a great occasion for a glorious bunch of champions. But 'twas only infield practice for Saturday night's "City of Champions" banquet at Masonic Temple.

—Bob Murphy, *Detroit Times*, 4/16/36

IMPORTANCE OF THE RED WINGS WINNING CHAMPIONSHIP IN 1935–1936

By triumphing over Toronto's blue horde, the Red Wing's gave Detroit a "grand slam" in sports. The three major team titles—baseball, football, and hockey—are claimed by this dynamic "City of Champions."

—Bob Murphy, *Detroit Times*, 4/13/36

A quick look up at the rafters in Joe Louis Arena shows the importance of this first championship. Had not the first championship banner been hung, it is quite possible that none of the others would have been hung. Though

the franchise had existed in Detroit for ten years, it had been in a state of flux; changing its name twice and going through up and down years as it fought to carve a niche in the city's sports consciousness. Winning the championship in the same year as the Tigers and Lions elevated the Red Wings onto the same pedestal, cementing the franchise in the hearts and minds of Detroit's community of fans. Like a tower being built, this championship provided the foundation for its stability, allowing the franchise to add story upon story of future successes.

One issue that was definitely answered was the question of Jim Norris Sr. possibly buying up another franchise. Until this championship, Norris did not have any particular attachment with the Red Wings, as an owner he was always more or less a "free agent." If he had grown weary with this team not winning, or maybe a more established franchise had sought out his patronage, would he have possibly moved on to give his financial support to another team—such as his hometown Chicago Blackhawks? If he had left, would the team have continued to grow and develop into the NHL power that it did without his backing? Had he not developed a bond with this team and left, would a new owner have come in and changed the name to suit his particular taste, the iconic "Winged Wheel" logo fading into the realm of the forgotten? These are questions that need never be answered because the Red Wings did win this championship, and the franchise did become a stable power under the patronage of Norris.

On April 6th, 1936, a day after the first game of the Stanley Cup finals, the Detroit Times announced that a Testimonial dinner was going to be held for all of the champions in the city. The announcement was in the form of a newspaper article and the Red Wings were to be present after winning the American Division championship and the Prince of Wales Trophy which had accompanied it. But in reality, this dinner was not for division champions, it was for world champions. When this announcement came out, the Wings were put in an awkward position because now they *had* to win the Stanley Cup. They couldn't show up with the Prince of Wales trophy and expect that to be good enough, this would have been embarrassing for the franchise and possibly even had a detrimental effect on it. Anybody who was anybody at this party walked in wearing the mantle of world champions, and with their Stanley Cup win in 1935–1936; the Red Wings would not be the exception.

CHAPTER
5

CITY OF CHAMPIONS TESTIMONIAL

Champions Day!

Only one city in the whole world could hold such a holiday as Detroit is celebrating today. Detroit, the City of Champions! Detroit, the Capitol of the Sports World.

—Edgar Hayes, *Detroit Times,* 4/18/36

Shortly after the Red Wings' Stanley Cup victory the newspapers began to go crazy over the idea that Detroit was supreme in all three major sports. Each team had celebrated their championships and received Testimonial dinners. Now it was decided to have one major Testimonial dinner which would bring all of the teams together in one giant celebration. Along with the three teams, Joe Louis would be the guest of honor as the "uncrowned champion" of boxing. In addition to the major sports and Joe Louis, this Testimonial would honor the other Detroit Champions of the 1935–1936 sporting season, of which there were many.

Gar Wood, nicknamed the "Gray Fox of the Algonac" was a major figure in the world of water sports at this time. He had first set the world record for speed on water in 1920 near the Isle of Wight [an island off of the coast of England], with a speed of 61.51 miles-per-hour. In 1932 he had beaten his own record. His new record of 124.86 miles-per-hour, set on the St. Clair River, left him still in possession of the Harmsworth Trophy, the award for the world record of speed on water.

Gar Wood is to the speedboat, what Lindbergh is to the airplane and Paderewski is to the piano. No individual or team in the world stands more supreme in its particular field than Detroit's Gar Wood.

For more than 15 years some of the best mechanical minds in the world have been plotting and scheming with a hope of lifting the Harmsworth Trophy from Gar Wood and America. This sly slender veteran of the roaring main was quoted by the International News Service as saying: "I'm always afraid some of these English, French or Italian boat builders will learn how to reduce the skin friction on a boat beyond anything we know now. If they do they are likely to come over here and lift the Harmsworth Trophy. This won't happen without a battle. You see I've become kind of attached to that darn thing since I won it over 15 years ago. I'd hate to think one of those foreigners could beat us at anything."

—Bob Murphy, *Detroit Times,* 4/16/36

Detroit was also home to one of golf's early legends, Walter Hagen, who was the first club professional at Oakland Hills Country Club in Bloomfield Hills, Michigan. In September of 1935, Hagen had captained the U.S. Ryder Cup team to victory over the British 9–3 in Ridgewood, New Jersey. Hagen had also teamed with Gene Sarazen to win one of the Scottish foursome matches.

The Dixie Oils were a professional fast-pitch softball team from Detroit and had dominated on their way to winning the George H. Sisler Trophy in September 1935,

In a sport in which pitching is supreme, the four Detroit pitchers William Dombrowski, Dick Zimmerman, Popeye Novak and Ralph Cook, showed

(Clockwise from top) Gar Wood Sr., the world record speed boat, "Miss America X" and his son Gar Wood Jr.

"Speed, they say, is more than a hobby with Gar Wood. It's his fetish, his religion. He walks, eats, sleeps and dreams motorboating. His father was a Duluth steamboat captain. So you might say he was born on the water.

Those who have been close to Gar Wood down through the years will tell you he has as much fight and determination as any man you could meet. He thrives on competition and loves a fight.

Since Gar Wood is the 'king of speed on water,' it is entirely fitting that his son, Garfield A. Wood Jr., should bear the title of 'crown prince.'"

—Bob Murphy
Photos courtesy of the *Detroit Free Press*

Walter Hagen, one of the all-time legends of golf, called Detroit home. He captained the victorious 1935 U.S. Ryder Cup team.
—Photos courtesy of the
Detroit Free Press
Obtained through the use of
the Alan Feldman Collection

The Dixie Oils, winners of the softball championship and the accompanying George H. Sisler trophy in September 1935.

—Photos courtesy of the *Detroit Free Press*
Obtained through the use of the Alan Feldman Collection

themselves masters of the art, striking out 119 during the series, an average of 19 a game. Their efforts were ably seconded by the other members of the team, Rollie DeChene and Milton Ludwig, catchers; Spike Waltz, John Clancy, Bill Slove, Frank Shields and Wallace Machon, outfielders, and Charles Bartus, Andy Jacobs, S. Spudzinski and Arthur Mueller, infielders. Ray Crout is the manager of the team. Teams from all parts of the United States were entered but the Dixie Oils, by the expedient of allowing their opponents very few hits and no runs, won all six games in the title series and returned home with the George H. Sisler Trophy, emblematic of the championship of the United States.

—John E. McManis, *The Detroit News*, 12/22/35

Detroit was also the home of the World Champion Stroh's bowling team. This team had won the American Bowling Congress championship at Peoria, Illinois in 1934, and had travelled to New York later that year to play against other national champions from around the world. They beat every country that competed, including: Germany, Sweden, Finland and Canada. As the 1935 season started they were still champions after their dominating performance. Joe Norris (captain and future bowling Hall-of-Famer), Phil Bauman, Walter Reppenhagen, Cass Grygler and Freddy Gardella were the five members of the squad and boasted truly outstanding career totals after winning this championship. Between the five of them they had bowled 47 perfect games and they held *"the city high single, (1251), and high series, (3481), records. [They] rolled 3 series over 3500, 12 over 3400, 24 over 3300, and 36 over 3200. Up until this year (1935) Stroh's held the highest average of any team competing in the world classic, 975.*

There were more champions at the banquet as well. In track, Eddie "the Midnight Express" Tolan, was world champion in sprinting. Tolan had won two gold medals at the 1932 Olympics (setting the record for 100 & 200 meters), and in 1935 won the world's professional sprinting championship during a tour in Australia.

Clark Haskins had won the senior A.A.U. championship in the 56-pound weight throw in 1934 and 1935, setting the record with a throw of 35 feet 1-2/3 inches. He was, *"the pride and joy of the Detroit police department; under whose banner he competes."*

Stanley Kratkowski had been national middleweight-

Eddie "the midnight express" Tolan was a native Detroiter and attended Cass Tech High School before his dominating college career at the University of Michigan. He won two gold medals at the 1932 Olympics and was the world's professional sprinting champion in 1935.
—Photos courtesy of the *Detroit Free Press* Obtained through the use of the Alan Feldman Collection

Clark Haskins, national A.A.U. 56-pound weight champion.

Stanley Kratkowski, national middle-weight lifting champion.

—Photos courtesy of the *Detroit Free Press* Obtained through the use of the Alan Feldman Collection

weightlifting champion for four years, setting eight records on his way to winning the national championship in 1935.

Besides Joe Louis were two other emerging boxers from Detroit who were champions in their own right. Al Nettlow was the national A.A.U. 126-pound champion, and Dave Clark, national A.A.U. 160-pound champion.

Esther Politzer (left) and Constance O'Donovan, (right) National Public courts doubles Champions, 1935.
—Photos courtesy of the *Detroit Free Press*
Obtained through the use of the Alan Feldman Collection

—*Detroit Times* photo/ Courtesy of *The Detroit News*

Dick Degener, " Fred Astaire of the Sports World," as well as its greatest diver (clockwise from top) showing the diving form that made him a champion, and in diving position.

Jake Ankrom, National amateur three cushion billiards Champion, 1935.
—Photos courtesy of the *Detroit Free Press*

Walter Kramer, rated number 1 badminton player in the United States in 1935.
—Photos courtesy of the *Detroit Free Press*

—Photo courtesy of the *Detroit Free Press* Obtained through the use of the Alan Feldman Collection

Bill Bonthron, holder of the 1,500 meter world's track record.
—Photos courtesy of the *Detroit Free Press*

Jimmy Gilhula (left) and the rest of the Detroit Athletic Club's outdoor swimming team. They captured the A.A.U. National Championship in 1935.

—Photos courtesy of the *Detroit Free Press*
Obtained through the use of the Alan Feldman Collection

Another speed boat racer was Herbert Mendleson of Detroit. His boat, the Notre Dame won the Presidents Cup after a race on the Potomac River.

—Photos courtesy of the *Detroit Free Press*
Obtained through the use of the Alan Feldman Collection

"Newell Banks, World's Match Checker Champion and keenest mind of the game in a generation."

—*Detroit Times* photo/ Courtesy
of *The Detroit News*

Harry B. Joy Jr., National 20-gauge skeet shooting Champion, 1935.

—Photos courtesy of the *Detroit Free Press*
Obtained through the use of the
Alan Feldman Collection

Dick Degener was considered the greatest diver in the world.

Degener is the Fred Astaire of the Sports World. His performance on the 10 foot board is the acme of grace, form and timing. To impress you the amazing ability of this Detroiter, he is a much greater favorite to beat the world's finest divers in the Olympics this summer at Berlin than Louis is to beat Braddock when they meet for the world's heavyweight title in September—which they will. And those who quote odds will tell you Louis is as high as 5–1 to beat Braddock. Degener has been awarded more "10's"—denoting flawless execution than any other diver in history. In 16 competitions off the 10-foot board in National A.A.U. competition, Degener has hit 158 dives. Another thing, at least one judge in every one of the dives has given him a rating of at least 9.

—Bob Murphy, *Detroit Times*, 4/9/36

"So great is his ability that he has lost but one championship in four years and when an American swimming team was picked for a tour of Japan [1935]. Degener was taken along for exhibitions, as the Japanese had no divers who could have competed against him."

—Bob Murphy, *Detroit Times*, 4/18/35

Sell Banquet Tickets At Two Places

Tickets for the City of Champions banquet, to be held at Masonic Temple April 18, may be purchased at The Detroit Times lobby or the cigar stand of the Book-Cadillac Hotel.

This banquet will honor all of Detroit's champions, including the Detroit Tigers, Red Wings, Olympics, Joe Louis, Detroit Lions and a score of individual titleholders.

The cost of tickets is $3. It is possible to reserve tables of 10 or 20 for groups. Reservations may be made by mail to The Detroit Times or by calling Cherry 8800, line 342.

Since April 6th various advertisements for the City of Champions Testimonial banquet had been appearing in the Detroit Times Newspaper.
—*Detroit Times* photo/Courtesy of *The Detroit News*

In swimming, the Detroit Athletic Club had sponsored the A.A.U. national team champions, with one of their swimmers, Jimmy Gilhula, winning the national 220-yard free style championship.

Constance O'Donovan and Esther Challova Politzer had won the women's national public courts-doubles championship in 1935. While another woman named Katherine Hughes-Hallet was the Michigan and Midwest fencing champion.

Jake Ankrom was the national three cushion billiard champion. Even the world champion checkers player, Newell Banks was from Detroit!

Newell Banks, keenest student of the checker game in a generation. It's your move—mention somebody who can beat him.

—Bob Murphy, *Detroit Times*, 4/18/35

One notable absence from the actual banquet was Azucar, the winner of the first Santa Anita Handicap (1935). But his absence was to be expected because they didn't allow horses in the building! In winning the race, Azucar had won $108,000 dollars for his Detroit owner, Fred M. Alger; and also the bragging rights that go along with winning the first ever $100,000 horse race.

The day of the Great Testimonial was forever etched on the calendar of Michigan, as Governor Frank D. Fitzgerald issued a proclamation setting aside April 18th, the date of the banquet, as "Champions Day." The Council followed suit by issuing a proclamation to the same effect for the city of Detroit. Everyone in the State was especially encouraged on this day to display flags, pictures, or anything else that would honor the teams and athletes. The Testimonial was held at the Masonic Temple in Detroit on April 18th 1936, and coverage of it was broadcast over the radio station WXYZ. Bud Shaver, the sports editor of the Detroit Times was master of ceremonies and also the voice of the broadcast.

Governor Proclaims Champions' Day

STATE OF MICHIGAN
EXECUTIVE OFFICE
LANSING

FRANK D FITZGERALD
GOVERNOR

April 15, 1936

To the People of the State of Michigan:

In view of the fact that Michigan has won such
an amazing total of athletic championships within the
past year as to earn the title of the "State of
Champions", I deem it fitting that a day should be set
aside to honor those who have brought this distinction
to our State. Therefore, I am glad to designate
Saturday, April 18, as the "Day of Champions". It is
my earnest wish that citizens of the state will observe
the day by a display of flags, banners and pictures of
our champions when possible.

Such champions as the Red Wings and Olympic hockey
teams, the Detroit Tigers, Detroit Lions, Gar Wood,
Dick Degener and Joe Louis, have contributed much to
the fame of Michigan. The prestige they have given
Michigan and Detroit cannot be over-estimated.

Therefore, I hope citizens in general will find
occasion to do honor to our outstanding athletes and
their matchless achievements on this day.

Governor

Governor Proclaims Champions Day.
—Detroit Times photo/Courtesy of *The Detroit News*

City Council Urges Champions' Day

City of Detroit
COMMON COUNCIL

By Councilman Van Antwerp

Whereas, the people of the City
of Detroit have during the last year had many
occasions to rejoice in the fame and glory brought
to the City through the winning of numerous sport
championship, especially the World's Championship
won by our Detroit Tigers, the Professional Football Championship, and

Whereas, the people of the City of
Detroit take great pride in the accomplishments of
Joe Louis who started his remarkable rise in the
sporting fraternity in the amateur ranks of our
city, and

Whereas, we are now celebrating the
winning of the Prince of Wales, Oke and Stanley
Cups by the two hockey teams representing our city,
namely the Olympics and Red Wings, therefore be it

Resolved, that this Common Council
does hereby designate Saturday, April 18th, as
Championship Day to be officially recognized as
such, in honor of the athletic teams of the City of
Detroit all of which have brought great renown to
our city.

Detroit City Council Proclaims Champions Day.
—Detroit Times photo/Courtesy of *The Detroit News*

BACK IN THE CITY OF CHAMPS

IT IS swell to be home again in the City of Champions. A citizen of Rome, howling for Caesar when Julius was fighting at his own weight, couldn't feel a fiercer pride in his hometown—and I hope you are the same.

This is the home of the Red Wings, the Olympics, the Lions, the Tigers, the Gar Woods, papa and son; Dick Degener and Joe Louis!

Yes, by gum, this is the home of Newell W. Banks, the checker king, and a lot of other champions!

This is Detroit, the City of Champions, and my home town. I'm proud to raise a cheer for it.

If this enthusiasm be small town, bush league stuff, I'll take the rap smiling. In fact, I'm so shame-less about it I give public thanks to my parents for rearing me in a small town, coating me with the provincialism which enables me to get a bang out of my town's triumphs.

It may be unintelligent, but its heaps of fun.

Town Makes Champs

THE TIMES is throwing a party for the champions tomorrow night, I understand, which is swell, but I wish there was some way the champions could put on a love-feast for Detroit. It's about time the champs return the compliment, kiss the hands which pat 'em on the back as it were.

I have that feeling about it because I'm convinced the town makes champions, rather than the other way around, although to date the town very generously has given all the credit the other way.

Winning championships is the biggest mass team play of its kind. When you have an entire town as big and energetic as Detroit behind you, you can't lose unless some other town puts up bigger and better backing, which hasn't happened since Detroit found its size and force.

Emphasizes Importance

THERE IS a lot of good in sports for the citizenry and Detroit was smart enough to find it. Some of the best things we do are done on the diamond, the gridiron, the hockey arena, in the ring, on the springboard, in the cockpit of a Miss America.

There are exhibited the qualities most to be admired in the human race, courage, determination, loyalty, self sacrifice and just plain git and go.

In a quieter way the same qualities are exhibited in the every day business of life, but sports, by putting them on public exhibition daily, emphasizes their importance and makes them fashionable.

That is a good thing for all concerned and it is especially good when sports and the citizenry are as closely welded as Detroit is to its champions.

Nearly All Transients

THERE IS little patience in this corner for those who scoff that our champions are not all home bred, are but transients set down here by chance and circumstance.

Nearly all of us are transients. Like the champions, we came here because it was a better place, offered opportunity, encouraged accomplishment.

That's the swell thing about Detroit in its attitude toward its professional and amateur athletes. It doesn't merely sit them down and say: "Well, let's see you do it."

It shoves them out there and says: "Go to it, kid. We're with you." There is a lot of difference, as any athlete can tell you.

—Bud Shaver, *Detroit Evening Times*, 4/17/36

GREATEST GATHERING OF CHAMPIONS UNDER SINGLE ROOF

As more than 600 fans thundered ovation after ovation, the heroes of Detroit's many stirring sports' conquests were feted Saturday night at Masonic Temple at the City of Champions' banquet, held under the auspices of the Detroit Times. It was an unparalleled gathering of illustrious champions. No one city has ever before had a chance to house so many of its bona fide crown wearers under one roof. It is quite possible this record may never be equaled. Worshipping at the most glamorous sports shrine in the world, the fans showed with cheers and applause just how grateful they are to the athletic warriors who have spread Detroit's fame to the remotest corners of the world.

Mickey Cochrane and his Tigers, individually and collectively, acknowledged the fans plaudits. The Lions of football, the Red Wings and Olympics of hockey, took their bows. Gar Wood, he of the long, white locks, was accorded one of the most heartfelt and sincere tributes of his long career as king of the watery speed main. Joe Louis, the tan leopard of the ring, was praised as a fighter and as a sportsman. Studded with magic names, the roll call of champions continued. Miss Constance O'Donovan and Esther Challova Politzer, national doubles tennis champions, and Miss Katherine Hughes-Hallett, Michigan and Midwest fencing champion, represented the fair sex at the table of honor. There was giant broad-shouldered Clark Haskins, national A.A.U. 56-pound weight champion, and Dick Degener, greatest diver in the world, and recognized by many as the greatest of all time.

Tom Haynie, national medley swim champion, and Stroh's bowling team, international match champions, took bows. Among the former champions now residing in Detroit, Tommy Milton, two-time winner of Indianapolis, and one of the immortals of racing, was introduced. Bud Shaver, Detroit Times sports editor, was toastmaster. Before

"The Greatest Gathering of Champions Under a Single Roof."
—*Detroit Times* photo/Courtesy of *The Detroit News*

(Left to right) Clark Haskins, Donnie Hughes (Olympics coach), and Orlin Johnson (Gar Wood's legendary mechanic).

(Left to right) Gar Wood, Albert E. Dale (Editor-in-Chief of the Detroit Times), and Joseph Carr (President of the NFL).
—*Detroit Times* photo/Courtesy of *The Detroit News*

Harry Kipke (University of Michigan coach), and Gar Wood.

(Left to Right) Jack Adams, Potsy Clark and Joe Louis look at the "commemorative edition" Detroit Times given to all the guests at the dinner.
—*Detroit Times* photo/Courtesy of *The Detroit News*

(Left to right) Dick Degener, Tom Haynie, Miss Kathleen Hughes-Hallett and Mrs. Esther Politzer.
—Detroit Times photo/Courtesy of *The Detroit News*

Elden Auker meets Glen Presnell   Cy Perkins with Mickey Cochrane   Bucko McDonald meets Gerald Walker
—Detroit Times photo/Courtesy of *The Detroit News*

"World Series, Stanley Cup Stars Meet at Champions' Fete"
(Left to right) Mickey Cochrane, Bud Shaver (toastmaster and Sports Editor of the *Detroit Times*), and Pete Kelly. Cochrane and Kelly "had something in common." They had both scored the final point for their respective championships.
—Detroit Times photo/Courtesy of *The Detroit News*

These two Tigers keep an eternal vigil in Southfield Cemetery for the man who guided Detroit baseball from its humble origins, to the pinnacle of success.

"And then one sad note, Memories of Frank J. Navin coming to the dressing room at the end of the final game, the happiest man in the World. And how the same night; in the zenith of his glory, after waiting a third of a century, Navin sought out Monsignor John M, Doyle, chancellor of the Detroit diocese, and confided: "I can now die in peace . . . "

"And how, from all walks of life, the same fans who had time and again stood in line to gain entrance to his ball park, stood in line a few weeks later on a cold-penetrating and wind-swept day to pay respects as the rose-colored casket of the late Frank J. Navin moved past. Here, indeed, is the only sad note as the parade of champions moves past."

—Bud Shaver 4/11/36
Photo by Kelly Karnesky

introducing Mickey Cochrane, the first speaker of the evening, Shaver paid tribute to the memory of the late Frank J. Navin. Saturday was the anniversary of Mr. Navin's death. Mrs. Navin sent her best wishes to the assembled athletic greats. Bronzed by Florida's hot suns, Cochrane stood to the accompaniment of a mighty reception. "We'll be in there swinging for another championship," he promised the fans. "I've got a tough job in attempting to carry on without Mr. Frank Navin. But I hope the fans will stick with me." From the roar that greeted this remark it was apparent just

where ruddy-faced Mike stood in this great city of champions.

The Tigers were introduced, starting with Gerald Walker and ending with Charles F. Navin, secretary and treasurer of the club. W.O. Briggs Jr. represented his father, the new Tiger owner, at the banquet. Al Simmons [newest Tiger acquisition], making one of his first appearances at an affair of this kind in Detroit was given an uproarious salute. Jack Adams paid high tribute to Mr. James Norris, his boss, and to the Red Wings and O's. Adams introduced the Wings. Donnie Hughes,

Olympics' coach, and described by Shaver as a "Cinderella man of sports," introduced the O's who were present. Potsy Clark, coach of the Lions called his 1935 world champions the greatest team ever assembled in football. Even greater than the Illinois team of 1914, on which Clark played. The Lions who were presented included: Sam Knox, Regis Monaghan, Glenn Presnell, Tom Hupke, Ace Gutowsky, Ernie Caddell, John Schneller, Red Stacy, Claire Randolph, Jim Steen, Ox Emerson, and George Christensen.

Praised for his sportsmanship in not hitting Max Baer when the latter landed blows after the bell had rung. Louis faced the crowd and briefly expressed thanks to the fans. "I'm not a champion yet," said Louis, "but I hope to be." And, incidentally, dead-pan Joe smiled as he faced his audience. A.E. Dale, editor-in-chief of The Detroit Times; paid tribute to the warring athletic heroes and welcomed the fans who turned out to honor the champions. Due to illness Gov. Frank Fitzgerald was unable to attend. He sent his greetings and congratulations to Detroit's great array of champions. Harry Kipke of Michigan received one of the best hands of the night, as did Gus Dorais of U. of D. Dick Degener declared he wouldn't feel satisfied until he had turned in a victory in the Olympic Games at Berlin this summer.

Joe Norris, captain of the Stroh bowling team, introduced his teammates—Cass Grygler, John Crimmins, Phil Bauman and Walter Reppenhagen. Gar Wood flew 2,800 miles from the Bahamas to be present at the testimonial. When the veteran speedboat king, first to bring honor and prestige to his town as a champion arose, there was a mighty demonstration, "It's been well worth the long trip to be here," said Wood. "This is a great community of champions. I'm proud to call Detroit my home." Wood introduced his famous mechanic, Orlin Johnson. Gar Wood Jr., national interscholastic champion, was unable to get away from school to attend. Herbert Mendelson whose Notre Dame won the President's Cup, was absent due to illness. Although he was absent, the mere mention of Eddie Tolan's name drew a burst of enthusiastic applause. The same was true when Shaver recalled some of the past exploits of one of the Tiger immortals, Harry Heilmann, one of the greatest batsmen of all time. Judge John D. Watts, George Dusette, light heavyweight wrestling champion, and newspapermen were among others introduced. It was a stirring occasion and one that Detroit fans can never forget.
—Bob Murphy, *Detroit Times*, 4/19/36

The significance of this banquet is pretty self-evident. Gathering all of the athletes in one place and recognizing all of the teams in the same breath, linked them together to an outstanding degree. Each were champions in their own right, yet all were part of the incredible achievements of this season. With Joe Louis as the guest-of-honor, it was another breakthrough in race relations. This great testimonial must have set some kind of a record for the most sports champions under one roof, and it is simply fascinating that such an event took place.

RISE OF
THE DETROIT FAN

It's What's 'Above the Ears,' 'in the Heart,' and 'in the Mob' that makes Detroit Great

Upon what meat does our city feed that it has grown so great? No symposium of viewpoints probably would go far in explaining why Detroit today—with its unduplicated distinction of supremacy in all major sports, in hockey, in baseball, in football and in boxing, and with its long list of champions and world records in more or less minor sports—is being called "The Sports Capitol of the World" and

"The City of Champions." Any symposium unless gathered from psychologists might miss the point, might be vain, might be carelessly unanalytical, might be wholly without an appreciation of the fine line that divides victory and defeat, success and failure—and what it takes to cross to the right side of the filament to fame. And what it takes are those intangibles that are "above the ears" and "in the heart" and "in the mob."

It would be as illogical as it would be provincial to say that Detroit's hockey players are faster,

Overflow crowds at Bennett Park in the early days of Tiger baseball. Here, Germany Schaefer and Harry Tuthill (trainer) do their best to keep fans in order. The wall dividing the field and stands is not visible because of the amount of people.

—Photos courtesy of *The Detroit News*
Obtained through the use of the Alan Feldman Collection

123

Navin Field, view from behind home plate in 1934.
—Photo courtesy of the *Detroit Free Press*

gamer and more skilled than the hockey players of other cities; or that Detroit's ball players can hit harder, field better or pitch more deceptively than the players of any other team in baseball; or that Detroit's football players can smash a line, kick a football or throw a pass without comparison; or that Joe Louis is a superman whose physical equal the world does not own; or—to conclude—that no man lives besides Gar Wood with the fortitude to drive a boat 125 miles an hour. [He] Who says those things or makes those claims is ridiculous. In a physical sense, Detroit's teams and individual athletes are but counterparts of the teams and individuals of other cities. They are no better and no worse. Silly as it may seem it is well to say this.

Wherein Detroit's teams and individuals differ from their rivals is in their clearer concepts of the mental attitudes needed to complement physical abilities, and (most important) in the encouragement Detroit, as a spending, sport-loving populace, has given its teams and individuals. Such an assertion immediately carries one into the intangibles but it is with the intangibles that one must deal if one is to tell why Detroit is supreme. Jack Adams

knows this; Mickey Cochrane knows it and so does Potsy Clark. In fact it is that about which they talk most. Also it is why they have brought their teams down in front. It is why they have had the jump, the psychological jump, on all other teams in hockey, baseball, and football. Jack Adams will tell you before the start of any season, 'If I can get this bunch 'up' if I can make them fight, if the fans will string along until we get going, we'll go places—we'll be in there at the finish.' Cochrane will tell you the same thing; so will Potsy Clark.

Yes, of the absolute necessity for applying the mind and heart to the physical: the encouragement of the fans having been a natural sequel to a realization that sincerity and determination were utilized factors.

What Adams, Cochrane, and Clark have done with their teams, other Detroit teams and individuals have done with themselves. Relatively, they have done it in swimming and diving, in softball in track, in tennis, in billiards and bowling, and in weight-lifting and relatively, they have had the encouragement of the groups interested in these sports.

Comerica Park, modern day. Though the location has changed, the spirit of the diehard Detroit fan still remains.
—Photo courtesy of Ilitch Holdings.

Just what part the mind, the heart, and the mob played in supplementing the physical is something, of course, that can not be assayed, but Detroit's records today are proof of the value of these attributes. Detroit is supreme because of what is "above the ears" and "in the heart" and "in the mob."

—Harry Leduc, *The Detroit News*, 4/13/36

This article by Harry Leduc must be considered the first newspaper article to ever discuss the importance and the uniqueness of a city's fans. It is extremely relevant in that it discusses how a city's fans could make a difference in the fortunes of the teams. The idea that the fans of Detroit "willed" their teams to this highest level of athletic achievement seems entirely plausible. The situation of the city at this time was one of tremendous suffering and deprivation. If ever a city needed hope, or reason to celebrate, this was it. It would have been only natural that a city that needed this hope would have done everything they could to get it. This includes getting excited about sporting events, and playoff races. The almost magical ability of the Detroit supporters to galvanize their teams and inspire them to victory helped to endear the fan support and solidify a fan base that would grow with every generation.

In Leduc's reasons for "why" Detroit became the "City of Champions," he points out that it was the fans which helped carry the teams. That it was a reciprocal exchange where the players gave everything they had out on the field, and the fans would give everything by way of support. The fans to this day are passionate about their teams, a fact that becomes obvious when attending any Detroit sporting event. When fans give their full support to a team, their spirit can lift that team to its highest potential, just as the inspiration by the team can carry the fans.

The joy that winning brought to these Depression-weary people came with a sense of pride that *they* were associated with winners and as such were winners themselves. This sense is one of the reasons that people follow sports today.

Taking this concept one step further is the idea that fans stick by their teams through the tough times *and* the celebrations. This concept is important because it is one that shares a parallel with life. Life, like the rising and falling fortunes of sports teams is never entirely happy. There are always rough stretches that must be ridden out in order to get to the happiness at the end. In these rough stretches a person, a fan, a city must persevere and not give up, because the happy times will eventually arrive. Championships and festivities that take place throughout the course of a team, or a person's life are actually the celebration of the fortitude which it took to get there.

This concept is the reason why "bandwagon" fans are so frowned upon [a bandwagon fan is the fan who cheers for whatever team in the city or country is winning at the moment, i.e. they "jump on the bandwagon" just for the celebration]. Anyone can follow only winners, but it's like the old saying goes, "anyone can be happy when everything is going well, it's how you conduct yourself when things are *not* going well, that is the true testament of a person's character." Let it be enough; to say that in life and sports there is far more satisfaction in "earning" your joy than it is to have it handed over on a silver platter.

Taking into account the article by Harry Leduc, the rare opportunity presents itself to identify a few more characteristics that make up modern Detroit sports fans. As mentioned earlier, fans of Detroit sports are loyal to their teams when they are winning and when they are not. They are knowledgeable about the important aspects of team play, cheering fine defense as loudly as they cheer flashy offense. They appreciate and embrace honest effort by players who may not necessarily have the greatest athletic skills, a tribute to the blue collar work ethic that embodies the people of Michigan. They never bring farm animals to a World Series game and then leave an eternal curse on their team when their livestock can't get in.* They never take a ball from one of their own fielders in the middle of an important game just to get a souvenir. And if something unforeseen does happen in a game, they don't give up

hope.** In fact, that is one of the primary faults of Detroit fans, we love our teams so much that we have hope for them every year—all year, until it is mathematically impossible for a championship to materialize. But at that point is when hope starts again, in the form of the familiar phrase, "there's always next year!"

Detroit fans are also united by the understanding that we are underappreciated and often slighted in the national media. For example, a certain ex-Mariner second baseman working for a certain national media network called for the elimination of the Tigers in 2003; essentially kicking the team while it was down [in 2003 the Tigers almost set the all-time loss record for a season after playing poorly for a decade]. Eliminate the Tigers for playing poorly? It might have been said as an innocent comment, but it is one that has never been excused; Detroit fans noticed and were insulted. There is also a question that arises, mainly—is this how other fans think? Eliminate the team because their win-loss record suffers? Is that a logical conclusion to make? A team has a few terrible years, so you eliminate it, and their history? With that type of mentality, I suppose that if your dog has an earache or gets sick, you simply take it out back and put a bullet in its head; and not give something that you love, a chance to get better. Not in Detroit, not with one of our teams.

We also don't appreciate athletes who come into our city and behave like prima donnas. A prime example comes to mind, of a few short years ago after a blockbuster trade brought in a supposed superstar slugger who was set to bomb home runs over the left field fence and usher in a new age at Comerica Park. There was only one problem, the fence was too deep! Instead of adjusting his game and waiting for the tweaks to be made at the new ballpark, he pouted his way out of Detroit. Well, Tiger fans laughed as he sulked out of town, and as he looked for a team who played in a "hitter-friendly" ballpark. We'd rather have a team of no-name players trying their best, than cater to the whims of a cry-baby.

A good friend of mine, Kevin Bush, recently told me in reference to the recent poor decade of play by the Tigers, "*You know; the losing seasons actually had a positive. It was much easier to get tickets!*" I need not say more.

. . . .

*Author's note: This refers to the Curse of the Goat (Chicago Cubs).

. . . .

**Author's note: This refers to the Bartman incident (Chicago Cubs).

CONCLUSION

The impacts of winning the trifecta of championships had a profound and far reaching effect on the teams, fans, people, and city of Detroit. In fact the impacts were so profound that this season must be considered the most important in the history of Detroit sports. Associating the two unstable franchises with one that was already established eased the transition of the Lions and Red Wings into the Detroit sports world. Winning their championships in the same season as the established and beloved Tigers, quickly cemented the two franchises into place. Having three successful teams in the city solidified Detroit as the center of Michigan sports. The attention that was focused on the accomplishments of the teams helped to increase the fan base for future seasons. The success also brought a measure of pride to the fans, who could now support their teams in expectation of the next championships. It also established a precedent, especially for the two new teams. It gave both of them a past, which future teams and fans could look upon fondly. Looking back proudly on past achievements gives fans a sense of nostalgia, an underappreciated sense that makes people feel that somehow people in the past were tougher, stronger, or more heroic. This sense can fire the imagination and inspire modern-day people to excel like the people in the past. This idea is not exclusive of sports but it certainly is inclusive.

Winning these championships was more important than just being the best in a particular year. Local newspapers around Michigan, such as the *Kalamazoo Gazette,* followed these events because it is what their readers wanted. This fol-

Russell A. Alger Memorial Fountain. This statue was erected in 1921 and honors the memory of one of the great early leaders in Michigan history. Located in Grand Circus Park, it symbolizes the State of Michigan in the classic pose of Victory. It seems appropriate that such a statue exists, and stands out like a beacon in the center of Detroit.

—Photo by Kelly Karnesky

lowing of people outside of the city would lead them to associate with Detroit and the sports teams they supported. Drawing in people from many different areas for one common interest has the happy side effect of tying them more closely together.

Sports teams are important to people and the community, they have money-making potential and can have tremendous commercial power. To fans they serve as unifying factors that cross cultural and ethnic lines, creating similar interests between different people. Teams (and sports) create entertainment and teach values. Many times, sports teams serve as an identity for people and the cities they live in. Sports teams are very important to the prestige and pride of their cities. In modern America, cities compete for the privilege of having a team, and fight to keep their teams from moving to other cities. It is a blessing that Detroit has such stable franchises and solid fan support. That this stability was created so quickly was another impact of the 1935–36 season.

The prestige gained by Detroit as a result of being "City of Champions" is impossible to measure. But that doesn't mean there wasn't a measure of increase in the prestige of the city—quite the contrary. The exposure gained by its dominance brought tremendous prestige and presented the city as a contributing and competitive part of the growing national phenomena of American sport. The steady stream of champions paraded across the pages of other city's newspapers, carrying positive publicity about a city that many may have previously known little about.

Further emphasis must also be placed on the importance of

Spirit of Detroit. Dedicated in 1958, the shining bronze sphere in the giant left hand represents God, while the right hand holds a "family group, symbolic of all human relationships." This statue has become one of the most endearing pieces of artwork in the city. It has become synonymous for its close relationship between the city, the fans, and the sports teams and is periodically decorated with the jersey of whichever team is competing in the playoffs.

Joe Louis at this time. Before starting this project, I knew that he was a good fighter, good enough to have an arena named after him, good enough also, to have a monument made for him. But I never knew how great he really was. Inside the ring the stories are incredible; he was the most dominant fighter ever; but it was outside the ring that he was better. He stood as a pillar of the community as he carried the weight of being a great unifier with a class and dignity like no man before or since. Despite the awful segregation of this era, he never seemed to hold a grudge; appearing at sporting events and being photographed with white athletes. In all the articles and books that I read about him, not once did anyone ever have any "dirt" on him, he was simply above reproach. In fact, his biggest flaw can be considered an inspiration to us all—Generosity. Throughout the course of his life, he donated so much money to helping people that by the end of his life he was so riddled with debt that he could never dream of paying it back. He may have, as the old saying goes, "been poor in money," but he was phenomenally "rich in spirit."

In writing this book, I have poured through countless statistics and records, and throughout the moments of excitement, frustration, and borderline insanity, one thing stayed in my mind. How could such an amazing sporting season have faded from our memories so badly? While

there are several possibilities, I believe that World War II (1939–1945), was the primary reason. When the United States entered the war in 1941, sports contests immediately became unimportant. An entire generation of fans were part of the effort that went into winning the war, and many of them never returned. When the war was over, the country looked forward to a new chapter in American history, and chose to shelve the stories of the Great Depression. Sports in turn entered a "Golden Age," as many of the pre-war sports' memories were also filed away. It is my sincere hope that this story never fades away, and that this book contributes to bringing this story back to the forefront where it belongs. It is a story that should stand out prominently in the minds of every Detroit Sports fan, and definitely one which should be celebrated.

I have often thought about the many ways in which this story could be celebrated by modern fans. One possibility would be for the Governor of Michigan, and Mayor of Detroit to dust off the proclamations issued in 1936 that called for April 18th as Champions Day. As it was back then, people would be urged to show their fan loyalty through banners, pictures, flags, clothes, decorated cars and any other outward signs of support for the teams. It is a day that would be extraordinary with perhaps a parade down Woodward Avenue, televised across the state. Another possibility is for the teams themselves to commemorate the events through a series of "turn back the clock" days. On these days, not only would the teams play in vintage jerseys but fans would be urged to dress up in their finest clothing. To encourage the fans to dress up and look "dapper," the team would sell their concessions at 1935 prices! A scene like that would really make a statement about the uniqueness of Detroit; media outlets would relay sights like these, and allow this story to be retold to people across the nation. Detroit was once loudly proclaimed the "City of Champions," but it has passed to us through a whisper and it is time for it to be shouted again.

The city of Detroit was the historical origin of the state of Michigan, and as such became its center for everything; including business, culture, arts, architecture, entertainment, and sports. The people of this time left us an important legacy. They gave us the teams we cheer for, amazing stories of perseverance, and the dream of Detroit as one of the premiere cities in not only America, but in the world. Over the course of the last several decades the city has fallen on hard times but the time of this decline is over. No more must people, especially in Michigan, slander this great city—to do so is the equivalent of being a "bandwagon fan." There is no longer any room for naysayers and negative-thinking people as ill talk does nothing but bring the city down. Many people may scoff at this claim that Detroit is turning a corner for the better; but to those people let it be enough to say that hope now permeates in and around the city, and that belief in its revival grows every day. It must also be said that citizens in the state of Michigan all have a responsibility in helping the city towards its revival and a new era; there can be no more of the idea that Detroit is some isolated city that has to sort its own problems out—all must contribute something, even if that contribution is as simple as one positive word instead of a negative. Every waterfall starts with a single drop, and if everyone contributes their drop, the stream of hope will become a powerful river and waterfall that carries Detroit into a new age.

In having such an outstanding array of sports in Detroit, the teams of today have led the way in drawing people and revenue to the city, much as they did during the last major economic hardship of the Great Depression. Let us look to this time for inspiration; roll up our sleeves, and go work to continue the dream of making Detroit one of the premiere cities in the world.

When I first started working on this project in 2005, what drew my attention was the fact that no city has won three major professional championships in the same season since this time. That statistic alone seemed amazing to me. How was it; that after all the years has it not happened again? For the last few years I have watched as a couple of cities have won two titles, nervously hoping that a third team would not complete the trifecta, that Detroit alone would continue to be the only "City of Champions." But it was while reading the numerous stories in newspaper articles that I realized the importance lay not in the statistics. It was about the people of this time, and the joy that it gave to them at such a hard period in history. There is no unit of measurement that can quantify the laughter, celebrations, and excitement which was what these people needed most.

I am no longer worried that another city may become "City of Champions" because no other city could hope to achieve what Detroit achieved at this time. It's first three championships, all in the same season, a championship caliber boxer and great social unifier, and a myriad of other champions, all in the middle of the Great Depression. It is my sincere hope that any city hoping to make a claim as the new "City of Champions," will read this book before making such a bold statement.

We now have a unique opportunity; to draw inspiration and hope from the people and teams of this time, to use the legacy they left to us, and shout with the sound of one voice, and one human race—that despite the passage of time; Detroit was, is now, and will forever be, the City of Champions.

"Detroit the Dynamic. Detroit, the Champion of the Sports World."
—Photo courtesy of the *Detroit Free Press*

APPENDIX

From the very beginning of this project I wanted to make an Appendix which would be a one-stop source for the fan who is interested in the specifics of these championships. That is to say, throughout the course of the text, the games and events of each team/person's season were summarized to allow for a free flowing story.

This appendix I hope, will allow for an easy reference of the details. In 1935 television was in its infancy, and the radio had nowhere near the coverage of sporting events as is the case today. The result was that play-by-play analyses were written in the newspapers for sports fans not in attendance to still follow the action. The articles contained within this appendix are transcribed original documents, but completely unaltered.

A spelling mistake or two may present itself, and one writer may have spelled the same player's name slightly different than another. I kept these mistakes in order to present the material in its original form, as a fan of this time would have had to read it. These play-by-play accounts were invaluable for me to understand the sporting events of this period, and I can easily say that this book would not have been possible without them. It is my hope that modern fans can appreciate the rich detail, and the important legacy that the writers of this time left through their thorough coverage of these events.

Contents

· Birth of a Fight Extra (How play by play newspaper coverage was made possible)

· Runyon Story of Joe Louis Victory (Joe Louis vs. Primo Carnera)

· Louis' Own Story of his Victory in Sixth Round

· "Bob Tales" (Life in Joe Louis' camp on the eve of his fight with Max Baer)

· "Stop Playing Catch," Jacobs Tells Joe

· Runyon Calls Detroiter the Greatest Fighting Machine of Ring (Joe Louis vs. Max Baer)

· Joe Louis' Career Fight Record

BIRTH OF A FIGHT EXTRA

In Composing Room

HOW BOUT APPEARED OVER WIRE

SHAVINGS

Detroit Times, June 26th 1935

(Reprinted with the permission of *The Detroit News.*)

By Bud Shaver

CHICAGO, June 26—I saw the fight in the Times composing room before grabbing the train with the Tigers for Chicago.

Not a bad place to see a fight, my friend. Fights in the ring sometimes are dull. Those in the composing room never are. The birth of a Fight Extra is the most thrilling episode in the life of a daily newspaper, swift and calm as a shooting star.

It isn't at all like it is pictured in movies and fiction, with all hands rushing about like sailors in a shipwreck.

ALL BUT ON THE PRESSES

FIGHT EXTRAS are all but on the presses hours before the fighters get in the ring. It is a routine, practice has made perfect. Come with me and I'll show you. Let's go into the press room an hour before the fight.

That's the center of a web of machinery and electrical transmission which even sends its slim tentacles of telegraph wires thousands of miles into Yankee Stadium where sit Bob Murphy, Damon Runyon, Bill Corum, Davis J. Walsh and a whole army of Hearst sorts writers waiting for Joe Louis and Primo Carnera to come into the ring.

Every word is flashed over the wire a soon as it's written. It is transcribed in the composing room next to linotype machines and the linotype operator casts it in lead word by word as it comes over the wire by the simple process of reading over the telegraph operator's shoulder. Every blow Louis or Carnera lands is in type almost before they have time to start another.

CENTRAL STAGE OF DRAMA

IT IS no sooner in type than it is "in the paper" meaning Hughie Daly, the veteran printer who stands behind the "stone" claps sticks of type into their proper column with a neat flick of that little metal dingus he uses to drop in leads.

This is old stuff to Hughie and he goes about the business of "making up" the page while kidding and talking with the brass hats who stand around watching.

Hughie's page is the central stage of the drama. There gather Jack Stenbuck, the circulation director; Walter Aranoff, his city circulation manager; Ed Lapping, the city editor, and Al Carson, the news editor.

Al moves around chewing on a soggy cigar and grinning, although he already has made up 27 pages in preparation for the Extra. Near Hughie Daly's hands like cuts and headlines that can be slipped in like a magician pulls a rabbit out of your hat, only faster.

There is nothing which can happen that the little group in the composing room is not ready to handle. If the fight ends in one blow or one round the paper will be ready to go at that instant. If it goes 15 the paper will be ready to go without the loss of a precious second and every bit of news will be in it.

I've watched this birth of a Fight Extra many times. It never fails to fascinate.

PRESSES READY TO ROLL

THE TELEGRAPH operator's set stammers a few words in Morse code.

Sam McGuire, boss of the copy desk; who is handling copy looks up, says quietly:

"They're in the ring now."

Carson and Daly nod and go on talking to Dave Almond, the burly boss of the press room. His seven presses are ready to roll out 100,000 extras in a half hour. He is so little excited about it that he brought his troupe of kids to see the show like going to a picnic. They romp through the composing room, follow their dad downstairs to the cavern where the presses lie sleeping.

SENSE LOUIS' STRATEGY

THE FIGHT is on. A little group hovers around the telegraph operator's typewriter, reading every word as it comes to life beneath his keys. The linotype operator calmly and swiftly gets it into type a line at a time.

Round by round we watch the story unfold—Carnera rushing out at the beginning of each round. Louis circling away to avoid those crushing feet. Louis gliding inside Carnera's left leads, belting him alternately to the head and body. We learn he made Carnera's mouth bleed in the first round. We sense the strategy of Louis' fight in the fourth round when he induces the clumsy Carnera to lead to him.

A tense moment as the fifth round starts. That's the round Louis picked to flatten Primo. He doesn't, but he gives Carnera a good pasting, had him bleeding again.

The sixth starts. The operator breaks a sentence in the middle. "Flash—Louis Scores a Knockdown."

An excitable young man, new to the business misread it.

"Louis wins by a knockout," he yells. He was right, but slightly premature. Cooler heads corrected him. One flighty yell like that might start the presses rolling with misinformation.

Almost immediately comes the message which starts the presses rolling in earnest.

"Flash—Louis wins by Knockout."

HISS OF HOT TYPE METAL

THAT'S ALL that is needed. Daly already is pushing page one in its form to the stereotype machine. Twice it is squeezed through the big rollers and out comes two paper matrices. Down a Shute they drop. Both go into the bit plate caster. There is a hiss of hot type metal. Out come two half cylinders, each a front page. A few seconds to shave the edges and cool in a stream of water. They are shooting down the rollers to the gigantic presses. Pressmen seize them, bolt them on the rolls. Lights flash. The presses groan, whine and roar as a steady stream of extras stream out and up into the mailing room.

There is bedlam but no confusion in the alley as 100 trucks seize their cargo and whirl out into the night. More colored boys than usual riding the trucks. It's their big night. Crap games break up in a hurry. All downtown Detroit is blanketed with extras in a few minutes. Five thousand kids will be yelling, "Extra" in every part of town.

There is no fight as thrilling as its swift embalming in type.

RUNYON STORY OF LOUIS VICTORY

Detroit Times, June 26th 1935 (6/25/35)
(Reprinted with the Permission of *The Detroit News.*)
By Damon Runyon

NEW YORK, June 26, A bleeding, punch-bewildered giant, stumbling as he is led to his corner, a brown-skinned, boyish-looking Negro, whose fists have wreaked this terrible damage, staring after him with a cold, cruel, unchanging expression.

And 70,000 roaring spectators in the stands and bleachers of the Yankee Stadium, cheering Joe Louis, the new thunderbolt of the pugilistic world, conqueror of Primo Carnera, the Italian mastodian by technical knockout in the sixth round of their battle last night.

Carnera's huge bulk—280 pounds—drops to the stained canvas with a great noise three times under the smashes of the boy from Detroit they call "the Brown Bomber," the blows falling on the giant's chin with unbelievable rapidity.

GUSHING BLOOD

Carnera's mouth is gushing blood from a steady pop of lightning—like left hooks fired at him from the beginning of the battle. As he gets up the third time, his enormous legs are tottering under him, and Referee Arthur Donovan mercifully stops the fight and calls for Carnera's seconds to come in and get him.

The men have fought 2 minutes 30 seconds of the sixth round when the finish comes.

A right cross late in the round drops the giant the first time. He falls in a huge mass, that slowly resolves itself into the figure of a man posed on one knee. Carnera's eyes are glaring wildly. The blood trickles down his chin as he rests there, his great gloved paws on the canvas.

Louis keeping Carnera at bay with his straight left.
—Photo courtesy of *The Detroit News*

Louis, as cold as ice, his brown features expressionless is pushed into a neutral corner by Donovan. Then the referee glances around, sees Carnera upright and motions Joe to go ahead. The Negro moves across the ring without excitement and Carnera, dead game to the last, puts out the post-like arms with which he has been trying to fend off the attack of the brown boy from the start. Louis calmly whips a left hook to the bloody chin of the giant and Carnera goes down again.

He takes a count of four, his hands groping on the canvas, he gets up again. He is a sorry spectacle, this great fellow who started life as a circus freak, and was turned into a prize fighter because of his size. But he is dead game. He puts out his arms once more, and another left hook whips out of nowhere, and for the third time the huge man collapses to the floor.

He is up as the timekeeper hammers out three. His mouth streaming blood, and there are cries of "stop it," from all over the arena. The relentless Louis is crowding forward to deliver another blow when Donovan calls a halt.

It is just as well. The great Italian cannot cope with this strange, "dead pan" throwback to some other era of fighting men. From the opening bell, Louis stalks the giant like a tiger stalking an elephant, taking his time, wasting no motions, but always shuffling in, shuffling in, his gloves cocked, ready to explode punches.

He has an amazingly patient, deliberate manner and method. His punches in the opening round obviously startled

Carnera and made him very cautious. The huge man stands merely pawing at Louis at times, as he watches the merciless young fellow slowly circling him, each circle taking Louis in nearer to his prey.

WHIPS LEFT HOOKS

They said Louis would not be able to get inside Carnera's huge arms, and it is true for a time the vast barrier of bone and sinew baffled Joe. Then he began whipping left hooks over Carnera's arms, dropping them on the giant's chin with the accuracy of a crack horseshoe pitcher landing his shoes over the pegs. He would vary this by banging his right hand into Carnera's vast stomach.

Louis said he would knock out Carnera in the fifth. Carnera said he would knock out Louis in the sixth. After the fight, Louis in his dressing room, with thousands waiting outside greatly excited, remarks:

"I couldn't get him in my round, so I thought I'd better get him in his."

Carnera's comment is Louis is a hard hitter, a sharp shooter, though he says he thinks he hurt Louis in the fifth. The crowd, which pays close to $400,000 to see the battle, according to Mike Jacobs, promoter of the Twentieth Century Club, which conducted the affair, goes out babbling it has at last seen a great young fighter, a hitter like the beloved Dempsey of old.

FORGETS MOUTHPIECE

Some one in Carnera's corner forgets to give him his mouthpiece as he goes out for the first round, it is said, and this accounts for the damage in Carnera's mouth from the first left hook Louis lands. He bleeds and bleeds, and they are unable to stop the gore, especially as Louis keeps re-opening the wound round after round.

Rise of Joseph Barrow, called Joe Louis, is as sensational as the comeback of James J. Braddock. A year ago this Detroit boy, a former employee in Ford's factory, got $50 for his first professional bout. Today he is the most talked-of figure in the pugilistic world. But amid all the hubbub he is perhaps the calmest of all.

The idle talk, an insult to the sporting spirit of millions of Italians and Negroes of New York City, [that] this fight might cause racial trouble becomes a joke before the orderly behaviour of the greatest assemblage for a pugilistic presentation in years. There is not a ripple of disorder. The whites applaud the amazing performance of this youthful Negro even more than the blacks, though Harlem celebrates last night in its cafes and in the streets.

There is only one round in which the actions slows down to where it bores the crowd, but this is only because Louis is following his system of fighting—taking his time. His punches have reduced Carnera to a statuesque pose, with his long left extended, and Joe is maneuvering to get in close enough for his short, murderous punches to land.

BEGINS TO LET FLY

Joe doesn't like to miss punches. The crowd claps in derision for an instant, then suddenly it is aflame with excitement as Louis slips inside the tremendous arms of the Italian and begins letting fly.

Primo demonstrated his gameness under the battering of Baer. He demonstrated it again last night as he kept getting up from the knockdowns. He must realize as he gets up, if he is able to do any thinking at all, his finish is inevitable. This brown tiger is on the kill.

At the final knockdown there is a great sound from the huge crowd, a sort of combined "phew! They have seen something at last in the prize ring. They have seen a great fight between big men. They have seen a new "phenom." It is a relief after the dullness of the last heavyweight championship battle, after the inept fumbling of many huge men who promised action, and turned out to be great bores.

BAER WINS BY KO

The program from start to finish last night is a succession of thrills. With Gene Tunney, Jack Dempsey, Max Baer and Jack Johnson, all former heavyweight champions, in the ring, and Max's brother Buddy figuring in a sensational knockout, and a new Argentinian starring above the fistic horizon in Jorge Brescia.

Louis entered the ring last night a slight favorite due to the form he has displayed in his training camp, though this is his first 15-round bout, and Carnera is the best known opponent "the Brown Bomber" has yet faced. There is considerable betting on both men, as the fistic talent thinks Carnera's experience will prove too much for the boy. Experience is not worth a dime a ton against punching such as Louis disclosed last night.

"It is likely Louis will now be matched with Max Baer" or Max Schmeling for a fight in September by the Twentieth Century Club.

LOUIS' OWN STORY OF HIS VICTORY IN SIXTH ROUND

Detroit Times, June 26th 1935
(Reprinted with the permission of *The Detroit News*.)
By Joe Louis
(As Told to Bob Murphy)

NEW YORK, June 26—It was in the fifth round that I knew I had Primo Carnera licked.

All the way through this fight the fifth round has been bobbing up. I predicted I would win by a knockout in that round, but I feel wonderful about the way it turned out.

I cut Carnera's lip in the first round. He never had me worried, but he did have me puzzled a bit until the fifth. Then when I caught him full tilt on the face and the blood started coming I knew I had him.

In the sixth round, after he went down the first time, it was all over, so far as I was concerned. For the first five rounds I had a hard time making Primo drop his hands. But in that sixth he dropped them and then I had him.

The first time I dropped him it was a straight right hand punch to the face. On the other two occasions it was left and right crosses.

He didn't hurt me at all, but in the fourth round Primo came close to hitting me a good 'un. He whacked straight at my head and fortunately, I took it going away. It turned out to be only a glancing blow.

Carnera tried twice in the first three rounds to rough me up in the clinches. With his strength he naturally tossed me around, but once I caught him in the stomach just right. He said, "oh."

That was the only thing Carnera said, so far as I know, during the entire bout until the sixth when he finally asked the referee to "Give it to heem."

I am so happy and so thankful that I don't think what I am saying makes sense. I'll never forget this, my first fight in New York, and always the Yankee Stadium fight of June 25, 1935, will be something I can't forget.

If people are saying nice things about me as a fighter they should direct part of toward Jack Blackburn; my trainer, who has taught me what I know, and to my advisors, John Roxborough and Julian Black, for all the things they have done for me.

I am going to try hard and be a credit to boxing and to the people who have shown faith in me.

Joe Louis.
—Photo courtesy of *The Detroit News*

BOB TALES

(LIFE IN JOE LOUIS' CAMP, ON THE EVE OF HIS FIGHT WITH MAX BAER)

Detroit Times, September 20th 1935
(Reprinted with the permission of *The Detroit News.*)
By Bob Murphy

POMPTON LAKES, N. J., Sept. 20.—Brothers and sisters, I comes before you on this auspicious occasion to inform you the camp of Joe Louis presents a new study in relaxation as known to the hustling, bustling sports world.

In kicking about this country I have held the crying towel for some of our best football coaches on the eve of important games. I've heard them moan louder than a 90-mile Alaskan wind on Christmas Eve.

The football coach of an undefeated team knowing he has a cinch, will sob on your shoulder and tell you the boys are over-confident. The guiding genius of an already defeated outfit will howl with the mournful notes of a chained hound dog and assure you the game on the morrow means his job. The Alumni Wolves are coming—why, man, don't you hear them?

You travel with a ball club like the Tigers. You see them leave the dressing room chattering and backslapping and counting their World Series dollars. They lose a game and back they come with the pleasantness of an enraged landlord who corners you after a diligent two-months search.

Scowling Mickey Cochrane, his club leading by something like nine or ten games, will tear out his hair by the roots while expounding that the pennant is slipping away. All is lost save virtue!

The thing can be carried along to almost any sport you mention, that is, any sport except boxing as dished out by Joe Louis and his training camp sides.

Here is relaxation at its best. A stranger could drop into the camp and never know that a 21-year-old warrior is almost on the eve of his greatest moment—a moment that comes to few men during an eternity.

The same lazy, carefree atmosphere that would attend a watermelon cutting or foot washing in Alabama hangs over the camp. There is nothing tense, no one seems unduly excited and no one is in a hurry.

There is philosophic pleasantry about all the remarks passed back and forth. The crowd is usually made up largely of Joe's own race.

When the time arrives for Joe to fight they climb up trees and scamper atop surrounding house roofs.

Then the impromptu minstrel show begins. The boys combine the laughing nonchalance of the old south with the hi-de-ho and "let's-swing-it" of Harlem.

"Where yo' all want your flowers sent?" one colored gent yelled at Lou (Tiger) Flowers, one of Joe's spar partners. The crowd joined in the laugh.

Then from the top of the trees will come a booming message: "Give 'em the left in the basement and then land you' right in the attic, Joe Loose. Yeah, man!"

On and on it goes. Everybody laughs, except the Bomber and his harassed spar partner. No one seems tense. It's all fun and merriment and a Harlem holiday.

When the day's work is over, the hosts from Harlem trail back to New York and Louis and his clan settle back in a thoroughly relaxed atmosphere.

"How'd them Tigers come out?" is usually Joe's first question when he gets back to his quarters after a workout. Incidentally, Hank Greenberg is no longer Louis' favorite ball player. He has switched to Gerald Walker.

"Why do you like Walker?" someone asked.

"Don't know," Joe replied. "I jest likes him, that's all."

An incident typical of the whole camp is the manner in which Joe keeps his tooth brushes. He has four of them hanging from a rack. Over the brushes, printed in large letters is the name

"Joe Lewis." Someone suggest that it was a fine state-of-affairs when one of Joe's helpers misspelled his name. The answer to this was a set of wide grins and a few peals of laughter.

"STOP PLAYING CATCH," JACOBS TELLS JOE

Detroit Evening Times, September 20th 1935.
(Reprinted with the permission of *The Detroit News.*)
By Bob Murphy

POMPTON LAKES, N.J., Sept. 20.—Through no fault of their own, the Detroit Tigers yesterday played an extremely nervous role in the fistic drama involving Joe Louis and Maxie Baer.

This correspondent was seated in Promoter Mike Jacobs' office at 1610 Broadway. The boys were chewing the rag, and Mike was prancing about as nervously as a bridegroom.

"Louis is nuts about the Tigers," someone suggested."

"Yeah," said another, "plays catch out at camp every chance he gets.'

"Gerald Walker is his favorite Tiger," another volunteered. "He's postponing his honeymoon so he can see the Tigers in the World Series," still another injected.

All this time Mike Jacobs is pacing the floor. Mentally he was counting his money and wondering if it will rain Tuesday night, or whether Tuesday will ever come and if the newspaper boys will ever quit asking for passes.

SCARES JACOBS

"Be too bad if Louis broke his finger playing catch and your million-dollar gate went up in smoke," this correspondent, blessed with the soul of a devil, threw into Mike. It registered. Jacobs quit pacing the floor. He went into 16 different tantrums at one time.

"Hey, there," he yelled at a girl stenographer, "get me Pompton Lakes. Get 'em quick. Tell that Louis to lay off baseball. No, wait a minute. Let me talk." For the next several minutes Michael Jacobs burned up the wires to Pompton Lakes. "Don't let him so much as touch a soft ball," admonished Jacobs to John Roxborough. "Your Tigers may be all right, but this is a prizefight. Say, how long has this been going on anyway?"

With that Mr. Michael Jacobs snapped up the receiver, mopped a wet brow and resumed his floor walking. "Baseball," he snorted. "Who are them Tigers to get a guy's finger broke, anyway." He paced and he paced. And the best part of the story is that John Roxborough had to rouse Sleeptime Joe from his slumber and inform him as to how he shouldn't play any more baseball, or fool with any more policemen's motorcycles, or anything.

RUNYON CALLS DETROITER
THE GREATEST FIGHTING MACHINE OF RING

(JOE LOUIS vs. MAX BAER)

Detroit Times, September 25th 1935 (9/24/35)
(Reprinted by permission of *The Detroit News.*)
By Damon Runyon

NEW YORK, Sept. 25—Bridegroom Joe Louis, married at 7 o'clock last evening, gives his bride a wedding present of $250,000 and a four-round knockout victory over Max Baer a little over three hours later.

The California ex-champion sinks to the canvas after taking a frightful hammering from the fists of the "Brown Bomber" of Detroit, and is counted out resting on one knee.

Baer's face is a smear of blood. It spouts from his nose and mouth, damaged by the cutting left hooks of the Negro.

A crowd of upwards of 84,831 men and women who pack the great Yankee Stadium paid a gross of $ 932,044 ($805,725 net) to see this fight, which is partly for the benefit of the free milk fund for babies, boo the man who has been called "The Hollywood Harlequin" as he leaves the ring.

Some of them seem to feel Max offers a spiritless defense, standing almost inert under the blistering fire of Louis as long as he can, grinning a bloody grin of braggadocio but rarely making a real effort to fight back.

Louis, cold, cruel, relentless as always relaxes his "dead pan" features just once in a fleeting grin as he stalks the former heavy weight champion of the world.

Joe is almost slow-motion in his deliberateness at times. He seems to feel he can make the "kill" any time he desires, but he takes no undue chances.

Just once, in a fierce mixup against the ropes, does Baer fight back with real fury, but Louis stands toe to toe with him and it is Baer who finally pulls up and clinches.

Whatever the crowd may think of Baer, it tenders amazing sporting tribute to Louis, at the finish as the greatest fighter of modern times.

In the other corner Jack Dempsey who once held the same distinction, stares goggle-eyed with amazement at Louis.

He knows he has seen a tremendous gratification. Dempsey serves as Baer's chief second, an office that will, perhaps cost him many explanations and apologies in the future.

He does his best to instill into Baer some of the desperate Dempsey ring spirit that cause Dempsey to climb back into a ring one night and get his man—Louis Angel Firpo. But no such flame burns in the Baer bosom. He stands still in the center of the ring while Louis pegs his nose to a bloody pulp. Max is supposed to be a good puncher with his right hand, but he does not swing that right and keep swinging it, as a Dempsey would.

TAME AS PUSSY CAT

After one taste of the Louis blast in the opening round, the bragging Baer, who came down out of his mountain retreat breathing death and defiance to the Louis camp, is as tame as a pussy cat. He apparently has no zest for battle.

It is no new fistic characteristic to followers of the ring game for a fighter to display what passes for gameness by staying in there and stoically taking a hammering without fighting back, and Baer seems to be of this type.

Max is like a horse that will not run from behind. But it is doubtful if he, or any other man, could have long survived the magnificent mechanism of the Louis attack last night, but another man might have gone down with his colors flying.

Possibly the answer is Baer's legs, on which the famous comedian of the ring has run through many night clubs between the coasts declined to answer the call of his spirits as he kneels on the canvas after 2 minutes and 50 seconds of fighting in the fourth, listening to the count.

Damon Runyon was one of the legendary writers of the early 1900's. He covered a variety of subjects including sports, and was a frequent contributor to the Hearst Newspapers including the *Detroit Times.*

EYED DISDAINFULLY

Louis, from a neutral corner, eyes him rather disdainfully. Perhaps some of Louis' tiger-like attack on Baer may be explained by the rancor smouldering in the Louis bosom over "wise cracks" made by Baer about the Bomber's marriage that took place last evening long before Louis went into the ring. His bride, Marva Trotter, is supposed to be at the ringside, perhaps spellbound by the prowess of her new husband.

On quitting his new bride earlier that evening, Joe Louis turned to her and said:

"See you later, honey. Ah got an appointment with Mist' Baer."

Baer, who lost the heavyweight title last June to James J. Braddock in one of the greatest fistic upsets in history, claimed his hands were bad in that bout. He can have no such alibi for last night, as he did not use his hands sufficiently to determine their status. He trained faithfully for this bout, making many threats and promises.

NOT WORTH NICKEL

Baer enlisted the services of Dempsey as his chief second, feeling Dempsey might add to his confidence, Dempsey claims he was in there last night because he has long had a financial interest in Baer anyway.

He whispers much in Baer's ear between rounds, but his advice is not worth a nickel to Max if the Baer hears it. He never comes out of his corner with any of his old swashbuckling confidence. He seems under the spell of the strange man in the other corner, who acts as unconcernedly as if he were fighting [a] fistic tramp instead of the "great" Baer.

The time Louis grins is when Baer tags him lightly at the bell as Joe is leaning against the ropes near Baer's corner. It is a tough night for the Baer family all around as Ford Smith of Montana whips Buddy Baer in a bout that goes on after the main event, although Buddy looms over Smith like a factory over a hovel, as far as size is concerned.

NO MATCH FOR JOE

Max Baer is at no stage of the game any match for Louis. He is out-boxed, out-hit, out-roughed. Louis handles him with ease in the clinches. After Louis tags him a few, mild punches in the first round, Baer leaks gore continually and even the great Dempsey cannot stop that.

In their first exchanges in the first round Baer lands his right flush on Louis' chin several times and it does not phase the colored boy. As a matter of fact, Baer stands up at this moment under a battering that makes it look as if his boast that his chin is impregnable is correct.

Thereafter, under the advice of cool-headed old Jack Blackburn, his chief second, Louis starts blasting at Baer's body to save his hands from damage, and to bring Baer down gradually.

This system is successful. When Baer raises his hands to protect his chin he gets a smack in the stomach. Then he drops his hands he gets hooked across his sore face.

NO REST FOR BAER

There is no rest for the weary Baer. His grin becomes the weirdest expression imaginable. His white teeth show through the bloody smear across his mouth.

However, he never attempts any of the usual clowning. He was a serious man last night and booked for a serious beating.

There is no telling what ultimate damage Louis might inflict if Baer gets up off his knees from the last knockdown, the third of the battle and due to a smashing right-hander.

The two other knockdowns are in the third round. Baer sinks to the first knockdown like a suddenly deflated balloon.

As a spectacle, the thing is a great thrill for the 90,000 spectators. As a fight, it seems too one-sided to the experts to be called a great contest.

SAYS HE'S THROUGH

Baer says after the fight he is through, he will go back to his cattle ranch." He says Louis is "a great kid," but he thinks Eddie Simms punches harder. Eddie Simms is a Cleveland heavyweight who hit Baer so hard in an exhibition bout Max saw stars for weeks afterwards.

Someone asks:

"Why didn't you get up?"

Baer says:

"I was in a daze."

The crowd and receipts last night probably come close to the record for a non-title bout, set by Sharkey and Dempsey on this very field. Baer and Louis each get 30 percent, plus $5,000 for training expenses.

So ends the great spectacle that makes New York live again the palmy days of the gold rush.

JOE LOUIS CAREER FIGHT RECORD

(Totals: **69 Wins**, 55 Knockouts, 13 by Decision, 1 Disqualification; **3 Losses**—2 by Knockout, 1 by Decision)

Opponent	Type	Round	Time	Date	Location	Result
Jack Kracken	KO	1(out of 6 possible)		7/04/34	Chicago, Illinois	Win
Willie Davics	KO	3(6)		7/12/34	Chicago, Illinois	Win
Larry Udell	TKO	2(8)		7/30/34	Chicago, Illinois	Win
Jack Kranz	Decision	8(8)		8/13/34	Chicago, Illinois	Win
Buck Everett	KO	2(8)		8/27/34	Chicago, Illinois	Win
Al Delaney	TKO	4(10)		9/11/34	Detroit, Michigan	Win
Adolph Wiater	Decision	10(10)		9/26/34	Chicago, Illinois	Win
Art Sykes	KO	8(10)		10/24/34	Chicago, Illinois	Win
Jack O'Dowd	KO	2(10)		10/31/34	Detroit, Michigan	Win
Stanley Poreda	KO	1(10)	2:40	11/14/34	Chicago, Illinois	Win
Charley Massera	KO	3(10)		11/30/34	Chicago, Illinois	Win
Lee Ramage	TKO	8(10)	2:51	12/14/34	Chicago, Illinois	Win
Patsy Perroni	Decision	10(10)		1/04/35	Chicago, Illinois	Win
Hans Birkie	TKO	10(10)	1:47	1/11/35	Pittsburgh, Pennsylvania	Win
Lee Ramage	TKO	2(10)	2:11	2/21/35	Los Angeles, California	Win
Don Barry	TKO	3(10)		3/08/35	San Francisco, California	Win
Natie Brown	Decision (unan.)	10(10)		3/29/35	Detroit, Michigan	Win
Roy Lazer	KO	3(10)	2:26	4/12/35	Chicago, Illinois	Win
Biff Bennett	KO	1(6)	2:26	4/22/35	Dayton, Ohio	Win
Roscoe Toles	KO	6(6)		4/25/35	Flint, Michigan	Win
Willie Davies	KO	2(6)		5/03/35	Peoria, Illinois	Win
Gene Stanton	KO	3(6)		5/07/35	Kalamazoo, Michigan	Win
Primo Carnera	TKO	6(15)	2:32	6/25/35	Yankee Stadium, New York	Win
King Levinsky	TKO	1(10)	2:21	8/07/35	Chicago, Illinois	Win
Max Baer	KO	4(15)		9/24/35	Yankee Stadium, NY	Win
Paulino Uzcudun	TKO	4(15)	2:32	12/13/35	Madison Sq. Garden, New York	Win
Charley Retzlaff	KO	1(15)	1:25	1/17/36	Chicago, Illinois	Win
Max Schmeling	KO	12(15)	2:29	6/19/36	Yankee Stadium, New York	Loss
Jack Sharkey	KO	3(10)	1:02	8/18/36	Yankee Stadium, New York	Win
Al Ettore	KO	5(15)	1:28	9/22/36	Municipal Stadium, Philidelphia	Win
Jorge Brescia	KO	3(10)	2:12	10/09/36	Hippodrome, New York City	Win
Eddie Simms	TKO	1(10)	0:26	12/14/36	Cleveland, Ohio	Win
Steve Ketchel	KO	2(4)	0:31	1/11/36	Buffalo, New York	Win
Bob Pastor	Dccision (unan.)	10(10)		1/29/37	Madison Sq. Garden, New York	Win
Natie Brown	KO	4(10)		2/17/37	Kansas City, Missouri	Win
James Braddock*	KO	8(15)		6/22/37	Chicago, Illinois	Win
Tommy Farr	Decision (unan.)	15(15)		8/30/37	Yankee Stadium, New York	Win
Nathan Mann	KO	3(15)		2/23/38	Madison Sq. Garden New York	Win
Harry Thomas	KO	5(15)	2:50	4/01/38	Chicago, Illinois	Win

....

Won World Heavyweight Title

Opponent	Type	Round	Time	Date	Location	Result
Max Schmeling	KO	1(15)	2:04	6/22/38	Yankee Stadium, New York	Win
John Henry Lewis	KO	1(15)	2:29	1/25/39	Madison Sq. Garden, New York	Win
Jack Roper	KO	1(10)	2:20	4/17/39	Wrigley Field, Los Angeles	Win
Tony Galento	TKO	4(15)	2:29	6/28/39	Yankee Stadium, New York	Win
Bob Pastor	KO	11(20)		9/20/39	Detroit, Michigan	Win
Arturo Godoy	Decision (split)	15(15)		2/09/40	Madison Sq. Garden, New York	Win
Johnny Paychek	TKO	2(15)	0:41	3/29/40	Madison Sq. Garden, New York	Win
Arturo Godoy	TKO	8(15)	1:24	6/20/40	Yankee Stadium, New York	Win
Al McCoy	TKO	6(15)		12/16/40	Boston, Massachusetts	Win
Red Burman	KO	5(15)	2:49	1/31/41	Madison Sq. Garden, New York	Win
Gus Dorazio	KO	2(15)	1:30	2/17/41	Philadelphia, Pennsylvania	Win
Abe Simon	TKO	13(20)	1:20	3/21/41	Detroit, Michigan	Win
Tony Musto	TKO	9(15)	1:36	4/08/41	St. Louis, Missouri	Win
Buddy Baer	Disqualification	7(15)		5/23/41	Washington, D.C.	Win
Billy Conn	KO	13(15)	2:58	6/18/41	New York City	Win
Lou Nova	TKO	6(15)	2:59	9/29/41	New York City	Win
Buddy Baer	KO	1(15)	2:56	1/09/42	Madison Sq. Garden, New York	Win
Abe Simon	TKO	6(15)		3/27/42	Madison Sq. Garden, New York	Win
Johnny Davis	TKO	1(4)	0:53	11/14/44	Buffalo, New York	Win
Billy Conn	KO	8(15)	2:19	6/19/46	Yankee Stadium, New York	Win
Tami Mauriello	KO	1(15)	2:09	9/18/46	Yankee Stadium, New York	Win
Jersey Joe Walcott	Decision (split)	15(15)		12/05/46	Madison Sq. Garden, New York	Win
Jersey Joe Walcott	KO	11(15)		6/25/48	Yankee Stadium, New York	Win
Ezzard Charles	Decision (unan.)	15(15)		9/27/50	Yankee Stadium, New York	Loss
Cesar Brion	Decision (unan.)	10(10)		11/29/50	Chicago, Illinois	Win
Freddie Beshore	TKO	4(10)	2:48	1/03/51	Detroit, Michigan	Win
Omelio Agramonte	Decision (unan.)	10(10)		2/07/51	Miami, Florida	Win
Andy Walker	TKO	10(10)	1:49	2/23/51	San Francisco, California	Win
Omelio Agramonte	Decision (unan.)	10(10)		5/02/51	Detroit, Michigan	Win
Lee Savold	KO	6(15)	2:29	6/15/51	Madison Sq. Garden, New York	Win
Cesar Brion	Decision (unan.)	10(10)		5/02/51	San Francisco, California	Win
Jimmy Bivins	Decision (unan.)	10(10)		8/15/51	Baltimore, Maryland	Win
Rocky Marciano	KO	8(10)		10/26/51	Madison Sq. Garden, New York	Loss

Contents

Detroit Times Advertisement.
—*Detroit Times* photo/Courtesy
of *The Detroit News*

IN TRIBUTE TO BILLY ROGELL . . .

"Baseball? I hear [these guys] talking about the Yankees. Don't those fellows *ever* remember our infield of 1934–1935? We drove in more runs than any infield in the history of baseball. Greenberg, Gehringer, myself, and Owen. Those two years we drove in more than any infield they ever had. I mean from the start of baseball, but you never hear anything about it. What the hell, there's nobody to talk about the great Tiger teams. We had a helluva ball club and don't forget it."

—Billy Rogell to Joe Falls in a 1975 interview.

1934 Tigers
Player RBI's

Player	RBI
Greenberg	139
Gehringer	127
Rogell	100
Owen	96
TOTAL	462

· · · · · · ·

* This statistic was verified by the Baseball Hall of Fame as being still the most by an infield in one season.

1935 American League Final Standings

Team	Win	Loss	GB
Detroit Tigers	93	58	—
New York Yankees	89	60	3.0
Cleveland Indians	82	71	12.0
Boston Red Sox	78	75	16.0
Chicago White Sox	74	78	19.5
Washington Senators	67	86	27.0
St. Louis Browns	65	87	28.5

1935 National League Final Standings

Team	Win	Loss	GB
Chicago Cubs	100	54	—
St. Louis Cardinals	96	58	4.0
New York Giants	91	62	8.5
Pittsburgh Pirates	86	67	13.5
Brooklyn Dodgers	70	83	29.5
Cincinnati Reds	68	85	31.5
Philadelphia Phillies	64	89	35.5
Boston Braves	38	115	61.5

Billy Rogell.
—Photo courtesy of *The Detroit News*

PLAY BY PLAY OF
FIRST WORLD SERIES GAME

1935 WORLD SERIES, GAME 1: DETROIT TIGERS VS. CHICAGO CUBS

Detroit Times, Oct.2nd 1935 (Tues. 10/1/35)

(Reprinted with the permission of *The Detroit News.*)

FIRST INNING

CHICAGO—Augie Galan was the first batter. A turn-around batter, he hit .315 in 154 games. He stepped into the left batter's box as he faced Rowe. Schoolboy's first pitch was a called strike. Galan fouled the next one into the stands. He slugged the next one over Rowe's head for a two-base hit. Rogell tried for a diving stop and Galan took the extra base as White raced in to pick up the ball. Herman, a right-handed hitter with a .340 betting average, was the next batter. Rowe got the first two over for strikes. Herman foul tipping the second. He hit a slow roller to Rowe near the third base line. Rowe's throw to first was on the wrong side of the bag and Herman knocked the ball out of Greenberg's hand as he raced across the bag, Galan scoring from third on the error, which was charged to Rowe's bad throw. Lindstrom sacrificed, Rowe to Greenberg. Harnett slugged a single to the right, scoring Herman. Demaree, a right-handed hitter, let one ball go by and then popped to Rogell in front of second. Cavarrctta, batting from the left side of the plate, fouled the first pitch. He foul-tipped the next one for strike two. He grounded to Gehringer on the next pitch, forcing Hartnett, Gehringer to Rogell. Two runs, two hits, one error, one left.

DETROIT—After fouling four pitches with a count of two and two, White looked at a third strike through the middle of the plate. Cochrane let the first one go by for a ball, the second for a called strike, he swung and missed a fast ball, foul-tipped the next one and then raised an easy fly to Galan in left field for the second out. Gehringer took the first strike and fouled the next pitch for strike two, Jurges went back on the grass in back of second for his pop fly. No run, no hit, no error, none left.

SECOND INNING

CHICAGO—Hack, a left-hand hitter, was the first batter to face Rowe. The first pitch was a ball inside and high. Gehringer raced out into short center field for his pop fly.

Rowe's first pitch to Jurges, a right hand hitter, was a called strike. He hit the next pitch for a single and took second on Goslin's fumble. His ground ball was just out of Rogell's reach and Goslin stumbled fielding the ball. Fox made a nice running catch of Warneke's fly and his perfect throw chased Jurges back to second. Rowe pitched two balls to Galan before he got a strike over. Galan fouled the next one down the left field line for strike two. Galan struck out, swinging at a wide curve. No run, one hit, one error.

DETROIT—Greenberg got a tremendous ovation when he came to the plate. He stepped away from an inside pitch for a called ball. He fouled the next one into the dirt for strike one. The next pitch was a ball, high. He hit a slow bounder to Hack, who threw him out. Goslin looked at the first one for a called strike. The next was a ball, outside. He swung and missed a curve for strike two. The next pitch was low for ball two. He fouled the next one down the first base line. He hit a slow bounder near first base and was thrown out. Warneke's first pitch to Fox was a ball. Pete fouled the next one back of the plate. The next one he banged off the screen of the left field bleachers for a double, the first Tiger hit of the game. Rogell flied high to Galan on the first pitch. Waving Lindstrom away, Galan almost misjudged the fly. No run, one hit, no error.

THIRD INNING

CHICAGO—Herman let two balls go by and swung and missed the next one. He fouled the next one back into the stands for strike two. Hank made a perfectly timed leap to spear Herman's line drive in the webbing of his big mitt as the crowd roared. Lindstrom singled on the first pitch, looping a short fly over Rogell's head. Harnett swung and missed the first pitch and then looked at a fast ball on the outside corner for strike two. The third pitch was a ball, outside. Gabby fouled the next one over the press box. The next pitch was a ball, low. A pitch out made the count three and two. Rowe made an easy toss to first. Hartnett fouled the next pitch over the right field pavilion. He took the next pitch for a

Mickey Cochrane, Babe Ruth, and Charlie Grimm posed for this picture before the first game of the 1935 World Series.

—*Detroit Times* photo/Courtesy of *The Detroit News*

called strike and Cochrane doubled Lindstrom stealing with a peg to Gehringer. The throw was high and Lindstrom slid into the bag hard, but Gehringer blocked him off and put the ball on him. No run, one hit, no error.

DETROIT—Owen hit a bounder back at the box on the first pitch. Warneke knocked it down with his bare hand but picked up the ball in time to throw out the runner. Rowe looked at a ball and poked the next one back to Warneke who threw him out. White swung and missed the first pitch. The next was a ball. Warneke's next pitch was low for ball two. White lined the next one into right field

for a single. Cochrane looked at a slow curve for a called strike. He bounced an easy grounder to Warneke, who tossed him out. No run, one hit, no error.

FOURTH INNING

CHICAGO—Demaree lined Rowe's first pitch past Rogell for a single. Rowe tried to pick him off first before he pitched to Cavarretta. Caverretta sacrificed, dragging a bunt which Rowe had to pick up bare handed and threw while down on one knee. Hack grounded to Gehringer, Demaree moving to third. Rowe's first pitch to Jurges was a ball. He fouled the next one into the right field stands. He fouled the next one back against the screen for strike two. A high pitch made the count two and two. He fouled a curve into the dirt back of the plate. Jurges struck out, swinging at a high fast ball. No run, one hit, no error.

DETROIT—With a count of one and one Gehringer hit an easy bounder back to Warneke, who threw him out, his fifth assist. Warneke got behind Greenberg, pitching three balls and one strike. He walked on a low inside pitch. It was the first base on balls of the game. Warneke was wild and also walked Goslin on four pitches, bring up Fox. Fox looked at the first pitch for a called strike. He hit a slow grounder to Jurges who threw him out with a fine peg, both runners advancing. Rogell swung and missed the first pitch for a strike. The next was a ball and Goslin had to slide into second when Hartnett tried to pick him off. The next pitch was a ball, inside. Rogell hit a slow roller down the first base line to Cavarretta, who took the ball and fell on the bag, retiring the side. No run, no hit, no error.

FIFTH INNING

CHICAGO—Warneke got applause when he came to bat. He hit the first pitch hard on the ground to Greenberg, who beat him to the bag. Rowe's first pitch to Galan was low for a ball. Galan swung and missed a fastball for strike one. He looked at the next one for strike two and then grounded to Gehringer. Schoolboy's first pitch to Herman was a ball and the second was outside for all two. He swung on the next pitch, raising a high fly to Goslin, ending the inning, the first time Row has kept the bases bare. No run, no hit, no error.

DETROIT—Owen looked at a wide one for ball one and took the next one for a called strike. He lined to Demaree in front of the bleachers. Rowe also got a hand when he came to bat. The first pitch was a called strike over the outside corner. Rowe fouled the next one back against the screen for strike two. He banged the next pitch over second for a double. Jurges, racing after the ball, kicked it into right center and Schoolboy by fast running and a slide turned it into a two base hit. White looked at a called ball, and fouled the next one into the stands for strike one. The next pitch was ball, outside. He grounded to Herman, Rowe moving to third. Warneke's first pitch to Cochrane was a ball, high and outside. The next was low for ball two. The third pitch was a called strike on the outside corner and Cochrane looked at the next one in the same place for strike two.

He hit a bounder toward Warneke who made the putout at first unassisted. No run, one hit, no error.

SIXTH INNING

CHICAGO—Rowe was slow coming to the mound. He took four practice pitches before he faced Lindstrom. Lindstrom popped the first pitch to Gehringer in back of second. Hartnett looked at the first one for a called strike. The next was a ball, outside. The second was a low curve in the dirt for ball two. Hartnett banged the next one past short for a single. Rowe's first pitch to Demaree was low for a ball. His next was through the middle for a called strike. He swung and missed a curve for strike two. The next was a low ball, making the count two and two. Demaree struck out swinging at a fast ball through the heart of the plate. Cavarretta swung and missed the first pitch for strike one. He swung and missed a wide curve for strike two. The next pitch was high for ball two. Cavarretta struck out swinging at a fast ball in around his wrists. No run, one hit, no error.

DETROIT—Gehringer grounded to Herman. Greenberg swung on the first pitch, a high fly in the back of third. Goslin looked at the first pitch, a ball, outside. He banged the next one back at Warneke, who deflected it to Herman, whose throw beat Goslin to first. No run, no hit, no error.

SEVENTH INNING

CHICAGO—Hack was called out on strikes. Rogell ran into short left field for Jurges' pop fly. Warneke hit a hard grounder to Gehringer, who threw him out. No run, no hit, no error.

DETROIT—Warneke tossed out Fox. Jurges ran far into the left field foul territory for Rogell's pop foul. Owen walked. Rowe flied high to Lindstrom in front of the bleachers in deep left center. No run, no hit, no error.

EIGHTH INNING

CHICAGO—Greenberg fumbled Galan's roller. Herman sacrificed, Rowe to Greenberg. Galan went to third on Cochrane's short passed ball. Lindstrom tapped to Rowe. He bluffed Galan back to third before throwing out the runner. Hartnett flied to White. No run, no hit, one error.

DETROIT—White swung and missed the first pitch. He bunted down the third base line to Hack and was thrown out on a close play, the crowd booing Quigley's decision and one fan threw a toy wooden bat out on the field. The first pitch to Cochrane was a ball. He fouled the next two back to the screen. Warneke grabbed his slow bounder and threw him out. He was Warneke's eighth assist and tied the world series' record for assists by a pitcher in one game, set by nick Altos of the Chicago White Sox on Oct. 12, 1906. Gehringer walked. Warneke pitched two balls to Greenberg and Hank foul tipped the next one for strike one. He hit on the ground to Hack who threw him out. No run, no hit, no error.

NINTH INNING

CHICAGO—Demaree hit a home run high into the left field bleachers. Cavarretta struck out. Hack flied to White. Jurges struck out. One hit, one run, one error.

DETROIT—Goslin flied to Lindstrom. Fox poked a single over second. Rogell grounded to Cavarretta, Fox moving to second. Jurges threw out Owen. No run, one hit, no error.

World Series Box Score—FIRST GAME

CHICAGO	BATTING												FIELDING		
	G	AB	R	H	TB	2B	3B	HR	BB	SO	SB	Avg.	E	TC	Avg.
Galan, lf	1	4	1	1	2	1	0	0	0	1	0	.250	0	2	1.000
Herman, 2b	1	3	1	0	0	0	0	0	0	0	0	.000	0	3	1.000
Lindstrom, cf	1	3	0	1	1	0	0	0	0	0	0	.333	0	2	1.000
Hartnett, c	1	4	0	2	2	0	0	0	0	1	0	.500	0	1	1.000
Demaree, rf	1	4	1	2	5	0	0	1	0	1	0	.500	0	1	1.000
Cavarretta, 1b	1	3	0	0	0	0	0	0	0	2	0	.000	0	17	1.000
Hack, 3b	1	4	0	0	0	0	0	0	0	1	0	.000	0	4	1.000
Jurges, ss	1	4	0	1	1	0	0	0	0	2	0	.250	0	4	1.000
Warneke, p	1	3	0	0	0	0	0	0	0	0	0	.000	0	9	1.000
Totals		32	3	7	11	1	0	1	0	8	0	.219	0	43	1.000

DETROIT	BATTING												FIELDING		
	G	AB	R	H	TB	2B	3B	HR	BB	SO	SB	Avg.	E	TC	Avg.
White, cf	1	4	0	1	1	0	0	0	0	1	0	.250	0	2	1.000
Cochrane, c	1	4	0	0	0	0	0	0	0	0	0	.000	0	9	1.000
Gehringer, 2b	1	3	0	0	0	0	0	0	1	0	0	.000	0	7	1.000
Greenberg, 1b	1	3	0	0	0	0	0	0	1	0	0	.000	1	10	.900
Goslin, lf	1	3	0	0	0	0	0	0	1	0	0	.000	1	2	.500
Fox, rf	1	4	0	2	3	1	0	0	0	0	0	.500	0	1	1.000
Rogell, ss	1	4	0	0	0	0	0	0	0	0	0	.000	0	3	1.000
Owen, 3b	1	3	0	0	0	0	0	0	1	0	0	.250	0	7	.000
Rowe, p	1	3	0	1	2	1	0	0	0	0	0	.333	1	5	.800
Totals		30	0	4	6	2	0	0	4	1	0	.133	3	39	.917

PLAY BY PLAY OF SECOND WORLD SERIES GAME

1935 World Series, Game2: Detroit Tigers vs. Chicago Cubs

Detroit Evening Times, Oct.2nd 1935 (Wed. 10/2/35)
(Reprinted with the permission of *The Detroit News*.)

FIRST INNING

CHICAGO—Manager Charley Grimm was in the third base coaching box and Joe Corridon in the first base coaching box for the Cubs when Galan stepped to the plate. Bridges first pitch was a ball, high. Galan fouled the next one into the press box. The next pitch was a ball, low and inside to a left-hand hitter. Tommy put another one in the same place for ball three. His next pitch looked good, but Umpire Quigley called it a ball. Galan taking first on a base on balls. Tommy's first pitch to Herman was a called strike. Herman grounded into a double play. Bridges to Rogell to Greensberg. Tommy's first pitch to Lindstrom was a ball. Lindstrom fouled into the press box for strike one. A fast ball for a called strike. Lindstrom struck out, swinging at a curve and the crowd howled its approval. No runs, no hit, no error.

DETROIT—With a count of three and two, White looped a single into left field. With a count of one ball and one strike, Cochrane smashed a double down the right field foul line, scoring White. No play was made on him at the plate. Cavarretta, who took Demaree's throw, slipped and fell before he could throw to the plate. Gehringer hit a terrific drive far over the right field fence, but it was foul by a couple of feet. Gehringer lined a single to the center. Cochrane scoring standing up. Herman and Hank had a conference with Root before he pitched to Greenberg. With a count of one ball and one strike, Greenberg hit a terrific line drive high into the left bleachers for a homerun. Gehringer scoring ahead of him. The entire Cubs' infield gathered around Root, who left the game. Roy Henshaw, a stubble little lefthander, replaced him.

Henshaw was nervous and wild. With a three and two count. He walked Goslin with a low, wild pitch. Fox lined into a double play. Herman grabbing his line drive and tossing to Cavarretta to double Goslin. Henshaw grabbed Rogell's hard grounder and threw him out. Four runs, four hits, no error.

SECOND INNING

CHICAGO—Gehringer came in on the grass to scoop up Hartnett's grounder and threw him out. With a count of two and two Demaree hit an easy grounder into the dirt to Gehringer. With a count of one ball, Cavarretta hit a bounder to Greenberg in back of first, Bridges taking his toss to make the putout. No run, no hit, no error.

DETROIT—Owen struck out on three pitches. Bridges hit an easy grounder to Hack, who threw him out. White walked on four pitches. Galan came in for Cochrane's fly. No runs, no hit, no error.

THIRD INNING

CHICAGO—With a count of three and two, Bridges walked Hack with a low pitch inside. With two balls and one strike Jurges flied to Fox in front of the scoreboard. Henshaw although a left hand pitcher, batted from the right side of the plate. He flied to Goslin, who had to chase the ball in the wind into center field. With a count of two balls and one strike, Galan lined to White in right center. No runs, no hits, no error.

DETROIT—Gehringer walked on a low outside pitch. Greenberg grounded into a double play. Jurges to Herman to Cavarretta. Goslin flied high to Galan in left center. No runs, no hit, no error.

FOURTH INNING

CHICAGO—Bridges got behind Herman, pitching three balls before he got a strike over, then he struck him out. Herman taking the third strike with his bat on his shoulder. Lindstrom worked the count to three and two and then popped to Gehringer back on the grass in short left field. With one ball and one strike, Hartnett slugged a single to center, the first hit off Bridges. With two strikes and no balls Demaree hit a fly into short right center. White plucking the ball right out of Fox's hand. No run, one hit, no error.

DETROIT—Fox popped to Hack near the left field foul

line, the wind blowing the fly fair. With a count of two and two, Rogell looked at the third strike over the inside corner. Owen was hit by a pitched ball. With a count of one ball and one strike, Bridges smashed a single off Henshaw's glove. Owen stopping at second. Henshaw pitched three balls to White before he got a strike over. With a count of three and two White walked on a wide pitch, filling the bases. Owen scored and the other runners advanced on a wild pitch. Cochrane worked the count to three and two, then walked, filling the bases again. After fouling one pitch, Gehringer lined a single to right center, scoring Bridges and White, and sending Cochrane to third.

The Cubs had another caucus in the pitcher's box. Kowalik replaced Henshaw. He is a right-hander. Greenberg smashed the first pitch back at Kowalik, who picked it up and threw him out. Three runs, two hits, no error.

FIFTH INNING

CHICAGO—Cavarretta grounded to Greenberg on the first pitch, but Greenberg fumbled the ball and threw badly to Bridges so Cavarretta was safe on first on the error. With a count of one ball and one strike Bridges tossed out Hack. Cavarretta moving to second. Jurges looped a low liner over Gehringer's head for a single. Cavarretta scoring. Kowik forced Jurges, Greensberg to Rogell, Greenberg starting a double play with a high throw that almost pulled Rogell off the bag.

Cochrane hopped out in front of the plate to pick up Galan's slow roller, but Greenberg muffed the throw and Galan was safe on the error. Herman lined to Owen. One run, one hit, two errors.

DETROIT—With a count of two and two Goslin grounded to Herman. The wind blew Fox' fly into Lindstrom's hands in short center. With a count of one ball and two strikes, Rogell singled to left, when Galan fumbled the

Bill Jurges scoring on Billy Herman's single in the seventh inning of game 2.
—*Detroit Times* photo/Courtesy of *The Detroit News*

ball momentarily. Rogell tried to take second but was thrown out. Galan to Herman. No run, one hit, no error.

SIXTH INNING

CHICAGO—With a count of three and two Lindstrom walked on a high pitch inside. With one strike and no balls Hartnett grounded into a double play. Rogell to Gehringer to Greenberg. With a count of two and two Demaree doubled to left center. With a count of two and two Cavaretta grounded to Gehringer. No runs, one hit and no error.

DETROIT—Owen popped to Hack, who collided with Jurges after making the catch. Kowalik tossed out Bridges. White was safe at first when Kowalik picked up his slow roller and hit him on the back with his throw and the ball bounded into foul territory and when White tried to take second Herman picked up the ball and threw him out with a peg to Jurges. No run, no hit, no error.

SEVENTH INNING

CHICAGO—Hack flied to Fox. Jurges worked the count to three and two and then walked Kowalik beat out a slow roller to Owen. Jurges stopping at second. Galan rolled to Gehringer, both runners advancing. Herman looped a single into left field, scoring Jurges and Kowalik and took second on Goslin's throw to the plate. Lindstrom popped to Greenberg near the pitcher's box. Two runs, to hits, no error.

DETROIT—Cochrane walked. Gehringer forced Cochrane, Herman to Jurges. Herman threw while down on his knees. Cochrane bumped into Jurges at second knocking him down and preventing a double play. Greenberg was hit by a pitched ball. Goslin flied to Galan. Fox smashed a single off Kowalik's glove the ball bounding into right field. Gehringer scoring but Greenberg was out at the plate. Demaree to Herman to Hartnett. One run, one hit, no error.

EIGHTH INNING

CHICAGO—Hartnett filed to Fox. Demaree fouled to Owen. Fox made a swell running catch of Cavarretta's short fly. No run, no hit, no error.

DETROIT—With a count of one ball and two strikes Rogell smashed a double past Cavaretta into right field foul territory. Owen sacrificed Hartnett to Herman. Bridges struck out on three pitches, swinging at a curve on the outside corner. White bunted and Harnett threw him out. No run, one hit, no error.

NINTH INNING

CHICAGO—Hack singled to center. Jurges popped to Rogell. Klein batted for Kowalik and filed to Goslin. Galan flied to Fox. No run, one hit, no error, one left.

RUNS BATTED IN—Herman 2, Jurges 1, Gehringer 3, Greenberg 2, Cochrane 1, Fox 1.

TWO-BASE HITS—Cochrane, Demaree, Rogell.

HOME RUN—Greenberg.

SACRIFICE HIT—Owen.

LEFT ON BASE—Detroit 8, Chicago 7.

DOUBLE PLAYS—Bridges to Rogell to Greenberg, Herman to Cavarretta, Jurges to Herman to Cavarretta, Rogell to Gehringer to Greenberg.

HITS—Off Root 4 in 0 innings (none out in first), off Henshaw 2 in 3 2-3 innings, off Kowalik 3 in 4 1-3 innings.

BASES ON BALLS—Off Bridges 4, off Henshaw 5, off Kowalik 1.

STRUCK OUT—By Bridges 2, by Henshaw 2, by Kowalik 1.

HIT BY PITCHER—By Henshaw (Owen), by Kowalik (Greenberg).

WILD PITCH—Henshaw.

LOSING PITCHER—Root.

UMPIRES—Quigley (N) at plate, McGowan (A) at first, Stark (N) at second, Moriarty (A) at third.

TIME—1:50.

World Series Box Score—SECOND GAME

CHICAGO CUBS

	AB	R	H	A	E
Galan, lf	4	0	0	1	0
Herman, 2b	4	0	1	6	0
Lindstrom, cf	3	0	0	0	0
Hartnett, c	4	0	1	2	0
Demaree, rf	4	0	1	1	0
Cavarretta, 1b	4	1	0	0	0
Hack, 3b	3	0	1	1	0
Jurges, ss	3	0	1	1	0
Root, p	0	0	0	0	0
Henshaw, p	1	0	0	1	0
Kowalik, p	2	1	1	2	1
*Klein	1	0	0	0	0
Totals	33	3	6	15	1

DETROIT TIGERS

	AB	R	H	A	E
White, cf	3	2	1	0	0
Cochrane, c	2	1	1	1	0
Gehringer, 2b	3	2	2	5	0
Greenberg, 1b	3	1	1	2	2
Goslin, lf	3	0	0	0	0
Fox, rf	4	0	1	0	0
Rogell, ss	4	0	2	2	0
Owen, 3b	2	1	0	0	0
Bridges, p	4	1	1	2	0
Totals	28	8	9	12	2

*Batted for Kowalik in ninth.

CHICAGO	0	0	0	0	1	0	2	0	0—3
DETROIT	4	0	0	3	0	0	1	0	x—8

DETROIT OVERCOMES ODDS TO DEFEAT CUBS IN 11TH, 6–5

1935 WORLD SERIES, GAME 3: DETROIT TIGERS AT CHICAGO CUBS

Detroit Times, Oct. 5th 1935 (Fri. 10/4/35)

(Reprinted with the permission of *The Detroit News.*) By Bud Shaver

CHICAGO, Oct.5—Detroit's 6 to 5 victory over Chicago Cubs in the third game of the World Series invited superlatives but doesn't need them.

The most barren factual account of the two-hour and a half 11-inning struggle in Wrigley Field could not but reveal it as the most dramatic production of all World Series history.

Players and fans unite in that appraisal. Mickey Cochrane, manager of the Tigers, Charley Gehringer and Goose Goslin, veteran actors in more than 1,000 ball games, including World Series and all-star contests, declared yesterday's game provided their greatest thrill.

The 45,532 fans who were locked in the tightening grip of its mounting tension, agree.

There have been games more skillfully, but none more dramatically. There was a quality of sustained and swelling drama about this one ball game which sets it apart from all others.

There were bad plays and bad pitches, sensational fielding plays and brilliant feats of pitching. There were brawls and bawdy talk, anger and disappointment, high courage and desperation.

EVERY HUMAN EMOTION BUBBLED TO THE SURFACE

Every human emotion which blood and brains can cook in the boiling pot of competition, bubbled to the surface.

It was a spectacle which leaves vivid and unforgettable pictures on the mind and endless arguments on the tongue.

In short, it was a ball game which so inflamed the minds it achieved the stature and dignity of a sporting epic.

Detroit entered the game a hopeless cripple, emerged a vain, glorious victor.

Hank Greenberg's stiff wrist and swollen glove hand not only deprived the Tigers of the services of baseball's greatest slugger and the American League's most valuable player, but his absence weakened the defense and attack at vital spots and shocked the morale of the club.

Odds on the Tigers' chance dropped like stock quotations in 1929 with the news Greenberg would not be able to play. The Tigers' spirits fell and the Cubs' confidence soared.

Marvin Owen went reluctantly to first base, dangling Greenberg's misshapen mitt upon his hand. Flea Clifton went eagerly to Owen's post at third and every other Tiger went to his position with sinking hearts.

Yet from somewhere the Tigers summoned a stubborn quality of resistance to the Cubs, and the cards which were stacked against them. That dogged rebelliousness smouldered to grim determination and burst finally into white hot flames of indomitable competitive spirit.

Four players were ejected from the ball game, three by Umpire George Moriarty of the American League, one by Umpire Ernie Quigley of the National League. Quigley banished Del Baker, Tiger third base coach, Moriarty chase Manager Charley Grimm of the Cubs out of the third base coaching box, Capt. Elwood (Woody) English and George Stainback off the bench.

Through all that turmoil and strife the Tigers battled against odds, the breaks, came from behind to take the lead in the eighth inning, only to lose it in the last half of the ninth and then came on again to win it in the eleventh.

Each team paraded three pitchers to the mound in the conflict and when the game ended, the Cubs lineup was as makeshift as the Tigers, riddled with substitutions.

Schoolboy Rowe emerged as the victor and Larry French the loser, yet Rowe almost brought the Tigers defeat instead of triumph. He was not a good pitcher yesterday, but he was a game one. And behind him he had a game, fighting team. The bats of Jo-Jo White, Charley Gehringer, Goose Goslin, Pete Fox and Bill Rogell thundered out the Tigers' complete attack. They provided all of Detroit's 12 hits, a brave barrage which even battered down the gods of chance who played hand in glove with one of the best defensive outfields in baseball.

TIGERS WOULD NOT BE DENIED, EVEN WITH BREAKS AGAINST 'EM

Augie Galan, Fred Lindstrom and Frank Demaree, racing like wraiths across the turf of the outfield, turned hit after hit into heartbreak. But the Tigers would not be denied, even with the breaks against them.

The Tigers' last turn at bat started as a replica of their most fruitless innings, except at the finish they broke through the web of mischance which bound them. It was an error by Fred Lindstrom which made the rent, a knifelike thrust by Jo-Jo White's bat in the eleventh inning which released the winning run.

French, a shopworn left-hander, was on the mound. Lindstrom had moved in from center field to play third base. Hack shifted from third to play short. Demaree moved from right to center field and Chuck Klein was in right field.

That had been the Cubs' revamped lineup since the ninth inning when Jurges was taken out of the lineup to let Klein bat for him and Jimmy O'Dea pinch hit for Lon Warneke. Each pinch hitter delivered a single off Rowe, following Hack's single with one out and those timely hits, with Galan's long fly, scored two runs and tied the score; sent the game into overtime and deprived Elon Hogsett of a World Series victory.

That was the lineup and infield defense when Rogell came to bat in the eleventh. He slugged a single past Hack in short. Owen bunted, but badly. He rapped the ball too sharply to Lindstrom, who charged in to scoop up the ball and force Rogell at second with a peg to Hack.

It was the old story of Tiger frustration, already more than 10 innings old. But Lindstrom provided the break on the next play. Clifton hit a grounder to his left. It was not a hard chance, but Lindstrom, unaccustomed to his infield job, botched it. The ball skidded off his glove, out of reach, and Owen reached second and Clifton first without a play being made on them. Rowe came to bat, but he seemed to lack his usual zest for the job. He fanned, swinging wildly at three pitches, the last two bad ones. That run on second seemed much smaller and more remote.

White's single was the blow which set the run in motion. He slugged a single to center, scoring Owen, the mercury footed Clifton racing to third and White took second on Demaree's panicky throw to the plate. Cochrane fouled to Hartnett and the inning was over. So was the game a little later.

This time Rowe was invincible when he faced the lower end of the Cubs' batting order. Clifton cooly scooped Cavaretta's grounder out of the dirt, took careful aim and threw him out. Rowe did the rest. He struck out Klein. Wally Stephenson pinch batted for French. He, too, struck out and baseball's most dramatic spectacle came to an end.

It almost ended an Inning earlier and with the Cubs victorious.

The last half of the tenth inning of the third game of the 1935 World Series will provide material for argument among the amateur tacticians and strategians of baseball.

Detroit was nearer defeat in that inning than at any time and the Tigers were close to the jaws of defeat throughout the game.

Lindstrom led off with a lusty double to the bleacher fence in right center. Gabby Hartnett, the "power" of the Cubs' batting order, the "cleanup hitter" strode to the plate.

Manager Charlie Grimm had been banished by Umpire Moriarty in the last half of the sixth inning. English, Chicago's non-playing captain, had been chased off the bench by Moriarty along with Stainback in the eighth. Joe Corriden and Roy Johnson, the coaches were on the field, but it is doubtful if either assumed authority.

If Hartnett received any orders they probably came from Lindstrom on second. It is not likely that Hartnett himself chose to sacrifice. Hitters like Hartnett like to hit, not bunt.

But bunt he did. Rowe was wary. He could not believe Hartnett would bunt even after he attempted and missed for the first strike. Rowe charged in with every pitch as did Owen, but Clifton played back in case Hartnett crossed Rowe with a swinging cut at the ball. He didn't. Hartnett dragged a beautiful bunt down the first base line. Were he as fast as any other man in the Cubs lineup he would have beaten it out, but Hartnett is slow. Cochrane leaped out, chased the rolling bunt down the line and threw Hartnett out as Lindstrom sped into third.

IT WAS UP TO CAVARETTA, BUT ROWE WAS TOO MUCH

Rowe was still in a tough spot, but he was much relieved that Hartnett had bunted instead of hitting. One man at least was out and Lindstrom was still 60 feet from home plate. Demaree hit a grounder to Rogell. Bill juggled it, but Lindstrom never moved from third and Rogell threw out the runner. It was up to Cavarretta and Rowe was too much for him. Gehringer smothered his grounder and threw him out.

The incident provides the second guessers with an inexhaustible source of argument, pro and con, which is another reason the game reached the stature of a baseball epic.

Between the closing and climatical acts, and the beginning of the ball game was a drama of Tiger frustration which finally was dispelled by a four-run rally in the eighth inning.

But the drama really opened with a prologue behind the scenes.

Before the game Hank Greenberg sat dejected in the little cell reserved for Trainer Denny Carroll, baking a swollen fist and arm under a heat lamp. In the next room Cochrane, Baker and Cy Perkins were in earnest conference with the players.

A search was on for a substitute for Hank and Cochrane invited the players to join in it. In the end they came to no decision. Cochrane changed his mind a half dozen times between the opening of practice and the game which started with Owen on first and Clifton at third.

Auker started for the Tigers and Lee for the Cubs. An error by Herman put Cochrane on in the first and he got as far as second. Galan and Lindstrom singled off Auker but the slow footed Hartnett grounded into a double play to keep home plate clear.

Rogell beat out an infield single, took second on Cavarretta's wild throw but got no farther than third before the Tiger half of the second ended.

Auker made a bad pitch and Clifton a bad play to give Chicago two runs in their half of the second.

The bad pitch was one Auker grooved to Demaree when he had two strikes and no balls on him. Demaree banged it into the right field bleachers for a home run. With one out, Hack singled, stole second on the first pitch to Jurges. Clifton fumbled Jurges' grounder, Hack reaching third. He scored on Lee's slow roller to Gehringer.

Those two runs loomed larger and larger as the innings dragged on and Lee with the help of brilliant fielding kept the Tigers at bay.

Cochrane walked and Gehringer singled after two were out in the third but Galan flitted across in front of the center field bleachers, leaped high in the air to pull down Goslin's drive.

LINDSTROM ROBS CLIFTON OF AN EXTRA BASE HIT

Lindstrom robbed Clifton of an extra base hit with a running catch of his fly in the fifth. In the same inning White singled but Cochrane became the third out when De-

maree made a diving catch of his low liner, sliding along the turf to catch the ball just above the grasstips.

The Cubs added a run in their half of the fifth. Jurges walked, moved to second on a sacrifice by Lee and scored on Galan's single. Galan took second when Cochrane let Fox' throw bound away from him. Herman scratched a single off Owen's glove but nothing came of that because Lindstrom grounded into a close double play.

The sixth marked the production of Detroit's first run and the ejection of Del Baker from the game. With one out, Goslin singled. Fox scored him with a triple to the right field corner. When Hartnett picked Fox off third with a throw to Hack, Baker protested so hotly, Umpire Quigley sent him out of the game to cool off.

When Cavarretta was put out stealing by Gehringer's great play on Cochrane's throw to end the sixth inning, Grimm led the Cubs in a stormy protest meeting upon Moriarity. Moriarity retorted by putting Grimm out of the game. In the eighth inning came the big blow off.

Lee walked White, the first batter. The fine edge of Lee's control was wearing off. The strain had begun to wear on his nerves, too. When Moriarity held up his hand and stopped the game to go over to the Cub bench and dramatically order English and Stainback off the bench, Lee stood by fidgeting with the ball. He got out Cochrane with a fly to Jurges. But Gehringer rifled a double to right field, White halting at third.

Goslin drove a skipping drive at first base. It hit the bag, bounded over Cavarretta's head for a single and White and Gehringer raced across the plate with the tying runs.

WARNEKE SUMMONED TO STEM THE TIGER UPRISING

Lon Warneke was summoned to stem the Tiger uprising, but he couldn't stop them at once. Fox singled Goslin to second. Rogell poked a single over second, scoring Goslin and sending Fox to third.

The Tigers attempted a double steal. Rogell was run down and tagged out, but Fox sped across the plate with the fourth run that inning, making the score 5 to 3, Tigers.

There it remained until the Cubs tied it in the ninth. Hogsett pitched only the eighth for Detroit to give Rowe time to warm up. He hit one batter and walked another but kept the plate clear.

For a time, Hogsett seemed destined to be the victorious pitching hero of the drama, but that was reserved for Schoolboy, who almost muffed his lines.

PLAY BY PLAY OF FOURTH WORLD SERIES GAME

1935 World Series, Game4: Detroit Tigers at Chicago Cubs

Detroit Evening Times, Oct.5th 1935 (Sat. 10/5/35)
(Reprinted with the permission of *The Detroit News*.)

FIRST INNING

DETROIT—Del Baker was in the third base coaching box and Gerald Walker in the first base box when the game started. Carleton got behind White 2 and 1 but shot one over for a called strike. Stark then called out White on a wide pitch over the outside corner. With a count of two balls and one strike Cochrane fouled a long drive over the right field fence. Carleton deflected Cochrane's bounder to Herman, who threw him out. Gehringer looked at the first two strikes and then struck out, swinging at a low curve. No run, no hit, no error.

CHICAGO—Grimm was back in the third base coaching box and Corriden in the first base box when the Cubs came to bat. Hogsett and Auker went out and sat in the bullpen before Crowder made his first pitch. With a count of two strikes and one ball Galan hit a skipping bounder in back of first to Owen, who beat him to the bag. With the count two strikes and no balls on him Herman hit a hard grounder to Owen, who juggled the ball, but tossed underhanded to Crowder in time to put out the runner. Lindstrom fouled to Owen, who made a one handed catch against the rail of the right field boxes. No run, no hit, no error.

SECOND INNING

DETROIT—Goslin beat out a slow bounder to Herman for a single on the first pitch, the ball taking a bad hop. Gox's fly fell near the left field foul line out of Galan's reach for a double. Goslin stopping at third. Carleton got behind Rogell, 3 and 1 and he walked on a wide pitch and Hartnett tried to pick Goslin off third but Goose slid back safely. With the bases loaded and none out, French and Root started warming up hurriedly in the Cub bull pen. Owen popped to Herman, back on the grass in short right. The Cub infield played back for a double play. With a count 2 and 2, Clifton smashed a liner towards short. Timing his leap perfectly Jurges shot into the air and speared the ball with his gloved hand and tossed to

Herman, doubling Fox off second. No run, two hits, no error.

CHICAGO—With a count of 2 and 2, Hartnett poled an outside pitch into the right field bleachers for a home run. Fox ran up to the fence but the wind carried it over his head and into the crowd. Demaree, with a count of two strikes and no balls, struck out, swinging at a curve in the dirt. Cavarretta was the first batter. Crowder got behind with a 3 and 1 count, but he struck him out, swinging at a curve through the center of the plate. Hack was called out on strikes. Crowder making only three pitches, thus fanning the side. One run, one hit, no error.

THIRD INNING

DETROIT—Crowder poled a single past Cavaretta into right field. With one called strike. White tried to bunt but fouled the pitch for strike two. White bounced a single over Cavarretta's head, sending Crowder to third but White was out trying to stretch it. Demaree to Herman. Demaree fielded the ball quickly and made a perfect peg to Herman. Cochrane got behind Carleton 3 and 1, Hartnett making a diving stop to prevent a wide pitch. His next pitch was also low and inside and Cochrane walked. Gehringer lined a double to right center, scoring Crowder and sending Cochrane to third. Lindstrom tried for a running catch but the ball bounced off his glove and rolled into right field. Demaree picked up the ball and threw to third, the ball hitting Cochrane in the back as he slid safely in third. Goslin was intentionally passed, filling the bases. Fox forced Cochrane at the plate, Cavarretta to Hartnett, the bases remaining loaded. Cavarretta spoiled a chance for a double play by failing to get back to first for Hartnett's return throw and Gabby had to hold the ball. Rogell struck out, swinging at a low curve.

One run, three hits, no error.

CHICAGO—Jurges grounded to Clifton, Carleton worked the count to 3 and 2 and walked on a wide pitch. Galan popped to Rogell between first and second.

Herman swung on the first pitch and popped to Owen. No run, no hit, no error.

FOURTH INNING

DETROIT—Owen flied to Lindstrom in deep center. Clifton flied to Lindstrom. Carleton got behind Crowder 2 and 1 and made an angry gesture when Hartnett fired the ball back at him. Carleton got the next one over for a called strike and then walked Crowder with a wide pitch. Carleton also got behind White, 3 and 1 and Hartnett walked out and patted him on the back. White also walked on an outside pitch. French and Root pulled off their jackets and started warming up again. Carleton got the first two over to Cochrane for called strikes. Cochrane flied to Demaree in front of the right field bleachers.

No run, no hit, no error.

CHICAGO—Rogell threw out Lindstrom, who hit the first ball pitched. Clifton made a swell pickup of Hartnett's slow bounder. His throw was wide but Owen stepped off the bag and tagged Hartnett on the line. Demaree tried to bunt on the first pitch but popped a foul behind the plate. Cochrane making a great running catch near the rail. No run, no hit, no error.

FIFTH INNING

DETROIT—Carleton got behind Gehringer 3 and 1 and when the next ball looked low Charlie started for first base. Stark called it strike two and Gehringer had to come back to the batter's box. He hit a sharp grounder to Hack, who juggled the ball, but threw him out. Cavarretta making a swell pickup out of the dirt. Carleton was 3 and 1 on Goslin. The Goose hit the cripple, a fly to Jurges, who backed up in short left field. Fox popped to Jurges.

No run, no hit, no error.

CHICAGO—Cavarretta singled to right, his first hit of the series. Hack bunted the first pitch foul for strike one. He bunted a pop fly to Crowder. Jurges worked the count to 3 and 2 and walked on a low pitch. Carleton swung and missed the first two pitches for strikes and then Crowder pitched three balls to him. Carleton smashed a terrific drive to right but it was a foul. He then struck out, swinging at a low curve. Galan flied to Goslin. No run, one hit, no error.

SIXTH INNING

DETROIT—Rogell lined to Demaree in front of the right field bleachers. Owen lined to Demaree. Galan raced far back in left field for Clifton's long drive and then muffed the catch. Clifton reaching second on the error. Clifton's drive would have been a home run in Detroit. Jurges let Crowder's grounder roll past him for an error and Clifton scored all the way from second. Carleton was behind White 3 and 1 but got the next one over for a called strike. Moriarty called a balk on Carleton when he started his windup and then stepped off the rubber as if to throw to first. Carleton rushed furiously down to the plate to protest to Umpire Stark. Grimm and Hartnett joined him in the conference at the plate. Carleton then appealed to Umpire Quigley at second base but Umpire Stark's decision stood and Crowder went to second. White walked on a low pitch. Cochrane swung on the first pitch. Galan coming in to make the catch.

One run, no hit, two errors.

CHICAGO—Herman slugged a double off the wall in left field. Auker started warming up in the bull pen. Gehringer made a great running catch of Lindstrom's foul fly, but he was in a bad position to throw and Herman took third after the catch. The Tiger infield played in for a play at the plate when Hartnett came to bat. With a count of 2 and 2 Hartnett struck out swinging at a slow curve inside. Demaree fouled the first pitch back against the screen. He lined the next one to Gehringer. No run, one hit, no error.

SEVENTH INNING

DETROIT—Gehringer lined a single over Herman's head into right field. Demaree made a fine running catch of Goslin's fly in short right. Gehringer stole second. Fox protecting him by swinging at a pitch inside for strike two. Fox struck out on a wide curve on the outside. Rogell broke his bat fouling for strike two and went back to the dugout for a new one. Rogell worked the count to 3 and 2 and walked on an inside pitch. Carleton had started for the dugout and both he and Hartnett kicked on Stark's decision. Carleton knocked down Owen's bounder and threw him out. No run, one hit, no error.

CHICAGO—Cavarretta hit a bounder to Owen back of first and Owen beat him to the bag. Hack grounded to Clifton, Jurges worked the count to 3 and 2 and then walked on a low pitch. Klein batted for Carleton. He worked the count to 3 and 2 and Crowder knocked down his line drive and threw him out.

No run, no hit, no error.

EIGHTH INNING

DETROIT—Root went to the box for the Cubs. Clifton looked at the first two for called strikes. Clifton flied to Lindstrom. Crowder flied to Galan. White worked the count to 3 and 2 and then struck out swinging. No run, no hit, no error.

CHICAGO—Galan grounded to Gehringer on the first pitch. Herman poled a long drive but it was foul for strike one. He fouled the next one into the right field boxes out of Owen's reach for strike two. Clifton made a swell pickup of Herman's grounder and threw him out. Lindstrom grounded to Gehringer.

No run, no hit, no error.

NINTH INNING

DETROIT—Cochrane smashed a single past Herman into right center. Gehringer sacrificed, Root to Herman, who covered first. Goslin was walked intentionally for the second time. Fox popped to Herman near the pitcher's box. Rogell struck out. No run, one hit, no error.

CHICAGO—With two strikes and no balls Hartnett lined a slow pitch to Rogell. Demaree singled to right. Cavarretta singled to left, Demaree stopping at second. Hack grounded into a double play. Rogell to Gehringer to Owen. No run, two hits, no error.

Klein batted for Carleton in seventh.
TWO-BASE HITS—Fox, Gehringer, Herman.
HOME RUN—Hartnett.
SACRIFICE HIT—Gehringer.
STOLEN BASE—Gehringer.
LEFT ON BASES—Detroit 13, Chicago 5.
DOUBLE PLAY—Jurges to Herman.
HITS—Off Carleton 6 in seven innings.
BASES ON BALLS—Off Carleton 7, off Crowder 3,
    off Root 1.
STRUCK OUT—By Carleton 4, by Crowder 5, by Root 2.
BALK—Carleton.
UMPIRES—Stark (N) at plate, Moriarty (A) at first,
    Quigley (N) at second, McGowan (A) at third.

World Series Box Score—FOURTH GAME

DETROIT TIGERS

	AB	R	H	PO	A	E
White, cf	3	0	1	0	0	0
Cochrane, c	4	0	1	6	0	0
Gehringer, 2b	4	0	2	3	3	0
Goslin, lf	3	0	1	1	0	0
Fox, rf	5	0	1	0	0	0
Rogell, ss	3	0	0	2	2	0
Owen, 1b	4	0	0	13	1	0
Clifton, 3b	4	1	0	0	4	0
Crowder, p	3	1	1	2	1	0
Totals	33	2	7	27	11	0

CHICAGO CUBS

	AB	R	H	PO	A	E
Galan, lf	4	0	0	2	0	1
Herman, 2b	4	0	1	4	1	0
Lindstrom, cf	3	0	0	3	0	0
Hartnett, c	4	1	1	7	0	0
Demaree, rf	4	0	1	4	1	0
Cavarretta, 1b	4	1	2	3	1	0
Hack, 3b	3	0	0	0	0	0
Jurges, ss	1	0	0	4	2	1
Carleton, p	1	0	0	0	1	0
*Klien	1	0	0	0	1	0
Root, p	0	0	0	0	0	0
Totals	31	1	5	27	8	2

*Batted for Carleton in 7th

CHICAGO	0	0	1	0	0	1	0	0	0—2
DETROIT	0	1	0	0	0	0	0	0	0—1

WORLD SERIES GAME 5 PLAY BY PLAY

This play by play was pieced together by Charles Avison-Howell and is the only document in this Appendix that is not original. Due to the gap in information it was pieced together using two different sources. The Detroit Times, *and* The New York Times *from October 7th 1935.*

FIRST INNING

DETROIT—White was called out on strikes after a four pitch at-bat. The fourth time in five games that he led off with a strikeout. Cochrane's first at-bat resulted in a single to right field. Gehringer grounded out to Billy Herman, Cochrane advancing to second. Goslin bounced out to Herman at second. One hit, no runs, no errors.

CHICAGO—Galan flied out to White in center on a one and one count. Herman swung at the first pitch, grounding out to Rowe. With a one ball, two strike count, Klein singled into left field. Hartnett's single to right on a two-two count sent Klein to third base. Demaree then grounded to first, Owen throwing to Rowe who was covering the bag.

Two hits, no runs, no errors.

SECOND INNING

DETROIT—Fox popped out to Herman. Rogell then popped to Owen on the second pitch. With one ball, one strike, Owen grounded out to Jurges at short. No hits, no runs, no errors.

CHICAGO—Cavaretta was tagged out by Owen after bunting toward first. Stan Hack walked on Rowe's fifth pitch. Jurges was then struck out. Warneke singled to right on a two-two count, Hack advancing to second. Galan popped out to the shortop, Rogell.

One hit, no runs, no errors.

THIRD INNING

DETROIT—Clifton popped out to Herman. Rowe grounded to Warneke and was beat out in a foot race to first

Lynwood "Schoolboy" Rowe.
-Photo courtesy of The Detroit News

base. White grounded to first base, Cavaretta fielding it for the final out. No hits, no runs, no errors.

CHICAGO—Herman led off with a triple that left fielder White just missed. Rowe's intended outside pitch tailed over the heart of the plate, and Klein drove it into the right-field bleachers for a two-run homer. Gehringer threw out Hartnett for the first out of the inning. Goslin fielded Demaree's flyout. Cavaretta's fly to center was fielded by White. Two hits, two runs, no errors

FOURTH INNING

DETROIT—Cochrane drove a single straight through the middle of the infield, and into center, this hit coming with no balls and two strikes on him. Gehringer popped to Galan after working the count full. Goslin also worked the count full before flying out to Klein in right. Fox's single to center field advanced Cochrane to second. Rogell grounded out to first. Two hits, no runs, no errors.

CHICAGO—Hack lifted a fly ball to left which was fielded by Goslin. With one ball and two strikes, Jurges popped out to Cochrane. Gehringer fielded Warneke's grounder and threw to Owen for the final out of the inning. No hits, no runs, no errors.

FIFTH INNING

DETROIT—Owen's grounder was fielded by Jurges, throwing him out on a "nice play." Warneke struck out Clifton on five pitches. Rowe grounded out sharply to Jurges for the final out. No hits, no runs, no errors.

CHICAGO—Galan's fly ball to left

field was caught by Goslin. Herman also flied to Goslin, the count being two balls and two strikes when he swung at Rowe's fifth offering. Klein struck out after he had worked the count full. No hits, no runs, no errors.

SIXTH INNING

DETROIT—White grounded back to Warneke and was thrown out after the count had reached one ball and two strikes. With a full count, Cochrane flew out to Galan in left field. Gehringer then flew out to Klein in right. No hits, no runs, no errors.

CHICAGO—Hartnett popped out to Owen in foul territory, swinging at the first pitch. Demaree singled to right. Cavaretta's deep fly sent White to the warning track for the second out. Rogell fielded Hack's grounder and threw Demaree out at second.

One hit, no runs, no errors.

SEVENTH INNING

DETROIT—Lee came in to relieve Warneke, who left the game with a sore shoulder. Goslin led off with a walk. Fox flew out to Demaree, the Cubs' center fielder making a "sensational" catch on the run. Rogell grounded to Jurges at short, touched second and threw to first for the inning-ending double play. No hits, no runs, no errors.

CHICAGO—Jurges singled into left field on the first pitch he saw. Lee bunted, sacrificing Jurges to second, Owen throwing to Gehringer who was covering first. A ground ball that was missed by Owen gave Jurges a chance to score, but a "rifle-throw" by Fox in right reached home in time for Cochrane to apply the tag for the second out. Jurges arguing with home plate Umpire

George Moriarty. On the play, Galan advanced to second. Next up was Herman, who drove a two ball, two strike pitch, over White's head for a double, Galan scoring on the play. With a full count on him, Klein grounded to Owen, who threw over to Rowe for the final out of the inning.

Two hits, one run, one error.

EIGHTH INNING

DETROIT—On a two and two count, Owen was struck out. Clifton walked and advanced to second on Rowe's single to right. White then struck out. Cochrane grounded to Cavaretta who tossed to Lee to end the Detroit threat. One hit, no runs, no errors.

CHICAGO—Hartnett flew out to White in center field. Owen fielded Demaree's grounder and tossed over to Rowe. Rowe then struck out Cavaretta. No hits, no runs, no errors.

NINTH INNING

DETROIT—Gehringer hit a leadoff infield single, Hack knocked it down but couldn't field it cleanly enough to complete the play. Goslin followed with a single to right that advanced Gehringer to third. A single by Fox scored Gehringer, Goslin advancing to second. Rogell hit a short fly into right field that was caught by Klein for the first out. Walker was sent in to pinch-hit for Owen and grounded out to Herman. Goslin advancing to third and Fox second. Clifton popped out to Cavaretta, who ran a great distance to make the play, and end the ball game.

Three hits, one run, no errors.

HOW DETROIT WON FIRST WORLD CHAMPIONSHIP

1935 WORLD SERIES, GAME 6: DETROIT TIGERS VS. CHICAGO CUBS

Detroit Evening Times, Oct. 7th 1935 (Sat. 10/7/35)
(Reprinted with the permission of *The Detroit News*.)

FIRST INNING

CHICAGO—Strike one called after Bridges threw one called ball to the batter. Galen hit one through the box, Bridges knocked it down with his glove and Rogell came in behind him to pick it up and throw out the runner. With one ball and one strike Herman hit a slow bounder back to Bridges who threw him out. Klein, after getting one bad ball, fouled the next pitch to Owen. In front of the Cubs' dugout. No run, no hit, no error, none left.

DETROIT—Clifton took one strike and hit a slow roller to Hack who threw him out. Cochrane also had one strike when he poked a single to left. Gehringer lined the first pitch into right field for a single. Cochrane stopped at second. Goslin popped to Jurges. Fox drove a hard grounder through Hack's hands for a double, scoring Cochrane and sending Gehringer to third. Walker was purposely passed filling the bases. Rogell tapped the first pitch in front of the plate forcing Gehringer, French to Hartnett. One run, three hits, no error, three left.

SECOND INNING

CHICAGO—Hartnett was called out on strikes, looking at a high fast one through the middle. Bridges got behind Demaree 3 and 1, he flied to Fox on the next pitch. Cavarretta smashed a line drive past Owen for a single and he took second when Fox fumbled the ball. With 2 strikes and no balls, Hack rolled to Gehringer. No run, one hit, on error, one left.

DETROIT—Owen looked at the first two for called strikes and struck out swinging. With a count of two strikes and one ball, Bridges hit a slow bounder to Herman who threw him out. Cavarretta fell stretching for Herman's wide throw but held onto the ball and kept his foot on the bag. Clifton struck out. No run, no hit, no error.

THIRD INNING

CHICAGO—With a count of two balls and one strike, Jurges lined a single to center. French missed two strikes trying to bunt. He fouled the second one. He struck out swinging. Bridges got behind Galan three and one but came in with the next one for a called strike. Galan slugged a single past Gehringer, sending Jurges to third. Gehringer tried for a one-handed pickup but the ball skidded off his glove. With one ball and one strike Herman hit a single to right, scoring Jurges. Clifton grabbed Fox' throw and tagged Galan at third, pushing Galan's foot off the bag. Galan jumped up and protested so violently to Moriarty that Moriarty ordered him to the bench. Fox raced back to the scoreboard reaching over his head and grabbing Klein's terrific liner. One run, three hits, no error.

DETROIT—Cochrane worked the count to three and two and then went out. Cavarretta to French. Gehringer's fly bounded past Galan for a two-base hit. Galan tried for a shoestring catch but the ball dropped in front of him and bounded over his shoulder. Goslin fouled to right field boxes and then swung and missed strike two. Goslin hit a fast bounder back to French and Gehringer was trapped between second and third. In the run down Gehringer got back to second at the same time Goslin got there. Goslin raced back to first and was thrown out, French to Hack to Cavaretta, Gehringer remaining on second. With a count of three and two, Fox flied to Galan. No run, one hit, no error.

FOURTH INNING

CHICAGO—Goslin was hurt sliding into first but limped off to take his position in left field. Hartnett lined a single to center. With a count of two and two. Demaree looked at a third strike over the outside corner. With one strike Cavaretta popped to Rogell in back of second. With two strikes and no balls. Hack grounded to Gehringer. No run, one hit, no error.

DETROIT—Walker singled on the first pitch into right field. Rogell tagged the first pitch past Jurges for a single into left field. Walker stopped at second. Owen bunted down the third base line to Hack forcing Rogell at second, Hack to Herman. Walker going to third. Bridges worked the count to three and two and forced Owen, Hack to Herman, Walker scoring. It was a slow bounder and Bridges put on a great burst of speed going to first to prevent a double play. Clifton forced Bridges, Jurges to Herman. One run, two hits, no error.

FIFTH INNING

CHICAGO—Jurges flied to Fox. With count of one strike and one ball French poked a single to right. Galan was called out on strikes. Bridges pitched three balls to Herman before he got a strike over. He lined the next pitch into the left field bleachers for a home run, scoring French ahead of him. Klein lined a single to right center. With a count of two balls and one strike Hartnett flied to Goslin. Two runs, three hits, no error.

DETROIT—Cochrane was called out on strikes. Gehringer hit the first pitch on the ground to Herman who threw him out. Goslin popped to Hartnett.

No run, no hit, no error.

SIXTH INNING

CHICAGO—Rogell went back to deep short to scoop up Demaree's grounder and threw him out with a great peg. Cavaretta worked the count to three and two and then hit an easy grounder to Gehringer. Hack doubled to the right field scoreboard. Jurges hit a grounder to Clifton in the back of third. Clifton started to run down Hack and missed tagging him, but Umpire Moriarty called him out for running out of the base line. The Cubs again protested but the decision stood. No run, no hit, no error.

DETROIT—Fox flied to Galan. Walker popped to Jurges. Rogell doubled into the left field corner between the foul line and the bleachers. A fan reached out and touched the ball on the first bound and thus deprived Rogell of a three-base hit, ground rules holding Rogell at second. Owen lined the first pitch into the left field for a single-

scoring Rogell. It was Owen's first hit of the series. Bridges struck out.

One run, two hits, no error.

SEVENTH INNING

CHICAGO—French struck out. Galan grounded to Owen. Bridges got behind Herman, 3 and 1. Herman slugged the next ball pitched into left field for a single, his third hit in a row. Klein grounded to Owen. No run, one hit, no error.

Mickey Cochrane.
—Photo courtesy of the *Detroit Free Press*

H.G. Salinger. The sports editor of *The Detroit News*, contributed much to the city of Detroit through his columns and his contacts in the wider sports world. It was Salinger's advice that Navin took when he acquired Mickey Cochrane.

DETROIT—Clifton grounded to Jurges. Cochrane poked a single into center field. Gehringer popped to Cavarretta. Goslin grounded to Herman. No run, one hit, no error.

EIGHTH INNING

CHICAGO—Harnett singled to left. Demaree fouled the first pitch trying to bunt. Bridges curved the next one over for a called strike. Demaree grounded into a double play, Gehringer to Rogell to Owen. Cavarretta struck out. No run, one hit, no error.

DETROIT—Fox singled past Cavarretta into right field. Walker sacrificed Harnett to Herman, who covered first. Rogell stuck out. Owen was purposely passed. Bridges struck out. No run, one hit, no error.

NINTH INNING

CHICAGO—Hack tripled over Walker's head in center field. Jurges struck out on three pitches. French swung and missed the first two pitches and then tapped to Bridges, who threw him out, Hack holding third, first pitch to Galan was low and in the dirt but Cochrane went onto his knees to prevent a wild pitch. The next pitch was a called strike and Galan swung and missed the next one. He popped a short fly to left field, Goslin galloping in to make the catch. The crowd burst into a frenzy of cheers.

DETROIT—Clifton worked the count to 3 and 2 and then struck out swinging. Cochrane beat out a single to Herman. Herman made a one handed stop but too late to pick up the ball and throw him out. Cavarretta knocked down Gehringer's hard grounder and stepped on the bag retiring Gehringer, but Cochrane beat his throw to second. Goslin looped a single over Herman's head, scoring Cochrane with the winning run. One run, two hits, no error.

World Series Box Score—SIXTH GAME

CHICAGO CUBS

	AB	R	H	RBI	PO	A	E
Galan, lf	5	0	1	0	2	0	0
Herman, 2b	4	1	3	3	3	4	0
Klien, rf	4	0	1	0	0	0	0
Hartnett, c	4	0	2	0	9	1	0
Demaree, cf	4	0	0	0	0	0	0
Cavarretta, 1b	4	0	1	0	8	1	0
Hack, 3b	4	0	2	0	0	4	0
Jurges, ss	4	1	1	0	3	2	0
French	4	1	1	0	1	2	0
Totals	37	3	12	3	26*	14	0

*Two outs when winning run was scored.

DETROIT TIGERS

	AB	R	H	RBI	PO	A	E
Clifton, 3b	5	0	0	0	2	0	0
Cochrane, c	5	2	3	0	7	0	0
Gehringer, 2b	5	0	2	0	0	4	0
Goslin, lf	5	0	1	1	2	0	0
Fox, rf	4	0	2	1	3	1	1
Walker, cf	2	1	1	0	0	0	0
Rogell, ss	4	1	2	0	2	3	0
Owen, 1b	3	0	1	1	11	0	0
Bridges, p	4	0	0	1	0	3	0
Totals	37	4	12	4	27	11	1

CHICAGO	0	0	1	0	2	0	0	0	0—3	12	0
DETROIT	0	0	1	1	0	1	0	0	1—4	12	1

TWO-BASE HITS—Fox, Gehringer, Hack, Rogell.
THREE-BASE HIT—Hack
HOME RUN—Herman.
SACRIFICE HIT—Walker.
LEFT ON BASES—Detroit 9, Chicago 7.
DOUBLE PLAY—Gehringer to Rogell to Owen.
BASES ON BALLS—Off French 2.
STRUCK OUT—By Bridges 7, by French 7.
UMPIRES—Quigley (N), plate; McGowan (A), first;
  Stark (N) second; Moriarty (A), third.

A PRECEDENT IS UPSET

George Moriarty

PLAYERS, UMPS ACT STRANGELY

Detroit Times Sunday, October 13th 1935.
(Reprinted with the permission of *The Detroit News.*)

SHAVINGS
By Bud Shaver

AMONG THE oddities of sports must be listed the strange and unaccountable behavior of both players and umpires in the recent World Series.

The Cubs' complaint that Umpire George Moriarty was offending their ears with profanity is unprecedented in the history of baseball. It is the first time any ball player or group of ball players has ever admitted an umpire could outdo them in a mode of speech which may be said to be the ball players' native tongue.

Then, too, was the amazing bouquet of compliments tossed to another umpire of the American League by the Cubs after losing an 11-inning game to the Tigers, 6 to 5.

Mr. Willie McGowan is the gentleman who received this unprecedented accolade. Willie called balls and strikes that day and when Gabby Hartnett, the Cubs' catcher; Charley Grimm, the Cubs Manager, and virtually all of the Cub players congratulated Willie on what they called "a perfect job of umpiring," Willie was so surprised it was several hours before he could rid his mind of the suspicion he was being ribbed with deep sarcasm and really enjoy the praise.

This must be recorded as the first time in history a ball club has ever lost a close World Series ball game without declaring "We was robbed."

MADE HIM HERO, THEN A GOAT

WHILE ON the subject of that 11-inning game, it is perhaps timely to point out what might also be listed as an oddity.

What really lost the Cubs that game was the most sensational hit-killing catch of the the entire series. The catch was made by Frank Demaree on one of Mickey Cochrane's line drives, a paradox which needs some explaining.

It occurred in the fifth inning when the Cubs were leading 2 to 0. Two were out and White was on first with a single. Cochrane hit a looping liner to right field. Demaree ran in and dived on his stomach to make the catch just above the grass tops retiring the side.

The catch was rewarded with a great burst of applause by the Cub fans and Cochrane at the time displayed the proper chagrin, yet Demaree's catch really lost the ball game.

It was a lucky catch. He should not, by all the sound rules of outfield play, have tried to make it. The chances are almost 100 to 1 he wouldn't get the ball and, if he missed, it would get past him for an extra base hit which would be sure to score White and put the tying run in scoring position. Good judgment required that he play it safe and keep White from scoring. He took the one chance and made it.

THE PERCENTAGES PAY OFF

NOW TO explain how the catch lost the ball game. By making it, Demaree demonstrated to himself at least that he had played the ball well. It was a bad state of mind for him to get into.

Subsequently he was induced to try the same play again and that time the law of averages took its toll. He missed and it cost the ball game.

In the eighth inning, Gehringer came to bat with out and White on base. The Cubs were leading, 3 to 1, at the time.

Gehringer cracked a slow, twisting liner to right field and once again Demaree took the 100 to 1 chance, but that time he missed. The ball bounded past him for a double, sending White to third. Goslin bounced his famous single off the first base bag, scoring both White and Gehringer and tying the score as well as knocking Lee, the pitcher, out of the ball game.

Proving among other things, that the sensational catch is not always the wise one. Good players play the percentages.

1935 WORLD SERIES STATISTICS

1935 World Series Game 1 Box Score:

Team	1	2	3	4	5	6	7	8	9	R	H	E
CHICAGO	2	0	0	0	0	0	0	0	1	3	7	0
DETROIT	0	0	0	0	0	0	0	0	0	0	4	3

Pitchers:
Warneke (WP)   Rowe (LP)

1935 World Series Game 2 Box Score:

Team	1	2	3	4	5	6	7	8	9	R	H	E
CHICAGO	0	0	0	0	1	0	2	0	0	3	6	1
DETROIT	4	0	0	3	0	0	1	0	x	8	9	2

Pitchers:
Root (LP)   Bridges (WP)
Henshaw (1st)
Kowalik (4th)

1935 World Series Game 3 Box Score:

Team	1	2	3	4	5	6	7	8	9	10	11	R	H	E
DETROIT	0	0	0	0	0	1	0	4	0	0	1	6	12	2
CHICAGO	0	2	0	0	1	0	0	0	2	0	0	5	10	3

Pitchers:
Auker   Lee
Hogsett (7th)   Warneke (8th)
Rowe (8th WP)   French (10th LP)

1935 World Series Game 4 Box Score:

Team	1	2	3	4	5	6	7	8	9	R	H	E
DETROIT	0	0	1	0	0	1	0	0	0	2	7	0
CHICAGO	0	1	0	0	0	0	0	0	0	1	5	2

Pitchers:
Crowder (WP)   Carleton (LP)
Root (8th)

1935 World Series Game 5 Box Score:

Team	1	2	3	4	5	6	7	8	9	R	H	E
DETROIT	0	0	0	0	0	0	0	0	1	1	7	1
CHICAGO	0	0	2	0	0	0	1	0	x	3	8	0

Pitchers:
Rowe (LP)   Warneke (WP)
                   Lee (7th)

1935 World Series Game 6 Box Score:

Team	1	2	3	4	5	6	7	8	9	R	H	E
CHICAGO	0	0	1	0	2	0	0	0	0	3	12	0
DETROIT	0	0	1	1	0	1	0	0	1	4	12	1

Pitchers:
French (LP)   Bridges (WP)

1935 World Series Hitting Statistics

Name	Pos	G	AB	H	2B	3B	HR	R	RBI	Avg.	BB	SO	SB
Fox	Of	6	26	10	3	1	0	1	4	.385	0	1	0
Gehringer	2b	6	24	9	3	0	0	4	4	.375	2	1	1
Crowder	P	1	3	1	0	0	0	1	0	.333	1	0	0
Cochrane	C	6	24	7	1	0	0	3	1	.292	4	1	0
Rogell	Ss	6	24	7	2	0	0	1	1	.292	2	5	0
Goslin	Lf	6	22	6	1	0	0	2	3	.273	5	0	0
White	Of	5	19	5	0	0	0	3	1	.263	5	7	0
Rowe	P	3	8	2	1	0	0	0	0	.250	0	1	0
Walker	Of	3	4	1	0	0	0	1	0	.250	1	0	0
Greenberg	1b	2	6	1	0	0	1	1	2	.167	1	0	0
Bridges	P	2	8	1	0	0	0	1	1	.125	0	3	0
Owen	3b/1b	6	20	1	0	0	0	2	1	.050	2	3	0
Auker	P	1	2	0	0	0	0	0	0	.000	0	1	0
Clifton	3b	4	16	0	0	0	0	1	0	.000	2	4	0
Hogsett	P	1	0	0	0	0	0	0	0	.000	0	0	0
Totals			206	51	11	1	1	21	18	.248	25	27	1

Name	Pos	G	AB	H	2B	3B	HR	R	RBI	Avg.	BB	SO	SB
O'Dea	Ph	1	1	1	0	0	0	0	1	1.000	0	0	0
Kowalik	P	1	2	1	0	0	0	1	0	.500	0	0	0
Herman	2b	6	24	8	2	1	1	3	6	.333	0	2	0
Klein	Of	5	12	4	0	0	1	2	2	.333	0	2	0
Hartnett	C	6	24	7	0	0	1	1	2	.292	0	3	0
Demaree	Of	6	24	6	1	0	2	2	2	.250	1	4	0
French	P	2	4	1	0	0	0	1	0	.250	0	2	0
Jurges	Ss	6	16	4	0	0	0	3	1	.250	4	4	0
Hack	3b/Ss	6	22	5	1	1	0	1	0	.227	2	2	1
Lindstrom	Of/3b	4	15	3	1	0	0	0	0	.200	1	1	0
Warneke	P	3	5	1	0	0	0	0	0	.200	0	0	0
Galan	Of	6	25	4	1	0	0	2	2	.160	2	2	0
Cavarretta	1b	6	24	3	0	0	0	1	0	.125	0	5	0
Carleton	P	1	1	0	0	0	0	0	0	.000	1	1	0
Henshaw	P	1	1	0	0	0	0	0	0	.000	0	0	0
Lee	P	2	1	0	0	0	0	0	1	.000	0	0	0
Root	P	2	0	0	0	0	0	0	0	.000	0	0	0
Stephenson	Ph	1	1	0	0	0	0	0	0	.000	0	1	0
Totals			202	48	6	2	5	18	17	.238	11	29	1

1935 World Series Pitching Statistics

DETROIT TIGERS

Name	Win	Loss	G	GS	CG	S	Sh	IP	ERA	H	SO	ER	BB
Hogsett	0	0	1	0	0	0	0	1.0	0.00	0	0	0	1
Crowder	1	0	1	1	1	0	0	9.0	1.00	5	5	1	3
Bridges	2	0	2	2	2	0	0	18.0	2.50	18	9	5	4
Rowe	1	2	3	2	2	0	0	21.0	2.57	19	14	6	1
Auker	0	0	1	1	0		0 0	6.0	3.00	6	1	2	2
Totals	4	2	8	6	5	0	0	55.0	2.29	48	29	14	11

CHICAGO CUBS

Name	Win	Loss	G	GS	CG	S	Sh	IP	ERA	H	SO	ER	BB
Warneke	2	0	3	2	1	0	1	16.2	0.54	9	5	1	4
Carleton	0	1	1	1	0	0	0	7.0	1.29	6	4	1	7
Kowalik	0	0	1	0	0	0	0	4.1	2.08	3	1	1	1
French	0	2	2	1	1	0	0	10.2	3.38	15	8	4	2
Lee	0	0	2	1	0	1	0	10.1	4.35	11	5	5	5
Henshaw	0	0	1	0	0	0	0	3.2	7.36	2	2	3	5
Root	0	1	2	1	0	0	0	2.0	18.00	5	2	4	1
Totals	2	4	12	6	2	1	1	54.2	3.13	51	27	19	25

GREENBERG IS VOTED MOST VALUABLE

Detroit Evening News, October 21st 1935
(Reprinted with the Permission of *The Detroit News.*)

PHILADELPHIA, Oct. 21—For the second straight year a member of the Detroit Tigers has been voted the most valuable player in the American League. In 1934 it was Manager Mickey Cochrane and this year's choice is Henry Greenberg, slugging first baseman.

Eight members of the Baseball Writers' Association of America who participated in the voting all named Greenberg as their choice according to James C. Isaminger, head of the committee, who made the nomination public yesterday.

SIXTH LAST YEAR

Greenberg received 80 points, the highest possible number. Each writer named 10 players, with the first man receiving 10 points and so on down the list.

Big Hank, who played his third year as a Tiger regular, was named despite the fact he was kept out of the World Series due to an injured wrist. In the 1934 poll Hank was sixth with 20 points, Cochrane had 69 points to edge out Charley Gehringer for the top honor.

Wesley Ferrell, Boston Red Sox pitcher who won 23 games was second in the voting, receiving 62 points. Joe Vormik of Cleveland was third with 30 and Buddy Myer, Washington, fourth with 22.

24 ARE CONSIDERED

Twenty-four other players received consideration. They are Lou Gehrig, Yankees, 20 points; Charley Gehringer, Detroit, 28; Mickey Cochrane, Detroit, 24; Roger Cramer, Philadelphia, 18; Julius Solters and Rollie Hamaly, St. Louis, 18 each; Jimmie Foxx, Philadelphia and Tommy Bridges, Detroit, 11; Ted Lyons, Chicago, 10; Lefty grove, Boston, 8; Zeka Bonurn, Luke Appling and Luke Bowell, Chicago, 7 each; Johnny Allen, New York, 6; John Whitehead, Chicago, 4; Pinky Higgins and Johnny Marenum, Philadelphia, 3; Elden Auker, Detroit and Mel Harder, Cleveland, 2; and Lyn Lary, St. Louis 1.

Twenty-four players were placed on the honor list. They are: Tony Lazed, George Selkirk and Red Rolfa, New York; Rick Ferrell, Oscar Mellin and Mel Almada, Boston; Rabbit Warstier, Eric MoNair, Rob Johnson and Wally Moser, Philadelphia; Cecil Travis, Jake Dowell and Earl Whitehill, Washington; Pete Fox, Schoolboy Rowe, Al Crowder and Goose Gotlin, Detroit; Jimmy Dykes, Chicago; O'Dell Hale and Billy Knickerbocker, Cleveland and Jack Burns, Sam West and Ivey Andrews, St. Louis.

Hank Greenberg.
—Photo courtesy of the
Detroit Free Press

Appendix C: Detroit Lions

Contents

DETROIT GRID PROS WIN FIRST GAME

1935 NFL Season, Game 1:
Detroit Lions vs. Philadelphia Eagles

Detroit Times, September 21st 1935 (Fri. 9/20/35)
(Reprinted with the permission of *The Detroit News.*)
By Leo Macdonell

George (Potsy) Clark, coach of the Detroit Lions, today announced the release of three players in the wake of his teams' victory over Philadelphia Eagles, 35 to 0, in the opening game of the National Football League season in University of Detroit Stadium last night.

Those to go were Steve Banas, Gil LeFebvre and William O'Neill.

A crowd of approximately 12,000 saw Detroit's professional football team get off to a flying start in a spotty contest in which the local contenders for the 1935 championship had their big and dull moments.

Among the spectators was Joe Carr, president of the league.

Outstanding in the Detroit team's offense were Ernie Caddel, Dutch Clark, Buddy Parker and Frank Christensen. Defensively, Buster Mitchell, John Schneller, Elmer Ward and George Christensen rose to heights.

ALABAMA PITTS PLAYS

Alabama Pitts got into the Philadelphia lineup late in the final quarter and gave the fans a thrill when he just missed a forward pass for a nice gain for the visitors.

Defensively the Lions were impregnable, the Philadelphia team failing to gain a first down. Against the Eagles the Lions rolled up 16 first downs but wasted yardage by fumbling. Potsy Clark's warriors gained

Dutch Clark.

359 yards against but 15 for the Eagles. Both teams played wide open with comparatively few passes completed.

Turning in a brilliant individual performance, Caddel, fleet-footed Lion, scored three touchdowns on runs of 49 yards, 13 yards and 35 yards. On his first long run big George Christensen and John Schneller did the blocking in a pretty bit of footballing. Caddel clinging to the left side of the field on his stirring jaunt.

To start the fray the Lions looked none too good and fumbled around like a high school team, affected by the heat or stale from training. Twice in scoring position Henry Reese, Temple player with the Eagles, tried two field goals in the opening period.

Mitchell, playing bang-up football, blocked the first attempt.

Early in the second period the Lions reached Philadelphia's one yard line only to lose the ball when Pug Vaughan fumbled after Gutowsky had fumbled and Glenn Presnell lost seven yards.

With the ball back in the midfield Caddel, a little later, put on his 49-yard sprint for the first touchdown of the game. Clark kicked the extra point to give Potsy Clark's warriors a 7 to 0 lead.

To this margin the Lions added later in the period. With the ball on their own 345-yard line Caddel ran the ball to Philadelphia's 25-yard stripe.

Parker and Clark made it first down on the 13 from where Parker added nine more and Clark scored and converted to boost the total to 14 to 0.

In the third period the Lions reached the enemy's 19-yard line where Banas and LeFebvre failed to gain and the Phillies recovered the ball on the downs.

The fourth heat was still young when Clark zig-zagged his way through the center of the Eagles line to Philadelphia's 24-yard line. In two tries Gutowsky moved the ball to the 13-yard mark, from where Caddel, the antelope, skirted left end for another touchdown, making the score 21 to 0.

TA little later Clark intercepted Mike Sebastian's pass on the 35-yard line, from where Caddel raced for his third touchdown.

A the period faded Presnell, Parker and Vaughan advanced the ball to the four-yard line, from where Frank Christensen counted, and when Presnell converted the score was 35 to 0, at which it rested with the final siren.

The Lineups:

DETROIT		PHILADELPHIA
Mitchell	L.E.	Manske
Johnso	L.T.	Cube
Rupke	L.G.	Zyntell
Randolph	C.	Reese
Knox	R.G.	Wisner
G. Christens.	R.T.	Jorgensen
Schneller	R.E.	Carter
Clark	Q.B.	Kupcinef
F. Christensen	R.H.	Storm
Caddell	L.H.	Matesis
Gutowsky	F.B.	Leonard

Score by Quarters:

DETROIT	0	14	0	21	35
PHILADELPHIA	0	0	0	0	0

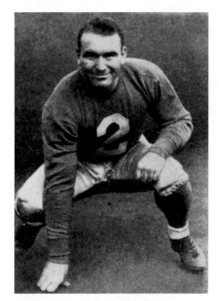

George "Tarzan" Christensen.

LIONS BATTLE CARDS TO 10–10 TIE

1935 NFL Season, Game 2:
Detroit Lions vs. Chicago Cardinals

Detroit Times, September 30th 1935 (Sun. 9/29/35)
(Reprinted with the permission of *The Detroit News.*)
By Frank Macdonnell

Detroit Lions and Chicago Cardinals today are tied for the leadership in the western division of the National Professional Football League.

Each team had won one game before yesterday when they clashed in U. of D. Stadium and the result was a 10 to 10 tie. Close to 12,000 persons watched the contest which was hard fought all the way.

The Lions appeared to be the better team even though the Cardinals put up a great exhibition. Detroit failed to dash in on scoring opportunities and a fumble by the peerless Dutch Clark put the Cards in position to tally a touchdown. Clark is the best quarterback in professional football but didn't' look like it Sunday.

Detroit came from behind twice. After a scoreless first period the Cardinals chalked up a field goal in the second session and the Lions came back in the next period with seven points as a result of a touchdown aid the so-called extra point. Cardinals moved into the lead again in the fourth quar4ter by scoring seven markers in the customary fashion and the Lions came back to tie the score by getting a field goal.

THRILLING GAME

It was a thrilling but not a spectacular game of football. Detroit outplayed the Cardinals in just about every department but errors cost the Lions the undisputed leadership in their division.

Detroit made seven first downs as against six for the cardinals and the Lions gained 234 yards while Chicago was making 173.

Potsy Clark's warriors four out of eight passes and the Cards five out of 12. Detroit fumbled five times and the Cards miscued the same way twice. Chicago was penalized 30 yards and Detroit only five yards.

The punters had a bad afternoon with each club averaging 30 yards per boot.

Play in the first period was slow and a trifle dull. The Cardinals made a first down in the early part of the period when Peterson gained 10 yards and it was the first first down made against Detroit this season.

DUTCH'S KICK SHORT

Dutch Clark gave the customers a thrill when he attempted a place kick form the Cards 45-yard line. It was a trifle short and sailed under the cross bar. He gave the boys and girls a headache a few minutes later by fumbling and Chicago recovered on the Lions' 30-yard line but lost the ball on downs after gaining nine and one-half yards. The first quarter closed a few seconds later with the score 0 to 0.

Detroit had the ball on the Cards' 37-yard line in the second period and after Schneller missed Clark's pass the latter tried to place kick from the 42. It was short.

Ernie Caddel received a pass from Clark, but the ball was tackled and after it bounced around a couple of Cards grabbed it on the Chicago 42.

PUTS CARDS IN FRONT

Chicago worked the ball to Detroit's 28-yard line on a series of plays and then Smith kicked a perfect field goal from placement from the 38-yard line to put the Cardinal's in front, 3 to 0.

Detroit missed a fine scoring chance a few minutes later. Glenn Presnell replaced Clark and tossed a bum pass but followed up with a beautiful throw to Caddel that was good for 42 yards and the ball was on the Cards' 25. Caddel was injured on the play.

Presnell then passed to Ebding for 14. Presnell hit the line a couple of times for a total of six yards and passed to Frank Christensen over the goal line, but Frank dropped the ball and deprived Detroit of a touchdown. Presnell tried to goal from placement and failed as the half ended with Chicago Cardinals leading, 3 to 0.

Play was much faster as the second half got underway and the third period didn't have whiskers when Nichelini fumbled and Frank Christensen recovered for Detroit on Chicago's 41. A determined drive for a touchdown followed. Clark scooted off right end for nine and Gutowsky added a half yard before Clark made a first down on the Cards' 25. Caddel went off left end for seven and Clark took the pigskin to the 15 for a first down. Caddel lost a couple and then the best play of the game occurred.

CLARK'S PASS CLICKS

Clark dropped back and after looking over a flock of receivers finally tossed a pass to Johnny Schnelle. The latter made a beautiful catch after a hard run. He was over the goal and of course it was a touchdown, putting Detroit in the lead, 6 to 3. Clark added the extra point by dropkicking the ball in perfect fashion. So the count was 7 to 3 in favor of the roaring Lions. And that's the way the third session ended.

Cardinals assumed command early in the last heat after the big break of the game. Sorboe punted over the Lions' goal. Dutch Clark attempted a run off right end and fumbled once more and Volos recovered for the Cardinals on Detroit's 16. Berry fumbled and again Volos pounced on the ball and this time it was on the Detroit's 12-yard stripe.

Nichelini failed at left end and then took a pass from Sorboe and the ball was on Detroit's 3-yard line. Nichelini shot off right tackle for a touchdown and Smith Added the extra point from placement to make the score 10 to 7 in favor of the Cardinals.

CLARK FUMBLES AGAIN

Following the kick-off, Clark fumbled once more but Hope recovered fro the Lions on Detroit's 34. Ernie Caddel passed to Johnny Schneller to the Cards' 36 for a gain of 34. Parker and Caddel cracked the line to the Cardinals' 10-yard chalk mark.

Presnell replaced Clark and turned each end for a total of 8 yards.

With three minutes to go Presnell knotted the count by kicking a field goal from the 20-yard line at an angle.

Presnell made a sensational return of Sorboe's punt, running the ball back about 40 yards to the Cardinal 20. Caddell picked up 3 yards and with a minute to play Presnell got off a hurried kick from placement from the 25-yard line but it was no go.

Ebding almost knocked the Lions into a victory when he belted Sorboe for a loss of 17 yards, downing him on the Cards 3-yard line. Had he hit him harder, which was impossible, it would have been a safety.

Detroit was penalized 5 yards for taking out too much time and the game ended at 10 to 10 as Berry reeled off 17 yards at right end.

The Lineups:

LIONS		CARDINALS
Morse	L.E.	Smith
Johnson	L.T.	Field
Knox	L.G.	Cuppolett
Ward	C.	Hughes
Hupke	R.G.	Tipton
G. Christensen	R.T.	Gordon
Ebding	R.E.	Neuman
Clark	Q.B.	Sorboe
F. Christensen	L.H.	Peterson
Caddel	R.H.	Nichelin
Gutowsky	F.B.	Mikulak

Score by Quarters:

DETROIT	0	0	7	3	10
CHICAGO	0	3	0	7	10

LIONS UPSET BY BROOKLYN ELEVEN

1935 NFL Season Game 3: Detroit Lions at Brooklyn Dodgers

Detroit Times, October 7th 1935 (Sun. 10/6/35)
(Reprinted with the permission of The Detroit News.)
Special to *THE DETROIT TIMES*

BROOKLYN, Oct. 7.—The vaunted Detroit Lions, professional football team, favored 2 to 1 in the betting, lost 12–10 to the Brooklyn Dodgers, yesterday, thereby surprising every one, including the Dodgers. Whereas the game did not decide conclusively whether a collegiate team is better than a professional outfit, it nevertheless added much to the arguments of the collegiate supporters, the Dodgers' squad being composed almost entirely of last year's college stars while Detroit's lineup included veterans of the old Portsmouth Spartans and several recent collegians.

Glenn Presnell, 100-pound Lion quarterback, formerly of the University of Nebraska, easily was the star of the afternoon, accounting for a 25-yard touchdown, scoring all of Detroit's points.

Brooklyn, on the other hand, depended on Ralph Kercheval's kicking for the two placements which they scored, and on "Red" Franklin's expert broken field running for their lone touchdown. Kercheval is from the University of Kentucky and Franklin claims Oregon State for his alma mater.

PRESNELL PLACE KICKS

The game opened slowly with the Dodgers receiving. They lost the ball on a fumble and Presnell kicked a placement from the 25-yard line, making the score 3–0 for the Lions. The Dodgers thought this was a good idea, so they sent in the capable kicking Kercheval, who tied the score with a placement from the 24-yard line.

This ended the first quarter. Place kicks being in season, Dutch Clark opened the action in the second quarter with a 41-yard placement kick which failed. The ball changed hands, and the Dodgers decided to try it again. Kercheval substituted for Sansen and delivered the goods with a kick from the 42-yard line which settled gracefully between the uprights.

A few incompleted passes by the Lions who could not gain through the line, and the ball was again with the Dodgers as Kercheval punted to the Lions 16-yard line. And, as the shivering 10,000 fans roared their approval of this strange sight, the half ended with the Dodgers ahead, 6–3.

Ralph Kercheval (left) and Cliff Montgomery (right) of the Brooklyn Dodgers.

DODGERS SCORE

The third period opened with the Lions receiving. Little progress was made bucking the heavy Dodger line, so Christenson kicked to the Dodgers 35-yard line. Punts were exchanged, and then Christenson's kick was returned by Franklin to the Lions' 24-yard line. Franklin circled right end for a touchdown, making the score 12–3 in favor of the Dodgers. The try for the extra point was wide. Then Glenn Presnell went into action and received Becker's kick on the Dodger's 40-yard line and ran for a touchdown. Not content with that, he kicked the extra point, making it Dodgers 12, Lions 10.

The last period witnessed an outraged and surprised group of Lions trying desperately to come out of what looked like grim defeat. Reckless forward passes were attempted, strange gods were called upon, but it was no use, and the last stanza ended to the mournful dirge of 12–10, with the Dodgers ahead.

The Lineups:

LIONS		DODGERS
Mitchell	L.E.	Riblett
Johnson	L.T.	Heidt
Monahan	L.G.	Croft
Randolph	C.	Oehler
Hupke	R.G.	Kirkland
Stacey	R.T.	Lee
Schneller	R.E.	Becker
Clark	Q.B.	Lumpkin
Presnell	L.H.	Franklin
F. Christensen	R.H.	Sansen
Parker	F.B.	Karcia

Score by Quarters:

DETROIT	3	3	7	0	10
BROOKLYN	3	0	7	0	12

LIONS HUMBLE REDSKINS

1935 NFL Season, Game 4:
Detroit Lions at Boston Redskins

Detroit Times, October 14th 1935 (Sun.10/13/35)
(Reprinted with the permission of *The Detroit News.*)

BOSTON, Mass, Oct.14—Playing before 25,000 rabid New England, under perfect weather conditions, the Detroit Lions eased back into the games won column of the National Football League by hanging a 17–7 defeat on the Boston Redskins yesterday at Fenway Park.

The Lions clicked better yesterday than they have at any time this season. The Redskins were noticeably stronger than a year ago, when they were swamped by Coach Potsy Clark's outfit at the U. of D. Stadium. Still smarting under the Brooklyn defeat, Detroit lost no time tearing into the Redskins. Their backs were against the wall and a victory was of vital importance especially in view of the fact owner George Richards was on the Detroit bench.

Ernie Caddel, Roy Gutowsky, Glenn Presnell and Dutch Clark featured in the backfield for the Lions, while the line play of Tommy Hupke, Jack Johnson and Elmer Ward was noteworthy. Caddel, always a threat, was closely watched by the Redskins and therefore did not shake himself loose until late in the final period, when a field goal would have tied up the ball game. Frank Christensen was a life saver on at least one occasion. With the ball on his own 20 and the score 10–7, he connected with a punt, which carried to the Boston 20.

Although the Redskins have improved they are still inferior to the Lions. Teddy Wright, who has been on the bench most of the season, was Boston's most effective player, furnishing the spark which resulted in the lone Hub tally. Charlie Malone was a dangerous receiver, finally nailing a Wright pass for a touchdown.

The Lions left for home immediately after the game.

Although the game was a bruising battle, there were no serious casualites, according to Doc Jacobs.

Glenn Presnell started the scoring early in the first period with a placement goal from the 35-yard line. About half way through the third quarter, the lions took to the air. Dutch Clark shot a pass to Frank Christensen for a first down on the Boston 22. Then Gutowsky heaved a long pass, from a spread formation, which Clark completed in the end zone after outrunning Shepherd.

LIONS EASE UP

Leading by a 10-point margin in the fourth quarter, the Lions let down and the Redskins began to fill the air with laterals. Twice they worked the ball down into scoring position but on both occasions Detroit managed to pull itself together and take the ball on downs.

Then Ted Wright, ace in the Boston attack, started a play in which the ball was lateraled three times, following a forward pass and the Redskins were again in scoring position. On the next play Wright shot a long pass right down the middle and Malone evaded Dutch Clark, got behind the Detroit safety man and scored the first touchdown Boston has hung on a Potsy Clark—coached eleven in four years.

Apparently well riled over the Boston touchdown, the Lions got down to serious football. Following the next kickoff, Caddel raced around Malone for 40 yards. On the ensuing play Clark tore outside tackle to the 9-yard stripe and then Caddel went the remaining distance around his own left flank for the second and final Detroit touchdown.

LIONS BEATEN BY PACKERS

1935 NFL Season, Game 5:
Detroit Lions at GreenBay Packers

Detroit Times, October 21st 1935 (Sun.10/20/35)
(Reprinted with the permission of *The Detroit News.*)
By Bud Shaver

MILWAUKEE, Wis., Oct. 21—Frank Christensen, Detroit Lions' fullback, saw one of his punts blocked for the first time in his career here yesterday and it cost the Lions their second defeat in the National Professional League this season. Green Bay Packers won 13–9. Ade Schwammel, mountainous 225 pound tackle of the Packers, blocked the punt with one ham-like hand when little Chris was punting from his 45-yard line early in the third period. The ball bounded squarely in the arms of Hutson, former Alabama end and the fastest man on the Packers' team. He gathered the ball in his arms near the sideline on the 25-yard line and streaked straight down the field to the Packers' only touchdown.

Little Chris, too late to cut him off, gave chase, but it was a hopeless pursuit. At the 5-yard mark, little Chris dived desperately for Hutson's heels, but the speedy end was out of his reach and stepped over the goal line. Ernie Smith place-kicked the point after touchdown.

NEVER CATCH UP

Hutson's touchdown put the Packers ahead, 7–3, and the lions never caught up.

Late in the first period Dutch Clark drop-kicked a 33-yard field goal to put the Lions ahead. For the entire first half the crippled Lions played valiantly to hold the Packers at bay. Not a substitution was made by Coach Potsy Clark during the entire first half for the reason his bench was loaded with cripples.

Ox Emerson, star guard; Jack Johnson, star tackle; Glenn Presnell, quarterback, and Buster Mitchell, an end, all were on the bench with injuries.

Long John Schneller, an end, was pressed into service as a guard, playing the position for the first time in his career, Red Stacy, as new tackle, and Clark played the full 60 minutes.

PACKERS OUTPLAYED

The injury riddled Lions suffered defeat, but not dishonor. Crippled, they outplayed the Packers, making 10 first downs to their 8 and except for that one tough break, would have won.

Schwammel kicked a 28-yard field goal late in the third period to make the score 10–3, but the Lions were

Ernie Caddel running his specialty play, the end sweep.

not daunted. Early in the final quarter Dutch Clark flipped a lateral backhanded to Ernie Caddel, who raced 13 yards for a touchdown. But Clark, who could dropkick goals from the 33-yard line, failed to dropkick one from the 2-yard line and Detroit missed the point after touchdown and a tie.

Later in the final period Schwammel place-kicked a 32-yard field goal, the last score of the game.

It was unfortunate little Chris should have had a punt blocked for the first time, one which cost a ball game, because he and Clark were the most valiant of a valiant team.

SAVES TOUCHDOWN

Time after time Little Chris sped down field to knock passes out of the fleet Hutson's hands. When Chris couldn't get to him Clare Randolph did. Once little Chris saved a sure touchdown by leaping high into the air to bat down a pass after Hutson had outrun him.

Clark played his heart out, but it just wasn't the Lions day. Buddy Parker, playing fullback furnished the Lions' first scoring opportunity when he pounced on Hinkle's fumble on the Packers' 23-yard line and ran to the 5-yard line before Michaelske dumped him.

Twice Buddy hit that big Packers' line and dented it, but the second time, when less than a yard from a touchdown, he fumbled and Evans recovered for the Packers on the 3-yard line.

Sauer punted to Clark on the Packers' 34-yard line. The Lions rushed on the first play, but gained less than two yards. Clark tried two passes, but both missed their mark. With the ball on the 33-yard line, Dutch dropped back to the 40-yard mark, and with a strong south wind at his back drop-kicked a field goal squarely between the uprights.

MUFF CHANCE

The Packers got their first scoring opportunity but muffed it at the start of the second quarter.

Sauer, with the wind now at his back, got off a 42-yard kick which hit out of bounds on the Lions 9-yard line. Little Chris kicked a low punt to Herber who caught it on the run, but was hauled down by Klewicki on the 37-yard line with a swell tackle.

After being thrown back eight yards. Herber finally threw a 21-yard pass over center to Hutson, who was knocked down on the 24-yard line. Hinkle banged through four Lion tacklers for 12 yards until little Chris finally stopped him. The Packers made only four yards

with two bucks and a pass to Hutson. Bob Monnett rushed in to take Sauer's place with the ball on the 17-yard line and tried to placekick a field goal from a bad angle. He missed.

Just before the half ended the Packers started from their 45-yard line. Herber got off a 20-yard pass to Hutson. Then one to Monnett for nine and Hinkle hit center for a first down on the Lions 25-yard line. Three of Herber's passes were batted down, but the Lions were offside on the last one and it cost them five yards and gave the Packers a chance to rush to a first down in two plays with Hinkle carrying the ball both times. Herber threw a pass to Bruder on the 4-yard line and Hinkle plunged to the 2-yard line. Monnett was stopped cold and time was almost up. Monnett tried hurriedly to kick a field-goal but missed as the half ended.

PLACE KICKS GOAL

The Lions were kicking against the wind in the third period and shortly after the half opened, Christensen's punt was blocked and Hutson ran for a touchdown.

After Caddel kicked off, the Packers marched 47-yards, making three first downs in succession, all by rushing. On the 28-yard line the Lions' defense held and Schwammel dropped back 10 yards to placekick a field goal with the wind at his back.

The Lions came right back and, starting from their 20-yard line, rushed the ball down to the Packers' 19-yard line, making four first downs in a row. Doug Nott went in to pass but when his first attempt was blocked, Clark tried for another field goal. The wind was against him and he missed it.

As the third quarter ended, Nott got off a beautiful 21-yard pass to Clark which put the ball on the Packers '38-yard line. As the final quarter opened, Nott threw another beautiful pass to Caddel, who was hauled down by Hank Bruder on the 13-yard line. On the second play Caddel took the backhanded lateral from Clark and scooted around left end for a touchdown, but Dutch missed the dropkick for the extra point which was needed to tie.

PASS INTERCEPTED

Bruder halted another Lions' march when he intercepted Nott's pass on the Lions' 34-yard line. It paved the way for the last score. The Packers rushed the ball to the 27-yard line, but lost five yards for stalling. Schwammel placekicked the 32-yard field goal against the wind.

Pro Grid Standings

WESTERN DIVISION

Chicago Bears	3	1	0	.759	86	28
Green Bay	4	2	0	.667	69	26
Chicago Cards	2	1	1	.667	33	33
Detroit	2	2	1	.500	31	42

EASTERN DIVISION

New York	4	1	0	.800	96	48
Pittsburgh	2	4	0	.333	54	139
Brooklyn	1	3	0	.250	36	51
Boston	1	3	0	.250	36	51
Philadelphia	1	3	0	.250	24	97

VICTORY PUTS LIONS IN RACE

1935 NFL Season, Game 6: Detroit Lions vs. Boston Redskins

Detroit Times, October 31st 1935 (Sun. 10/30/35)
(Reprinted with the permission of *The Detroit News.*)
By Leo Macdonell

Bouncing back into the championship running with a smashing victory over the Boston Redskins, 14–0, in University of Detroit's fog-enveloped stadium last night, an aroused and militant Detroit Lions football team today was preparing for an invasion of Chicago, where they will collide with the powerful and haughty Cardinals Sunday.

It will be the second meeting of two teams that played a 10 to 10 tie earlier in the season, teams fighting desperately for top honors in the western division of the National Pro League.

Tied with the Bears for third place as a result of last night's win, the Lions hope to overtake both Green Bay and the Cardinals.

A record night crowd of 17,000 saw the Lions pass and plunge to victory over a hard-fighting Boston eleven in a game played under weird weather conditions, a thick fog at times making it impossible for fans in the stands to see plays.

USED WHITE BALL

In the last half it was almost impossible for opposing players to see each other, and Lions and Redskins groped about like specters, as frantic officials tried to follow the progress of the ball. It got so bad that a white ball had to be put into play.

It was next to impossible seeing the brown ball, especially when it was hugged close to the bodies of the red jerseyed Boston players. "I have officiated for 16 years and never experienced anything like it," Bobbie Calin, the referee, said after the game.

John Schneller was on the receiving end of a pass

Hall-of-Famer Cliff Battles of the Boston Redskins.

from Ernie Caddel in a beautiful play late in the first period that scored the first of the Detroit touchdowns.

With the ball on Detroit's 40-yard line, Caddel, after receiving it from Ace Gutowsky, faded back 10 yards or more, started running to his left and spun around quickly and heaved the leather far to the right side of the field into the waiting arms of the lanky Schneller, who was standing on the 30-yard stripe, from where he all but walked across the enemy's goal line.

The bewildered Redskins were taken completely off their guard and there wasn't a Bostonian in speaking distance of Detroit's end as he nabbed the pigskin.

BALL "HUNG IN AIR"

"But, I thought the ball was never going to come down," Schneller described the play, "it seemed to hang in the air."

Frank Christensen converted the extra point to give the home guards a 7 to 0 lead.

Gurtowsky accounted for the second touchdown on a plunge across Boston's goal from the 1-yard mark in the middle of the fourth period and in the thick of the fog, after a 53-yard march down the field.

Besides the brilliance of those figuring in the scoring, Dutch Clark played standout ball in the Detroit backfield as did Frank Christensen and Pug Vaughn.

Taking a pass from Presnell, Clark weaved his way through a mass of Boston players for a touchdown in a spectacular 30-yard broken field run, but the ball was called back for offside.

He was on his way to what looked like another

touchdown when he was bumped by Gunner Elliott, one of the officials.

BLOCKED PUNT

Ox Emerson, making his first start of the season, blocked a punt at an important junction in the game and otherwise took care of his job in an efficient manner as did big George Christensen, Harry Ebding, Jackson Johnson, and the others in the line.

Their hard charging, both on offense and defense, figured mightily in the victory.

The statistics reveal that Detroit made 10 first downs to Boston's 7, which gained 297 yards and 140 yards, respectively. Each completed seven passes in 16 attempts by the Lions and 17 by the Redskins.

With the exception of Vaughn at quarter and Ed Klewicki at end it was practically last year's lineup that started the game for the Lions.

Turk Edwards, 260-pound tackle, kicked off for Boston and from the kickoff until Caddel and Schneller teamed for their sensational touchdown late in the opening period play was comparatively even with neither side threatening to score.

PUTS IN NEW TEAM

At the start of the second period, Coach Potsy Clark sent an entire new team of Lions into battle. It was early in this heat that Clark scored and the play called back and Detroit penalized five yards for offside.

An exchange of punts gave Detroit the ball on their own 44-yard line from where they advanced to Boston's 32-yard stripe, aided by a grand catch by Ebding from Presnell. Presnell tried another pass, this time over the line of scrimmage, which hit an official and on third down with five yards to go Presnell tried a place kick which was wide.

Taking the ball on their own 20-yard stripe the Bostonians rallied and marched to Detroit's 36-yard line, aided by a pass from Wright to Malone, which accounted for a sizable gain. There the Lions braced and forced the Redskins to punt, the ball going out of bounds on Detroit's 21-yard line.

As the end of the period neared Clark in two plays netted 17 yards and moved the ball into position for Presnell, hurried by time, tried his second placed and again was off line.

A few seconds later the gun sounded the end of the half.

LIONS' FIRST DOWN

Emerson blocked Shepherd's punt on Boston's 34-yard line from where the Lions carried the ball to their opponent's 23-yard line, making first down by inches.

At this point the fog had wrapped the players in a ghostlike pantomime.

Vaughn tore off three yards and it looked like Detroit was on the way to a touchdown when McPhail intercepted a Detroit pass on his own 15-yard line, from where Shepherd punted out of danger.

On the kick the ball was knocked out of bounds by Vaughn on Detroit's 37-yard line from where the Lions once again headed for the Boston end of the field and once again a Detroit pass was pilfered, Hokuf making the steal.

Turn about being fair play Gutowsky swiped Shepherd's pass and Detroit was in possession of the ball on Boston's 39-yard stripe. The Lions punted and Boston regained the ball on the Detroit's 44-yard mark.

From here the Bostonians advanced to a first down on Detroit's 20-yard line. The fog had gotten thicker and play was blotted out from the spectators' view.

The white ball was thrown out onto the field but declined by Boston.

Seven yards were ripped by McPhail but here the tide turned again and when Frank Christensen intercepted Shepherd's pass it was Detroit's ball on its own nine-yard line from where the same Christensen booted the ball out of danger.

OUT OF BOUNDS

Wright's return kick bounded out of bounds on Detroit's nine-yard mark and when Frank Christensen fumbled and recovered it was the Lions' ball one foot from their own goal as the fog horn sounded the end of the period.

The white ball was again thrown out and this time accepted by both teams.

With third down and 19 yards to go Clark punted to Wright on Detroit's 40-yard line, where the Boston player was downed by Ebding and Ward. Boston fumbled and Detroit recovered the ball and Clark, again punted.

In another exchange of kicks Clark's beautiful boot rolled out of bounds on Boston's 10-yard line. The Redskins kicked and Detroit took the ball on Boston's 47-yard line, from where the Presnell to Ebding pass put the home boys on Boston's 23-yard line.

Clark made it first down on Boston's 11-yard line after Presnell punched through for seven yards. A pass, Presnell to Clark, put the ball on the four-yard line.

It was third down for Detroit with three yards to go. Clark was run out of bounds on the one-yard spot and on the next play Ace smashed through center for his touchdown. Clark kicked the extra point and the score was 14 to 0.

Clare Randolph and Ward were the only casualties but they are expected to play Sunday. Randolph's nose was banged up and Ward hurt an arm.

The Lineups:

DETROIT		BOSTON
Klewicki	L.E.	Malone
Johnson	L.T.	Edward
Knox	L.G.	Kahn
Randolph	C.	Bausch
Emerson	R.	Olason
G. Christensen	R.T.	Brien
Ebding	R.E.	Collins
Clark	Q.B.	Shepherd
F. Christensen	H.	Pickert
Caddel	R.H.	McPhail
Gutowsky	F.B.	Hokuf

Score by Quarters:

BOSTON	0	0	0	0	0
DETROIT	7	6	0	7	14

LIONS DEFEAT CARDS, UPSET STANDINGS

1935 NFL Season, Game 7:
Detroit Lions at Chicago Cardinals

Detroit Times, November 4th 1935 (Sun.11/4/35)
(Reprinted with the permission of *The Detroit News*.)
By Leo Macdonell

Victorious over the Chicago Cardinals in a grueling game Sunday, the Lions returned home today to rest. Tomorrow they will resume work for the game with Green Bay Packers at Green Bay next Sunday.

Lions won 7–6, yesterday and caused a wholesale shaking up of standings in the torrid race in the western division of the National Professional League.

Besides pitching the haughty Cardinals from top to bottom in their section, the Detroit victory elevated Potsy Clark's men into a tie for second place with the Chicago Bears, who kept pace by defeating the New York Giants.

Benefiting also by the upheaval were the Green Bay Packers, now in first place. Their Sabbath triumph definitely put the Lions back into the championship running with more than ordinary accent on their next two games, contests with the Packers at Green Bay next Sunday and with the same eleven the week following in Detroit.

PLAY ON SOGGY FIELD

The game with the Cardinals was played under skies that dripped and on a soggy field that turned fancy-attired footballers into mud-bespattered objects not recognizable from the sidelines.

Besides that there were occasional outbursts of thunder, with spells of darkness that made electric lights necessary in the press box. All in all, it was a weird sort of an affair comparable with the fog-bound setting for the Boston game in Detroit recently.

Instead of an anticipated crowd of 25,000, there were less than 8,000 who braved the inclement weather.

The Lions outclassed the Cardinals in every department throughout the game and the close score falls to indicate Detroit's superiority over the former sectional leaders.

It was the Detroit team's answer to the tie game played between the two teams in Detroit earlier in the season.

With 10 first downs to four, the Lions gained many more yards than their opponents. Six first downs were made by Detroit in the first half and four in the last half against two each for the Cardinals.

Detroit tried three passes and completed two. The only one tried by the Cardinals was intercepted by Parker.

Fleet-footed Ernie Caddel, who played the entire 60 minutes of the game, scored the Lions' touchdown in the first period, sweeping 11 yards around left end after taking a shovel pass from Ace Gutowsky.

Dutch Clark's nimble toe converted the extra point, a point that later proved the margin of victory.

A fumble led the way to the Chicago touchdown in the second period, Bill Volok scoring for the home guards after Frank Christensen had fumbled a pass from center. When Frank fell to recover the ball, the slipper pigskin again escaped his reach and was scooped up by the Cardinal player, who, with nobody in front of him, ran 25 yards and across the Detroit goal line.

KICKED BALL CHARGE

Detroit players say Volok kicked the ball out of Christensen's hands.

Bill Smith's attempt to convert the extra point was blocked by Clare Randolph, who, like Caddel, played 60 minutes of great football. Frank Christensen, whose magnificent punting stood out, was another to play the full hour.

Besides the scintillating contributions of Caddel and Frank Christensen, the line plunging of young Buddy Parker featured in the Detroit backfield and from end to end the forward wall completely outplayed the opposition.

With Ed Klewicki turning in his best game in professional football, Detroit's ends were more alert than ever, tackled in deadly fashion and gave the enemy few chances to gain. Klewicki turned in plays constantly and dashed in and smeared plays before they could get under way.

Ray Morse and John Schneller distinguished themselves in the fourth period when the former blocked a place-kick from the 40-yard line attempted by Smith. The ball was recovered for Detroit by Schneller.

The Cardinals had reached the Lions' 32-yard line, the deepest point they had reached into the visiting team's territory excepting when they scored.

A penalty helped pave the way for the Detroit score when the ball was given to the Lions after Christensen had punted and Mike Mikulak was charged with clipping Klewicki.

From Chicago's 46-yard line the Lions marched to the score, a parade that included line smashes and sweeps by Caddel, Clark and Gutowsky. A pass, Clark to Klewicki, put the oval on the Cardinals' 12-yard line from where Ernie trotted around end to plant the ball behind the line.

After the fumble that gave the Cards their touchdown the Lions advanced to the home team's 30-yard line, mainly through Parker's stabs through the enemy's line. A fumble by Caddel halted the procession as the half ended.

START ANOTHER MARCH

The Lions early in the third period started another march from their own 26-yard line that ended when Christensen fumbled in holding the ball for Clark, who was attempting a place-kick from the 40-yard mark.

Punts were traded during the remainder of the period and it was at the start of the fourth stanza when Morse and Schneller messed up Chicago's try for three points.

As the end of the game neared, Parker intercepted a pass thrown by Ike Peterson, Cardinal halfback, and ran to the 10-yard line.

On the fourth down Clark recovered a Detroit fumble on the 5-yard line as the game ended, with 5 yards to go.

The Lineups:

DETROIT		CARDINALS
Klewicki	L.E.	Smith
Johnston	L.T.	Fields
Knox.	L.G.	Cuppoletti
Randolph	C.	Pearson
Emerson.	R.G.	Handler
G. Christensen.	R.T.	Gordon
Ebding	R.E.	Neuman
Clark	Q.B.	Pardonner
F. Christensen	L.H.	Russell
Caddel	R.H.	Nichelini
Gutowsky	F.B	Mikulak

Score by Quarters:

DETROIT	7	0	0	0	7
CARDINALS	0	6	0	0	6

LIONS HANDED WORSE DEFEAT IN HISTORY

1935 NFL Season, Game 8:
Detroit Lions at Green Bay Packers

Detroit Times, November 11th 1935 (Sun. 11/10/35)
(Reprinted with the permission of *The Detroit News*.)
By Leo Macdonell

GREEN BAY, Nov.11—Green Bay Packers, keyed to magnificent heights, combining an amazing ground and aerial attack here Sunday in grinding a helpless Detroit Team into the sand, 31 to 7. This strengthened the Wisconsin team's hold on first place and dropped the Lions to the cellar in the Western section of the National Pro-Football League.

When it is written "into the sand" it is meant literally.

To fill the deep ravines in Green Bay's gridiron after a heavy rain, 10 five-ton truck loads of sand were pyramided in selected sections.

PACKERS LIKED IT

The new-fangled turf did the Lions no good, as you might guess from the score. The Packers seemed to like it. There was talk that the GreenBays wore a special kind of sand cleat, but it was probably just talk.

After seeing Arnold Herber thread needles with the greatest pass throwing exhibition seen on any field and marveling at the sensational catching by Don Hutson, the former Alabaman, and Johnny Blood, who is supposed to be a fellow by the name of McNally from up around the Twin Cities, it is not haard to figure out why Green Bay won.

Green Bay won because they outplayed the Lions at every turn of the road.

Everything they did was brilliant and right, so an announced official attendance of 12,200 clients had their biggest football day in history.

LIONS WORST DEFEAT

It was the worst defeat ever suffered by the Lions, either at Detroit or Portsmouth. The closest to such a disaster happened some years ago and it was Green Bay that administered that shellacking at that time—something like18–0.

It is still possible for the Detroiters to rise from the depths but they will have to win all the rest of their games, somewhat of an assignment. It means whipping the Packers at Detroit next Sunday, taking two games from the Bears and licking Brooklyn in the windup of the regular season.

Three of GreenBay's four touchdowns came as a climax of spectacular passes for which the Lions had but a feeble defense. The other was achieved by George Sauer in a rush play, and three points were tossed in for good measure by a field goal, booted by Clark Hinkle, hard driving fullback from Bucknell.

Hall-of-Fame fullback Clark Hinkle of the Green Bay Packers.

KLEWICKI SCORES

Ed Klewicki scored Detroit's touchdown behind the Green Bay goal line on a pass from "Pug" Vaughn, one of the prettiest plays of the day.

Statistics reveal the Packers made 13 first downs to 8 for the Lions, gaining much more yardage than the Detroiters in their tremendous push. Green Bay grabbed an early lead with Hinkle's kick from placement at the start of the first quarter, dropping back from Detroit's 22-yard stripe to the 30-yard line to make the boot.

A fumble by "Dutch" Clark helped to put the Packers in position for the kick. The Detroit captain recovered the fumble on the 11-yard line, but Frank Christensen's punt was downed by Joe Laws on Detroit's 32-yard line. The Packers advanced the ball to make a first down by inches on the 22-yard mark.

PASS SLIPS

Spurred by this early success the Packers later in the quarter inaugurated a new drive which carried them to Detroit's 11-yard line, where the Lions braced and took the ball on downs. A pass, Herber to Hutson, just slipped off Hutson's fingers on the fourth down.

On their own 42-yard line at the start of the second heat, the Packers smashed and passed their way to Detroit's 5-yard line, from where Sauer, on a fake reverse (the play Northwestern used to make Notre Dame dizzy), circled right and for his touchdown.

The parade was made possible by some brilliant work on the part of "Swede" Johnston, a 200-pound pile-driving demon, who answers to the name Chester in politer society. Ernie Smith, a former Southern California performer, converted the extra point and the Lions were on the short end of a 10–0 tally.

LUCK AGAINST THEM

Undaunted, the Lions came back and with the aid of a sensational pass, Ernie Caddel to Klewicki , which was good for 41 yards, placed the ball on Green Bay's 25-yard line.

But luck wasn't with the Lions and the alert Johnston here intercepted another attempt in the air to spoil what looked to be a Detroit march to a touchdown. The Lions were not to be denied however, and before the half ended had a touchdown after Hank Bruder, former Northwestern star, punted out of bounds on Green Bay's 35-yard line and Vaughn, Gutowsky and F. Christensen moved the ball back to the home team's 12-yard stripe.

Once more, fate stepped in to annoy the Lions, Caddel dropping a pass behind the enemy's goal line. Then the Lions lost the ball on downs and Hinkle punted out of what he thought was dangerous territory, the ball coming into possession of the visitors on Green Bay's 28-yard line.

Once more Vaughn tossed to Klewicki and this time the former Michigan State star scored. Frank Christensen

converted and the Lions were in striking distance as the half ended, trailing 10–7.

REAL FIREWORKS

Now came Green Bay's real fireworks.

As the third period started, GreenBay took the ball from its own 32-yard line to Detroit's 21-yard line through some nice passing and snaring by Herber and Milt Gantenbein. Here Herber tossed to Blood and the score was 17–7 as the teams plunged into the final period.

As the fourth stanza started Detroit moved up to Green Bay's 32-yard line, only to lose the ball. Then came a tremendous pass from Herber to Blood over Vaughn's head for the third touchdown. Blood, after catching the ball, ran 33 yards unmolested.

The cheering for Blood's touchdown had hardly died away before Herber hurled another, this time to Hutson, who ran 15 yards for the final touchdown.

Just by way of keeping in practice, Blood threw to Hutson to add the extra point and make the total 31–7.

A pass from Presnell to Parker put the ball on Green Bay's 16-yard line, but Johnston intercepted another attempt and Detroit's last chance to close the gap was lost.

The Lineups:

DETROIT		GREEN BAY
KlewickiL	E.	Rose
Johnston	L.T.	Smith
Knox	L.G.	Michaelske
Randolph	C.	Barrager
Emerson	R.G.	Evans
G. Christensen	R.T.	Hubbard
Schneller	R.E.	Gantenbein
Clark	Q.B.	Bruder
F. Christensen	L.H.	Sauer
Caddel	R.H.	Laws
Gutowsky	F.B	Hinkle

Score by Quarters:

DETROIT	0	7	0	0	7
GREEN BAY	3	7	7	14	31

LIONS DEFEAT GREEN BAY

1935 NFL Season, Game 9:
Detroit Lions vs. Green Bay Packers

Detroit Times, November 18th 1935 (Sun. 11/17/35)
(Reprinted with the permission of *The Detroit News.*)
By Bud Shaver

The ghost of Dutch Clark today had donned flesh. It was the brilliant work of the veteran Detroit Lions' quarterback which inspired Detroit's entry in the National League to beat the Green Bay Packers 20–10, yesterday at University of Detroit Stadium.

Clark was a misty, impalpable figure which floated like smoke through opposing tacklers, once for a 50-yard run back of a punt which led to a touchdown, twice to scoring position where Bill Shepherd could trip hammer his way over for touchdowns.

The Clark, whom everybody said was through, was resurrected so sensationally one of the 10,000 customers' heart stopped and he was carried out lifeless.

For the rest, Clark so inspired his teammates they bottled up the most dangerous passing team in the country, ran hog wild and unleashed the most baffling passing attack any National league team has looked upon this season.

PACKERS BAFFLED

With Clark threading his elusive way through the line in old time fashion, Shepherd pounding the line and Frank Christensen hurling passes, the Lions hung on to the ball most of the afternoon and completely baffled the Packers.

Shepherd banged his way over for two touchdowns in the last quarter and Harry Ebding caught a pass to score the other Detroit touchdown in the second quarter.

Ernie Smith place-kicked a field goal from the 20-yard line in the first quarter to give the Packers a 3–0 lead. After Ebding grabbed Clark's pass for a Detroit touchdown late in the second quarter to put the Lions ahead, 6–3. Milt Gantenbein caught a pass from George Sauer in the end zone and Smith place-kicked the point after touchdown to put the Packers in the lead again 10–6.

In the final period the Lions came to life, pulled a flock of new plays out of the bag and passed their way to two touchdowns.

HALF ON PASSES

The Lions made 10 first downs to the Packers' 4, half of them on passes. Detroit threw 18 forward passes and completed 11 for a total gain of 123 yards.

Arnie Herber's passing was completely bottled up by the savage rushing Lion forwards and the persistent dogging of receivers by the secondary. Don Hutson never got under a single pass from Herber or Johnny Blood.

The Packers threw 15 passes and completed only four, two of them for first downs. They gained 62 yards passing and only 52 rushing. The Lions outgained them with a total of 250 yards to the Packers' 114.

Only in kicking did the Packers show any superiority, averaging 36 yards to the Lions 34.

FUMBLE SETS STAGE

Glenn Presnell's fumble of Sauer's punt early in the first quarter set the stage for the Packers' first score. Alfred Rose pounced on the ball on the Lions' 16-yard line. On the Statue of Liberty play, Sauer grabbed the ball off Joe Laws' hand and ran to the 12-yard line. It was a third down play, so Swede Johnston held the ball on the 20-yard line and Smith booted it over the cross bar.

The Lions didn't get a scoring chance until the second period. Clark tried a placement kick for a field goal from the Packers' 45 and a little later one from the 17-yard line but missed both of them.

When the Packers started from their 20-yard line a fumble gave the Lions their scoring chance. Sauer fumbled on the first play and Regis Monahan, Lions' guard, recovered on the 16-yard line. Clark took the ball from center, started running to his right, when the Packers' defense was drawn to that side of the field, he wheeled suddenly and threw a pass to the left side, which fell in Harry Ebding's arms on the 5-yard line. He slid over the goal line without a hand being laid upon him.

Frank Christensen fumbled the pass from center and the Lions had no chance to kick for the point after touchdown.

PASS TO TOUCHDOWN

A fumble by Frank Christensen which he recovered on his 5-yard line, forced him to punt from behind his goal line early in the third quarter. Blood lugged it back to the Lions' 34-yard line and the Packers passed their way to a touchdown. Sauer threw a 25-yard pass into the end zone, but the Packers' halfback, undismayed, threw a bullet pass over center into the hands of Gantenbein to put the Packers' ahead, 10–6.

Early in the fourth period the Lions unleashed their dazzling pass attack. One of Sauer's punts went out of bounds on the Packers' 40-yard line. Shepherd hit left tackle for 6 yards. Frank Christensen threw an 18-yard pass to Shepherd for a first down on the 16-yard line.

Dutch Clark threaded his way inside his right tackle for 11 yards and a first down on the 5-yard line. Once more he pranced inside right tackle to the 2-yard line. Then Shepherd took the ball and hit center, missing a touchdown by inches. He took the ball again and dived over center for a touchdown and Clark place-kicked the extra point, which put the Lions in front, 13–10.

They were never headed. Clark put the Lions in scoring position again with a beautiful 50-yard run-back of Johnston's punt. He caught the ball on his 28-yard, line, ran diagonally for the sidelines on the left side of the field as a wall of blockers formed for him. Near midfield he pivoted and raced toward the center of the field, finally being brought down on the Packers 23-yard line.

Shepherd hit center for 3 yards. Clark cut inside his right tackle for 12 yards and a first down. Through the same hole he went for 5 more yards. Then he fumbled but recovered for a 3 yard loss.

It was fourth down but Clark managed to squirm through to a first down with the ball only inches from a touchdown. Shepherd dived over his left guard for the last touchdown and Clark place-kicked the extra point.

The Packers had the ball only twice after that and took to the air, but the Lions broke up there aerial attack. Ernie Caddel finally intercepted one of Herber's passes and ran it back to the Packers 30-yard line. The Lions were trying to pass their way to another touchdown from inside the Packers' 25-yard line when the game ended.

The Lineups:

DETROIT		GREEN BAY
Klewicki	L.E.	Rose
Johnson	L.T.	Smith
Knox	L.G.	Michaelske
Randolph.	C.	Barrager
Emerson	R.G.	Evans
G. Christensen	R.T	Hubbard
Schneller	R.E.	Gantenbein
Presnell	Q.B.	Goldenberg
F. Christensen	L.H.	Sauer
Caddel	R.H.	Laws
Shepherd	F.B.	Hinkle

Score by Quarters:

DETROIT	0	6	0	14	20
GREEN BAY	3	0	0	7	10

BEARS BATTLE LIONS TO TIE

1935 NFL SEASON, GAME 10:
DETROIT LIONS AT CHICAGO BEARS

Detroit Times, November 25th 1935 (Sun. 11/24/35)
(Reprinted with the permission of *The Detroit News.*)
By Bud Shaver

CHICAGO, Nov. 25—Detroit's Lions today are nursing honorable wound stripes that come from the turmoil of bitter conflict.

Potsy Clark's steel-bodied and stout-hearted men battled the rugged Chicago Bears to 20-20 tie in a free scoring battle that gagged, stuttered and bewildered a crowd of 14,624 at Wrigley Field yesterday afternoon.

It was a game in which spectacular passes, long runs and discouraging penalties at critical moments were interwoven into a brutal slashing fabric of football that often found fights raging both on and off the field at one and same time.

REMAIN IN TIE

The Lions today are still tied for second place in the National Professional Football League with the Bears and Chicago Cardinals. All three are a full game behind the Green Bay Packers, and either of the three with a perfect record the remainder of the way might claim the western division title provided the Packers lose one of their remaining games.

Never in the history of pro-football has a more harsh or pulverizing battle been played. Men collided as if shot from springs of steel. Several from both teams were carried off the battlefield, and most of them later returned to the sanguinary struggle to help sway the fast-changing gridiron drama that the football fates decided should end in a deadlock.

The Lions scored first and were never behind. At one stage early in the second period, they led by 13–0. But the Bears were battling with the fury of wild men on the prowl.

They tied the score before the end of

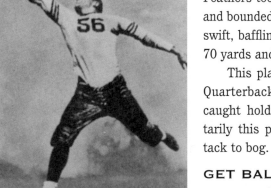

Chicago Bears and University of Michigan star, Bill Hewitt.

the first half 13–13, and overcame another Detroit touchdown in the third period to again deadlock the count.

The last quarter was played under a cloak of darkness that found the Lions putting on a desperate march that carried to the 9-yard line in the final minutes only to have a penalty called on Bill Sheppard for illegal use of hands as he led interference for the gallant Ernie Caddel.

It was heartbreaking to reach for the victory nectar and then be slapped so rudely in the face by an unkind break.

Bill Carr, right end for the Bears was poison in Detroit's bubbling cup of joy. He scored all three of the Chicago touchdowns on passes.

Dutch Clark, Bill Shepherd and Ed Klewicki carried the Lion colors into the touchdown sector. Clark added two extra points from placement for the Lions and had his third try blocked. Twice Jack Manders rushed on the field for the Bears to convert extra points from placement. On another occasion he was ineligible to re-enter the game and Gene Ronzani's try was blocked by John Schneller.

Penalties played played a villainous part in the game from beginning to end. On the third play of the game, Beattie Feathers took Frank Christensen's punt and bounded through the Lions with the swift, baffling strides of an antelope for 70 yards and a touchdown.

This play was called back because Quarterback Bob Dunlap had been caught holding Harry Ebding. Momentarily this penalty caused the Bear attack to bog.

GET BALL ON 1-YARD LINE

In the third period, Gene Ronzani was penalized 15 yards for sticking his knees in Glenn Presnell after the Lion back had carried the ball to the 14-yard line. Detroit was given the ball on the 1-yard line and Bill Sheppherd plunged over.

And then, the most heart breaking play of all, was the one which denied Detroit's thump on the victory gates in those last minutes after Caddel had raced and twisted around end to the Bear 9-yard line.

Detroit never played with more willingness and courage. Once the line repulsed the vaunted attack of the Bears on the 1-yard line, including even the vicious assaulting bronco, Nagurski, only to have Masterston a few plays later whip a 42-yard pass to the ever present nemesis, Billy Karr.

KICKS AGAINST WIND

Ox Emerson stood out like a blazing beacon in the Lion line, and Frank Christensen, even with the wind against him, was booming out kicks that ranged from 45 to 61 yards. The tougher the pressure, the better Christensen's toe delivered.

The younger members of the Lion squad played as if inspired. "Butch" Morse covered punts brilliantly, and hounded the Bear ball-carriers continually. Ed Klewicki, Bill Sheppard, Stacy and Buddy Parker flirted with the moments of glory.

The Lions received and, after battering futilely at the Bear forewall three times, punted. Beattie Feathers took Christensen's long toe explosion on his own 30-yard line, and wheeled 70 yards down the field through the entire Lion team.

DETROITERS GET BREAK

But the blue-shirted Detroiters got a break here. Dunlap was caught holding on the 37-yard line, which nullified the touchdown, and drew a 15-yard penalty from that point for the Bears.

Sam Knox a few seconds later pounced on a fumble on the Bear 48-yard line. Two passes, Sheppard to Presnell, for 17 yards, and another, Presnell to Caddel, for 18 yards, carried the ball to the 11-yard line.

But the grim fighting Chicago line rose up in all its might and tossed back the challenge at this point, Karr breaking through to spill Ernie Caddel for a 12-yard loss as he attempted a wide end sweep.

Detroit did not become discouraged. After Frank Christensen had kicked 50 yards to the Bear 15-yard line, Dunlap tried a pass and the alert Bill Sheppard roared in to pull it out of the air and battered down the field to the Bear's 13-yard line.

DUTCH CLARK SCORES

Dutch Clark entered the game at this stage, replacing Glenn Presnell. Sheppard bucked center twice to the 3-yard line and Clark knifed his way over the bulky form of Art Bush for the score. Dutch made good, placement.

Just before the first quarter the first quarter ended, the Lions took the ball on their own 48-yard line following Feathers' short kick. Just as the gun brought to a close the first period, Ernie Caddel took a pass from Dutch Clark and went to the Chicago 35-yard stripe.

On the first play in the second quarter, Ernie Caddel started to his right as if he intended a wide end sweep. Instead he faded back to his 50-yard line and whipped a pass 50 yards to Ed Klewicki, who took it unmolested across the goal. Clark missed his try from placement.

Amid much cheering, Bronko Nagurski led a new backfield quartet on the field composed of Masterson, Ronzani, Molesworth, and the old bucking, busting, bronco himself.

CHANGED WHOLE GAME

Trailing 13–0, Nagurski started with the kickoff and in a few seconds changed the whole complexion of the game.

Masterson mixed in two well-executed passes with Nagurski's running to drive to the first touchdown. A 26-yard heave, Masterson to Molesworth, placed the ball on the Lions' 20 yard line. Then followed a 22-yard pass across the goal from Masterson to Karr for the touchdown. Old "Dead-Eye-Dick" Jack Manders went back to the backfield to kick the extra point.

Carrying the fight to the Lions, the Bears tied the score in the second quarter after Gene Ronzani intercepted George Christensen's pass on the Lions' 42-yard line and raced down the field to the 16-yard marker. Ronzani passed to Karr for the touchdown. John Schneller broke through to block Ronzani's try from placement.

Just before the half the Lions drove to the Bears' 28-yard line, but on finding the scoring gates locked by land and air, Glenn Presnell dropped back to his 39-yard line and attempted a place kick. It was important, the score stood 13–13 as the players retired for the intermission.

The second half was under way only a few minutes before Frank Christensen stuck his toe into the pumpkin and it sailed 57 yard to be downed on the Bears' 3-yard line by "Butch" Morse.

Feathers kicked out to the Bears' 39, Bill Sheppard and Glenn Presnell started a drive down the field that placed the ball on the Bears' 14-yard line. Some vicious Bear roughed and the Lions were given the ball on the 1-yard line. They hauled off the heroic Presnell. But he heard the mingled cheers and groans a moment later as Bill Sheppard plunged over and Dutch Clark added the extra point to shove Detroit ahead, 20–13.

The Bears lost no time tieing the score. Feathers broke loose on a brilliant 48-yard run to the Lions' 10-yard line. The valiant Detroiters repulsed this drive on the 1-yard line and Christensen kicked out to his 42-yard line. But it was a glittering wasted. Masterson shot a pass to Karr which was good for the 42 yards and a touchdown. Manders went in and kicked the goal that tied the score.

The fourth quarter was played under a blanket of darkness with the Lions going to the 9-yard line in the final minutes only to be denied a scoring opportunity due to a 15-yard penalty.

LIONS DEFEAT BEARS TO TIE FOR LEAD

1935 NFL Season, Game 11: Detroit Lions vs. Chicago Bears

Detroit Times, November 29th 1935 (Thanksgiving) (Thurs. 11/28/35)
(Reprinted with the permission of *The Detroit News.*)
By Leo Macdonell

Very definitely in the championship running as a result of their smashing victory over the Chicago Bears, 14–2, at University of Detroit Stadium yesterday, the Lions today turned to Brooklyn Dodgers, who come to town Sunday.

Yesterday's victory enabled Detroit to tie the Chicago Cardinals for first place in the western division of the National Pro League.

Brooklyn will help the Lions wind up the regular season, and the result of the game will have an important bearing on the three horse race in the western division, in which the Lions, Cardinals and Green Bay Packers are battling for the right to meet the New York Giants for the national championship.

The championship game will be played in the city of the western division winner.

By their defeat yesterday the Bears, last year's champions in the western section, were eliminated.

STRONG CONTENDER

By their win over the Packers yesterday the Cardinals now become Detroit's most serious contender for the sectional honors. Because of a postponed game the Cardinals have two games left to play, both with the Bears, their ancient and most cordially hated enemy.

If the Lions beat Brooklyn, the Packers will be out, but Cardinals can win the title with a sweep against the Bears in their two games. If Detroit beats the Dodgers and the Cardinals split even with the Bears the title comes here.

A victory and a tie for the Cardinals will result in a deadlock with the Lions for top position.

In that case a playoff would be necessary, a situation that brings up visions of games played in snowstorms.

As it stands, the regular games will not be concluded

Ace Gutowsky grinds his way through the Chicago Bear defense.

until a week from Sunday because of the postponed game to be played off by the Bears and Cards. The game was pushed ahead because of the World Series.

If Detroit wins the divisional championship it is slated to play the Giants here, as the national championship game last year was decided in New York. The games are alternated. The Giants are the present national champions.

Sunday's game with Brooklyn will be played for the Old Newsboys, who will receive all the money from 3,000 tickets sold.

WON TROPHY

Whether or not they capture a championship, the Lions will not be without honors. When they defeated the Bears Sunday they won the Harold (Red) Grange trophy, a trophy donated annually to the winner of the games between the Lions and the Bears.

The victory was the first that the Lions have won over the Bears since the team was transferred from Portsmouth to Detroit and was a sweet morsel. A year ago the Chicagoans whipped the Detroiters twice to go on and play the Giants.

A crowd of approximately 20,000, cut down by the inclement weather, saw Dutch Clark, Detroit's brilliant captain, again rise to supreme heights to score both of Detroit's touchdowns in a grueling game that was bitterly fought, if not as spectacular as the one between the same teams on the same gridiron last Thanksgiving Day.

To win, the Lions played smartly, combining a ground and air attack that for the excepton of a brief time in the final period dominated the game.

Both of the touchdowns were the result of perfectly executed passes after brilliant marches had put the ball in scoring position.

Taking the ball from midfield to the Bears' 11-yard line, Bill Shepherd and Ernie Caddel, in a series of line smashes and end runs, paved the way for Clark's first touchdown in the first period. Shepherd tossed the pass, Clark snaring the ball behind the enemy's goal line, where the Detroit quarterback was standing all alone while bewildered Bears looked elsewhere for the play. It was fourth down and two yards to go when Shepherd passed.

Clark also kicked the extra point.

In the same period Glenn Presnell missed a kick from placement on Chicago's 45-yard line after Presnell had run a punt back 40 yards and Caddel had skirted right end 22 yards in a pair of pretty performances.

Chicago scored its two points on Buddy Parker's safety in the second period after Parker had intercepted Gene Ronzani's pass on the Lions' three-yard line. The ball was kicked out of Parker's arms and the Bears claimed a touchdown when Bill Hewitt fell on the ball but Referee Bobbie Cahn had blown the whisle while Parker still had possession of the oval.

Twice before in the period the Bears had threatened. On one occasion Ronzani carried Johnsos' pass to Detroit's six-yard line, a gain of 44 yards but the Bears lost their scoring chance when penalized 15 yards for illegal use of the hands.

LOOKED LIKE TOUCHDOWN

A second time the Bears reached the three-yard line and on fourth down with two yards to go Clark batted away Bronko Nagurski's pass to Johnsos, which looked like a sure touchdown.

Clark's second touchdown came in the third period after the Liions had worked the ball to the Bears' 20-yard line. Taking Ace Gutowsky's pass, Clark dodged prettily through a mass of Chicago players to cross the line. He kicked another point, concluding the scoring for the day.

With Ronzani throwing passes, the Bears rallied in the fourth period and advanced the ball to within the shadows of the Detroit goal posts only to lose it when Presnell intercepted a pass, the Lions punted out of danger and the visitors' last chance withered.

The Lineups:

BEARS		LIONS
Hewitt	L.E.	Klewicki
Buss	L.T.	Johnson
Richards	L.G.	Knox
Kawal	C.	Randolph
Kopcha	R.G.	Emerson
Musso	R.T.	G. Christensen
Johnsos	R.E.	Schneller
Masterson	Q.B.	Presnell
Molesworth	L.H.	Christensen
Ronzani	R.H.	Caddel
Nagurski	F.B.	Shepherd

Score by Quarters:

BEARS	0	2	0	0	2
LIONS	7	0	7	0	14

LIONS DEFEAT BROOKLYN

1935 NFL Season, Game 12:
Detroit Lions vs. Brooklyn Dodgers

Detroit Evening Times, December 1st 1935 (Sun. 12/1/35)
(Reprinted with the permission of *The Detroit News.*)
By Leo Macdonell

Overwhelming Brooklyn, 28 to 0, in a scintillating display of football, Detroit's roaring today, all alone, glittered atop their division and pointed to a national championship.

While the Detroit juggernaut, in all its fury, was grinding helpless Dodgers into a frost-bitten gridiron at University of Detroit Stadium, Chicago Bears were holding the Cardinals to a tie and smashed the deadlock in which the Lions and Cards were locked at the top of the western division of the National League prior to yesterday.

The score in Chicago was 7 to 7.

12,000 SEE VICTORY

Twelve thousand hardy souls, swathed in heavy sweaters, minks and other odds and ends fashioned to battle Winter's icy touch, witnessed the Lions in a glorious finish to the regular season.

As a result of the victory, the worst the Lions can now get is a tie with the Cardinals for first place in the red-hot divisional scrap, in which event a playoff will be necessary to determine which team plays the New York Giants for the National title.

The defeat of Brooklyn assured the Giants of first place in the eastern division.

PLANS PLAYOFF

With a victory over the Bears in their final game of the regular season in Chicago next Sunday the best the Cardinals can hope for is a tie. Defeat means elimination, leaving the Lions champions of the section with the right to play the Giants in Detroit, December 15.

George A. Richards, owner of the Lions, said today that he was waiting word from Joseph Carr, president of the league, as to plans for playoffs.

Two of three Detroit touchdowns were born of line plunges, the other was paved by a forward pass, two safeties scored points and one field goal was kicked in the greatest assortment of scoring seen in a local football game.

PRESNELL STARS

The touchdowns were scored by Captain "Dutch" Clark, Ace Gutowsky and Glen Presnell and Presnell kicked the field goal.

Outstanding in the day's labor was the performance of Presnell, who rose to supreme heights, running, kicking, and passing in a superb display. Aiding him were Gutowsky and the reliable Clark in the back.

On defense Ed Klewicki put on another show. Sharing with him in the glory were Ralph Morse, George Christensen, Jim Steen and Ox Emerson. Steen and Regis Monahan each played the entire 60 minutes.

Emerson emerged from the conflict with a pair of bruised ribs.

AMAZING PUNTING

For the Dodgers, Ralph Kercheval, kicker supreme stood out. The Brookynite uncorked amazing punting. Gil Bergerson, guard from the Oregon Aggies, who starred on defense for the Dodgers, had four stitches taken in a wound over his eye.

Jack Johnson and Sam Knox, Detroit forwards, were out of the game with injuries but are expected to see action in the next game.

Thirteen first downs for Detroit against but three for Brooklyn reveal the superiority of the Lions. The statistics further reveal that the Lions made 227 yards rushing against 62 for the Brooklynites.

With the one exception—punting—the Lions outplayed the Dodgers.

STARTS WITH FIELD GOAL

The first scoring of the game came in the second period when Presnell booted his field goal from placement after Emerson had recovered a fumble and the Dodgers had been penalized for holding.

With the ball on Brooklyn's 28-yard line Presnell

dropped back to the 36-yard line stripe and kicked true between the uprights and over the cross-bar for three points that sent the Lions on their way to victory.

A safety early in the third period increased Detroit's lead to 5–0 when Kercheval, back of his goal line slipped and then threw the ball for a pass and hit the goal post, the pigskin bounding back of the Brooklyn goal line. A fumble by Jack Grossman and a clipping penalty had shoved the Dodgers back to their 1-yard line just before Kercheval attempted to kick out of danger.

CLARK SCORES

Before the period ended, Clark made his touchdown, sliding off right tackle on the fourth down after he and Gutowsky had smashed their way from Brooklyn's 36-yard stripe to within inches of the goal line. Clark also converted to give the Lions a lead of 12–0 going into the fourth period.

Two more touchdowns and the second safety came in the final period. Presnell made the first on a beautiful in which he caught Gutowsky's pass on Brooklyn's 20-yard line and ran for a touchdown.

Pop Lumpkin, former Detroit player made a heroic attempt to catch him from behind, diving and missing Presnell by a few feet at the goal line. Presnell kicked the extra point to give the Lions a 19–0 lead.

Two more points were added when Kercheval fumbled the ball back of his own goal line when hit by Morse and Stacy.

To pave the way for the final score, Presnell intercepted a pass in Brooklyn territory and ran it back from the 40-yard to the 23-yard mark. From there Presnell and Gutowsky, in a series of line bucks, advanced the ball to the 3-yard line from where Ace plunged over for a touchdown on a spinner at left tackle.

Presnell kicked to make the count 28–0, the final scoring of the day.

LIONS ATTAIN WORLD GRID LAURELS

1935 NFL SEASON, CHAMPIONSHIP GAME:
DETROIT LIONS VS. NEW YORK GIANTS

Detroit Evening Times, December 15th 1935 (Sun. 12/15/35)
(Reprinted with the permission of *The Detroit News.*)
By Leo Macdonell

The Tigers and Joe Louis today moved over to make room for some more celebrated Detroiters—the Lions, new national professional football champions by virtue of a smashing victory over the New York Giants, 26–7, at University of Detroit Stadium Sunday afternoon.

Braving rain and snow that would chill hearts less stout, 17,000 hardy fans sat in a picturesque Christmastime setting and roared acclaim as the brilliant Dutch Clark and his cohorts marched to another great triumph for a city already knee-deep in honors on the field of sport.

To win their first championship the Lions combined an air and ground attack that gave them an early lead which they never lost, a marked superiority reflected in the statistics of the game.

GIANTS ARE UNSEATED

Besting the Giants, the Lions uncrowned the defending champions, who last year whipped the Chicago Bears in the playoff and again this year topped the eastern division.

To many of the Lions it marked the end of a long struggle to reach the top, a fight that for some of them started seven years ago when they first jointed the Portsmouth Spartans, who last year became the Detroit Lions.

Four players shared in Detroit's scoring, six plays netting the first touchdown within three minutes of actual playing time after the opening whistle, and two coming within three minutes of the end of the contest.

PASSES PAVE WAY

Two brilliantly executed passes, Glenn Presnell to Frank Christensen and Ace Gutowsky to Ed Klewicki, paved the way for the first touchdown, Gutowsky crashing over the New York goal line. Blinded by the sudden and unexpected air assault, the Giants were still in a daze when the powerful Gutowsky hurled his massive frame over the line as the great crowd roared and shrieked delight.

A spectacular, broken field run that was good for 38 yards, another of Clark's sensational achievements accounted for the second touchdown later in the period.

Ernie Caddel, fleet even on a soggy field, raced around end and Buddy Parker drove over center for the final Detroit markers to make victory all but irrevocable. There was less than a half minute left to play when Buddy scored.

New York's lone touchdown was fashioned with a forward pass. Ed Danowski to Ken Strong, and came in the third period. With New York in possession of the ball on Detroit's 41-yard line, Strong snared the pass on the 30-yard stripe and ran for the score. There was an element of luck in the touchdown inasmuch as Gutowsky seeking to knock the pass down tipped it into Strong's outstretched arms.

Three of Detroit's touchdowns—all save Parker's—were scored with the ball toter standing up. Gutowsky, Oklahoma's favored son, walked through on a spinner that had the Giants fooled completely. The passes, Presnell to Frank Christensen and Gutowsky to Klewicki, that greased the way to the touchdown, put the ball on the 7-yard line.

From there Presnell gained 2 yards, and Gutowsky topped it off when he trotted through his own left guard while the Giants were looking elsewhere for the play.

When Presnell kicked the extra point the Lions were off to a flying start, 7–0.

Six minutes had elapsed, three of them actual playing time.

A little later the Giants reached Detroit's 25-yard line, and failing to gain, Strong dropped back and on the fourth down tried a placement for a field goal, a kick that failed. A pass from Danowski to Goodwin had put the ball in scoring position.

Once again the Giants were deep in Detroit territory when Bill Morgan, tackle, recovered Gutowskky's fumble on the 21-yard stripe. Goodwin took Danowski's pass for a 10-yard gain and hurt on the play, had to retire. The Giants were held for downs and the Lions took the ball, Frank Christensen punting out of danger.

Here, Frank Christensen intercepted Danowski's pass for a 26-yard gain that put the ball on New York's 44-yard line. The ball was advanced to the 38-yard mark from where Clark weaved through the demoralized Giants for his run of 38 yards to a touchdown, the prettiest run of the day.

Clark missed the kick after the touchdown and shortly afterward the period ended with Detroit leading, 13–0.

It was at the start of the second period that Ebding's fumble robbed that capable gentleman of a touchdown.

After this the Giants put on a rally, a pass, Danowski to Milt Singer, former Syracuse end giving the visitors a first down on Detroit's 23-yard. Harry Newman, the old University of Michigan star football flinger, and Danowski moved the leather to the 9-yard line for another first down.

In two plays Danowski gained 5 yards and Elvin Richards added two more. Then with the Giants seemingly on the way to a touchdown Bill Shepherd threw Richards for a loss and the Lions regained the ball on downs on their own 5-yard mark.

From behind his own goal line Frank Christensen booted the ball out of danger. Buster Mitchell once of Detroit was penalized for holding, and this lapse combined with a 25-yard dash at left end by Caddel placed the ball on Detroit's 46-yard line.

A series of plays advanced the ball to New York's 32-yard stripe and when passes failed, Frank Chritensen kicked and the ball was in mid-field as the half ended.

New York's 32-yard touchdown in the third quarter came in the wake of an exchange in punts which put the ball in possession of the Giants on their own 46-yard mark.

After one play, in which he made 4 yards through the line, Danowski hurled the ball to Strong, who ran 30 yards and crossed the Detroit goal line. Strong also booted the extra point to make the count13–7.

PARKER LEADS CHARGE

Before the quarter ended, Parker stepped into the spotlight with a series of gains that were mainly responsible in advancing the ball from Detroit's 34-yard line to New York's 37-yard mark. Here the Lions lost the ball on downs.

Trading kicks, with seven minutes to go, Frank Christensen booted the pigskin 60 yards on the fly, a tremendous kick over the New York goal line.

Two plays failed to gain and George

Christensen recovered a blocked New York punt on the Giants 25-yard line.

Once again Parker took the spotlight, knifing his way 13 yards. Clark took it to within a foot of a touchdown. Parker fumbled and lost three yards but on the next play Caddel skirted the end to score. Presnell added the extra point to make the total 20–7.

With the end of the game only seconds away. Parker plunged over from the 3-yard line after intercepting Newman's pass and taking the ball from the 22, to the 10-yard line.

The Lineups:

DETROIT		NEW YORK
Klewicki	L.E.	Frankian
Johnson	L.T.	Morgan
Knox	L.G.	Jones
Randolph	C.	Hein
Emerson	R.G.	Owen
G. Christensen	R.T.	Grant
Schneller	R.E.	Goodwin
Presnell	Q.B.	Danowski
F. Christensen	L.H.	Strong
Caddel	R.H.	Richards
Gutowsky	F.B.	Corzine

Score by Quarters:

NEW YORK GIANTS	0	0	7	0	7
DETROIT LIONS	13	0	0	13	26

Ernie Caddel.

Glen Presnell.

Appendix D: Detroit Red Wings

Contents

1935–1936 NHL REGULAR SEASON FINAL STANDINGS

Canadian Division	GP	W	L	T	Pts	GF	GA	PIM
Montreal Maroons	48	22	16	10	54	114	106	504
Toronto Maple Leafs	48	23	19	6	52	126	106	579
New York Americans	48	16	25	7	39	109	122	392
Montreal Canadiens	48	11	26	11	33	82	123	317

American Division	GP	W	L	T	Pts	GF	GA	PIM
Detroit Red Wings	48	24	16	8	56	124	103	384
Boston Bruins	48	22	20	6	50	92	83	397
Chicago Black Hawks	48	21	19	8	50	93	92	411
New York Rangers	48	19	17	12	50	91	96	381

*Note: GP=Games Played, W=Wins, A=Assists, Pts=Points, PIM=Penalties in Minutes

1935–1936 NHL Intersectional Playoff Bracket

Quarterfinals
Toronto Maple Leafs (vs.) Boston Bruins
New York Americans (vs.) Chicago Black Hawks

Semifinals
Montreal Maroons (vs.) Detroit Red Wings
Toronto Maple Leafs (vs.) New York Americans

Finals
Detroit Red Wings (vs.) Toronto Maple Leafs

1935–1936 NHL Awards

O'Brien Trophy:	Montreal Maroons
Prince of Wales Trophy:	Detroit Red Wings
Calder Memorial Trophy:	Mike Karakas, Chicago Black Hawks
Hart Memorial Trophy:	Eddie Shore, Boston Bruins
Lady Byng Memorial Trophy:	Doc Romnes, Chicago Black Hawks
Vezina Trophy:	Tiny Thompson, Boston Bruins

1935–1936 NHL All-Star Teams

First Team	Position	Second Team
Tiny Thompson Boston Bruins	G	Wilf Cude Montreal Canadiens
Eddie Shore Boston Bruins	D	Earl Seibert Chicago Black Hawks
Babe Siebert Boston Bruins	D	Ebbie Goodfellow Detroit Red Wings
Hooley Smith Montreal Maroons	C	Bill Thoms Toronto Maple Leafs
Charlie Conacher Toronto Maple Leafs	RW	Cecil Dillon New York Rangers
Sweeney Schriner New York Americans	LW	Paul Thompson Chicago Black Hawks
Lester Patrick New York Rangers	Coach	Tommy Gorman Montreal Maroons

1935–1936 NHL Scoring Leaders

Player Team	GP	G	A	Pts	PIM
Sweeney Schriner New York Americans	48	19	26	45	8
Marty Barry Detroit Red Wings	48	21	19	40	46
Paul Thompson Chicago Black Hawks	45	17	23	40	19
Bill Thoms Toronto Maple Leafs	48	23	15	38	29
Charlie Conacher Toronto Maple Leafs	44	23	15	38	74
Hooley Smith Montreal Maroons	47	19	19	38	75
Doc Romnes Chicago Black Hawks	48	13	25	38	6
Art Chapman New York Americans	47	10	28	38	14
Herbie Lewis Detroit Red Wings	45	14	23	37	25
Baldy Nortcott Montreal Maroons	48	15	21	36	41

WINGS ROOKIE SCORES
AFTER 176 MINUTES

1935–1936 NHL Stanley Cup Semi-Finals, Game 1:
Detroit Red Wings at Montreal Maroons

Detroit Times, March 25th 1936 (Tues. 3/24/36)
(Reprinted with the permission of *The Detroit News.*)
By Leo Macdonell

MONTREAL, March 25.—Modere (Mud) Bruneteau, slim and sleek French-Canadian lad, just turned 22 and playing his first season on big time, this morning emerged hero from the longest most bitterly fought game in the long and glamorous history of hockey.

The clock pointed to 22 minutes after 2 when the young Winnipeg boy's story book goal came, breaking up a thrill-packed, puck-pounding contest that smashed all records for time and sent the Red Wings flying out in front in the first game of their Stanley Cup series with the Maroons by a score of 1–0.

When Bruneteau ended the game two great and thoroughly game but exhausted teams had played 176 minutes and 30 seconds of hockey extending over nearly six hours, during which 10,000 fans were wrapped in amazement.

BREAK MARK MADE IN TORONTO IN 1933

Staggering up and down the ice on weary legs and feebly trying to check one another, the contest when ended was in its ninth period-sixth of overtime.

The old mark was 164 minutes 48 seconds, established in Toronto in 1933 when Ken Doraty's lone goal won for the Maple Leafs over Boston Bruins.

Sharing fame with Bruneteau was Hec Kilrea, veteran of many cup playoffs and still ranking as tops among money players. It was Kilrea who pushed the puck into Monteal territory and made the pass that was

scooped up by the alert Bruneteau and shoveled into the net past the startled Lorne Chabot, grizzled veteran who along with Normie Smith played amazingly in the nets.

Brilliant in a remarkable display of batting and kicking out pucks, Smith turned in his greatest game and one of the finest exhibitions in the history of Stanley Cup competition.

He more thanmaatched Chabot in a thrilling duel that had Montreal fans marveling, as one and then the other goalie squirmed, stretched and dived to smother and clear pucks rained in on them during the night's time-eating orgy.

While Chabot was turning back 80 shots, Smith saved 75, dozens of which were seemingly goal ticketed and coming in the hectic overtime heats when a goal meant victory in the sudden-death system used in the series.

Joining Smith in the distribution of glory were the Red Wing defensemen and Detroit's smart back checking forwards who teamed in a magnificent performance that sent the Red Wing stock soaring as they prepare for the second game of the set here Thursday.

By virtue of their victory they will go home Thursday night with no worse than an even break which should make them favorites in the third game on their home ice and games to follow, if more games are necessary.

WINGS SAY THEY'LL BE READY AGAIN

That the grueling test as it plunged into the early hours this morning, might have taken something out of

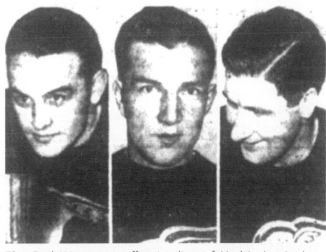

The Red Wings top offensive line of Herbie Lewis, Larry Aurie, and Marty Barry.
—*Detroit Times* photo/Courtesy of *The Detroit News*

the Wings, needed for the future in case they hurdle the Maroons was feared in some quarters though the Wings themselves overjoyed at their win, proclaimed that a day's rest is all that is needed to put them back in tip-top shape.

While the game was fiercely fought it was comparatively free from serious injuries. Scotty Bowman, hard luck member of the team, was once again nicked on the nose, suffering a gash that required five stitches, running the total of stitches taken in the young man's schnozzle to 33 for the season.

The injury came early in the game when he was accidentally struck by Russ Blinco but he returned to the game and turned in his best exhibition of the season.

CUTS ARE AMONG THEIR SOUVENIRS

The brothers Kilrea-Hec and Wally—also bear souvenirs of the fierce fray. The former had two stitches sewed over his left eye in a cut given him by Dave Trottier. Wally again was hit on the head.

There was only one penalty called in the six overtime periods—that on Hooley Smith for tripping. Hooley aggravated an ailing back early in the game but otherwise outside of fatigue, the Maroons came out of the melee in comparatively good physical condition.

They, like the Red Wings, played headsup hockey and there was little to choose in general play. The heralded first lines put on a great back-checking show and wound up in a deadlock as far as points were concerned.

Hooley Smith took Northcott's pass for the first shot on goal, a hard drive from the blue line, and in a second Maroon rush Ward tried a similar shot that Smith took care of with ease.

Ward rushed again and was unceremoniously spilled by the hard checking McDonald. As the Maroons continued the attack Northcott almost scored.

The Detroit shots were wide of the net.

Hooley Smith stormed down the ice and was met at the Detroit blue line by McDonald who bounced the Montreal star high in the air and broke his stick in doing so.

The forward lines were changed before Detroit got a threatening shot on the home team's net. With the change in players the second lines took up the burden. Pettinger, Howe, and Hec Kilrea facing Blinco, Trottier and Robinson.

DEFENSE CHECKS FORWARDS' CHARGE

As the two teams surged up and down the ice each in its turn was met by a powerful and determined defense that broke up the attacks near the blue lines.

With another change in lines, Marker rushed spectacularly and was spilled in like fashion by McDonald, following which Young pounced on a loose puck and steamed with lightning speed toward Maroons' goal but was checked as he crossed the blue line.

Bruneteau was teamed with Wally Kilrea and Sorrell on the Detroit line. As play flamed and the Red Wings attacked, Wally Kilrea and Sorrell almost scored.

With McDonald penalized for tripping Gracie, Maroons enjoyed the first big break of the game and pressed savagely as the short-handed Wings fought as viciously to hurl back the terrific assaults on the hard pressed Smith.

Evans rushed for a shot on goal in a sensational spurt down the center of the rink but the Detroit net minder saved nicely.

STAND AT GOAL HALTED MAROONS

The defense in front of the Detroit goal refused to yield and the Red Wings were again at full strength before the Maroons seriously threatened.

Trottier was sent off for cross-checking Hec Kilrea and Adams tossed out five Detroit forwards in a desperate effort to convert the advantage.

As they ganged on Chabot, Barry almost turned a loose puck into a goal at the corner of the net. Then as Howe whirled his way through the Maroons he was tripped by Shields, who joined Trottier in the penalty box, leaving the Maroons with only three men to protect Chabot.

Trottier came out of the box as Red Wings were storming the enemy's cage but the Maroons put up a gallant defense to hold them off.

Tearing into Montreal territory with tremendous speed, Goodfellow came within a hair of scoring and Barry snared the puck for a close-in shot but Chabot dived out to make a grand stop.

They were at full strength again as the period ended.

A magnificent stop by Smith of Northcott's close in shot from a pass off Ward's stick inaugurated the second heat, another blazing session marked by speed. Just after that came a near Red Wing catastrophe. Hooley Smith's puck rolled along the goal line, almost tottering into the net.

As play returned to the other end of the rink, Young almost tore off Chabot's pads with a wicked drive from off right wing. The Maroons' goalie had to stretch with magic speed to kick away the rubber.

As replacements took the ice, Pettinger smashed his way through Montreal's defense, but his shot was wide of the twine. Blinco broke through and was tripped by Hec Kilrea and with the Detroit man in the coop, the home guards once again had an advantage.

Marker and Cain teamed in a pretty play, but Goodfellow swept away Cain's shot from left wing. Young had switched over to left defense with Goodfellow holding down the right side. Combined with their mates' back checking the pair held off the Montreal rushes until the Wings were at full strength once again.

Shields was in for the only threatening shot.

As the teams battled on even terms in manpower Hec Kilrea threw the crowd into a near panic with a near goal. As players were switched Barry and Aurie almost scored.

BARRY AND WARD CHASED FROM GAME

The teams were warring at a high pitch when Barry and Ward were banished for roughing. Seconds later Hooley Smith came down left wing at breakneck speed to be dumped by McDonald, who was sent off for tripping.

As he tumbled to the ice Smith bounced 15 feet and was visibly hurt, but shook himself and skated off as relief was put out to fill his position.

There was a terrific jam up back of the net and Hec Kilrea skated off with blood pouring from a wound in his face.

Brilliant net minding by Smith and a stubborn defense in front of him held at bay the fierce fighting men of Gorman as they battled viciously to cash in on the advantage in numbers.

Trying to clear, Sorrell almost turned Conacher's pass out into his own net and seconds later the big crowd roared as they thought the Maroons had scored. The roar died out almost instantly as Smith stood up and shook the puck out of his pads.

Seconds later, Goodfellow hit the post in a scramble around the Montreal net which had Chabot bobbling from one side to the other like a jack rabbit.

Tumbling into the boards Wally Kilrea was hurt and skated off and as he did his brother, Hec, returned to the game with a patch over his left eye.

BOTH GOALIES KEPT BUSY SAVING

As Wings and Maroons resumed their bitter feud for the third period Barry made Chabot drop to his knees to clear a whistling shot, and when play surged to the other end of the ice Ward took Hooley Smith's pass for a drive that made Smith move fast.

Tremendous pushes by both teams were being shoved back as the Stanley Cup chasers tried to crash their way over each other's line. Bowman was hit in the nose by Blinco's stick and left the ice.

And soon after Blinco tore down the ice lanes and weaved his way through the Detroit defense for a wicked shot to the corner of the net on which Smith made a magnificent save, stretching his rubber leg clear across the mouth of the goal. The crowd gave the Detroit goalie a hand for the achievement.

Just in the nick of time, Chabot got his big glove out to ward off Pettinger's goal labeled drive from left wing. A second would have cost Montreal a goal.

The speed was blinding as the teams in electrifying movlements whirled through center ice from one zone to the other. Then in the end zones came scrambles in which sticks were high, and players were jammed into piles.

NORMIE'S STOP HALTS ROBINSON

And as the Red and Maroon clad ice warriors raced back Robinson burned a shot at Smith. He tried again and again and was beaten by a fine stop by the Detroit goalie. Blinco lifted a shot that Smith caught in his lap.

Then came McDonald in one of the most thrilling rushes of the night—his first—to almost score with a powerful drive off left wing that sent the startled Chabot back on his haunches. The crowd's Detroit sector [cheered] as the bell plunged the game into overtime.

To open the overtime Young and Ward traded shots on goal, efforts that were taken care of with no great stir by Chabot and Smith.

As the lines changed Robinson swept around left wing and just missed the corner of the net. With the players planly tired the tempo of the match subsided and rushes were less threatening.

On a beautiful play Goodfellow almost clicked the winning goal with Barry's smart pass to the mouth of the goal. Just after this play, and with five minutes left in the 20-minute session, lines changed.

Victory was almost in Detroit's grasp here as Wally Kilrea, trapping Maroon forwards, rushed and passed to the goal mouth where Sorrell swept in with a great burst of speed and almost jammed the rubber into the net. Chabot came out to smother the shot, stretched out across the front gate of his cage.

All but exhausted after 80 minutes of grueling puck pounding the two teams resumed the bitter tussle in another overtime period, playing cautiously and awaiting breaks.

FATIGUE SLACKS BURNING PACE

Up and down they moved—down and up. The pace kept slackening. They were fighting with their heads and hearts, two great, game hockey teams.

A great save robbed Ward.

Another brilliant save robbed Barry—a grim bitter struggle.

Cam the first lines Again. Speed came back. The crowd was brought to its feet roaring—for a Maroon goal of course.

A loose puck skimmed the ice a few feet in front of Aurie. Detroit's game little mite was too tired to chase it. Nor did a Maroon player want it very badly.

Fifteen minutes had passed in the second overtime stanza—and with it another switch in the personnel of the teams. Players not yet recovered from their previous hitch on the ice came back.

Almost a Detroit goal and victory. It came off Howe's stick. Five Maroons were in Detroit territory and Robinson almost scored with Evans' pass.

Tired athletes and 10,000 fans with frazzled nerves.

One minute to go. Will it go a minute?

Twenty seconds to go! Will it go 20 seconds?

It did. One hundred minutes played and the game is plunged into another period.

Young almost caught the corner of the net in the first threat as the teams staggered into their sixth period.

SCREECH OF WOMAN ABOVE THE ROAR

Howe and Hec Kilrea burned the iced in a stupendous rush. Howe weaving through a maze of players and passing to Hec who blazed a shot from left wing. But the shot was wide. The screech of a woman fan could be heard over the roar.

Kelley's in–Chabot makes a thrilling save as the great crowd gasps in one huge gasp. The play returns to the other end. Smith's defense cuts off the attack.

The players scramble around the Maroon net and the harassed Chabot jumps from one side to another, fearing a goal that would spell disaster.

Wally Kilrea reaches for the puck but his strength is almost gone. They skate off—both forward lines—reaching for the dashers for support, and tumble into their seats on the bench.

Down went Chabot. He was just in time to kick out Goodfellow's roaring shot that climaxed a fast bit of teaming with Aurie.

The first lines—the ace of trios—go to work again.

GETS LIKE 6-DAY BIKE RACE

And the crowd steams again—like the crowd during the sprints at a six-day bike race, only more so.

They surge—up and down—down and up. Tired athletes getting more tired. Somebody wishes somebody would get a goal. McDonald, younger than some of the rest and fresher, rushes. He's spilled after crossing the blue line.

Robinson tries to lift the puck after breaking around left wing. He comes back, swings around the same wing and almost scores—the puck just skimming the top of the net.

The crowd gave the players a big hand as each replacement was made. The crowd yelled as Lamb drove a hard shot from right wing, Smith going to his knees to block.

Two minutes to go in another period.

Will it go two minutes, the crowd wondered.

The first lines took the ice and were hardly in action when Hooley Smith swept in for what looked like a sure goal but Normie Smith turned in another wonderful save and was accorded an ovation by the fans.

Then in came Northcott fast and he too almost clicked.

They were battling in Maroon territory when the period ended and the teams were tossed into the fourth overtime heat.

WINGS SEND FIVE FORWARDS ON ICE

The seventh period was only seconds old when Hooley Smith was penalized for cross-checking McDonald and a big break came for the Red Wings.

Five Detroit forwards took the ice.

Intent on what might be the kill, the Wings pressed savagely. Diving out of his net, Chabot saved on Sorrell, then beat Lewis on the only other threat while Hooley was jailed.

The lines changed and Kilrea tore in from wing and passed to the goal mouth, but nobody was there. The ice was bad and the players had trouble handling the puck.

Conacher broke away but was checked crossing Detroit's blue line.

Once again the end almost came when Blinco and Trottier nearly scored. Normie Smith making an amazing stop. It took the combined efforts of big Conacher and the equally as powerful Shields to take the puck away from the usually mild Bruneteau in back of the Maroon net.

Gracie and Marker worked the puck in close on Normie Smith and almost scored. Again [the] Maroon's swept down the ice and Gracie got a shot on goal.

Another overtime heat was half gone when the first lines made their [?]teenth appearance on the ice and the anxious crowd hoped one of the aces would come through with the deciding goal.

At this juncture there was a delay while attaches cleaned the ice which was flooded with debris thrown by fans angry at fancied grievances against the referees. Players took advantage of the few minutes' lull to rest, sitting atop the rail boards.

Five minutes to go in another period! Would it go that long?

YOUNG MEN WITH WEARY LEGS

The first lines go back to their act as fans applaud another change. They were not long and there was another change of men.

One minute to go in the period and the shock troops return. Ward drills a long shot but it skims by the corner of the net and the whistle blows the jittery puck-chasers into their eighth period.

A long shot by Aurie opened the eighth period of the game, following which Ward tore down the boards but was bottled up in a corner. Snaring a loose puck 10 feet out, Aurie made Chabot come out of his net for a beautiful save

and immediately afterward, Northcott was in on Normie Smith and the Detroit goalie matched Lorne's skill with another marvelous stop.

Breaking through, Wally Kilrea was on top of Chabot and only another brilliant save prevented a tally.

The half of another heat was gone when first lines reappeared, but they were a well-spent aggregation of young men trying nobly to chase pucks with weary legs after more than two solid hours of hockey.

In a mixup around the Detroit cage, Northcott was accidentally struck over the head and laid on the ice until helped to his feet when he skated to the bench.

Three minutes to go in another period.

Two more marvelous saves by Normie Smith robbed Lamb and Gracie at the goal mouth just before another switch of players which brought back the top line with Northcott wearing a patch over his eye.

Ward almost jammed in the winning goal in a scramble at the corner of the net just before the bell.

With leg weary players all ready to drop in their tracks. The ninth period opened slowly in which was added a spark when Aurie drilled a hard shot just before the customary change in forwards.

Jamming the puck at the corner of the net Pettinger almost scored about the time the clock was spelling out a new world record for the length of a game.

The rushes got slower and slower and players fell without being checked. Catching the Detroit forwards in Maroon territory, Evans and Ward rushed. The latter all but scored, and when play moved in the other end Lewis forced Chabot to skate far out to save.

Five Maroons were hurled into the Red Wings' zone and gave Normie Smith lively seconds just before Bruneteau broke up the game.

A Record

DETROIT		MONTREAL
Smith	G.	Chabot
Young	R.D.	Wentworth
McDonald	L.D.	Evans
Barry	.C.	Smith
Aurie	R.W.	Ward
Lewis	L.W	Northcott

Scoring:

First Period: Scoring—None.

Penalty—McDonald, Trottier, Shields.

Goal Saves—Smith 8, Chabot 9.

Second Period: Scoring—None.

Penalty—H.Kilrea, Ward, Barry, McDonald.

Goal Saves—Smith 12, Chabot 12.

Third Period: Scoring—None.

Penalty—W.Kilrea.

Goal Saves—Smith 15, Chabot 8.

First Overtime: Scoring—None.

Penalty—None.

Goal Saves—Smith 5, Chabot 5.

Second Overtime: Scoring—None.

Penalty—None.

Goal Saves—Smith 10, Chabot 6.

Third Overtime: Scoring—None.

Penalty—None.

Goal Saves—Smith 13, Chabot 7.

Fourth Overtime: Scoring—None.

Penalty—Smith.

Goal Saves—Smith 13, Chabot 5.

Fifth Overtime: Scoring—None.

Penalty—None.

Goal Saves—Smith 7, Chabot 6.

Sixth Overtime: Scoring—Bruneteau (H.Kilrea), 16:30.

Penalty—None.

Goal Saves—Smith 8, Chabot 6.

. . . .

*Authors Note: The box scores don't add up to the article. According to the box scores Normie Smith saved 91 shots and Lorne Chabot stopped 64. In the article it says Smith saved 75 and Chabot stopped 80. I have seen other inconsistencies from other sources as well, In the text I went with the article but the exact number may never be known.

HOW HEC KILREA PASSED TO 'MUD' BRUNETEAU FOR HISTORY-MAKING GOAL

1935–1936 NHL Stanley Cup Semi-Finals, Game 1: Detroit Red Wings at Montreal Maroons

Detroit Times, March 25th 1936 (Tues. 3/24/36)
(Reprinted with the permission of *The Detroit News.*)
Detroit Times editorial

Two teams had battled for almost three hours. There seemed no chance for a score. Each trip up and down the ice saw the teams becoming more tired. It seemed that somehow a halt must be called.

Then all at once it was over. In a twinkling of an eye the end came. The third line was on the ice. The sixth overtime period was drawing to a close. Hec Kilrea, Mud Bruneteau and Wally Kilrea were on the ice. The Maroons using a power play. They wanted to end it. The thought of another short rest and then more work on the ice was not pleasant.

Three Maroons were inside the Red Wings blue line. Normie Smith, the sensation of his first playoff game was turning back shot after shot.

All at once out of a crowd of Maroons came Hec Kilrea carrying the puck. He stick-handled his way down the ice with Mud Bruneteau. At the defense he swung sharply to the left and passed both defensemen. Lorne Chabot, the goalie that was ticketed for the minors not many weeks ago, was ready for the attack. He moved over to block any attempt Hec Kilrea might make. Then right at the mouth of the goal Hec passed to Mud who lifted the puck gently past the disappointed goalie.

For a minute all were too tired to realize what happened. Then a lone red light flashed over the net and the first game of the playoffs was over.

The Red Wings were wild with joy over a great victory despite the fact it took three hours to accomplish. It was the Wings first victory over the Maroons on their home ice.

There was plenty of credit for every member of the team after this morning's brilliant victory. Tired as they were there was no compromise. The Red Wings wanted to win. The defense work of Goodfellow, McDonald, Bowman and Young won the praise of a hostile crowd. The forward lines skated until it seemed they couldn't skate another foot. A short rest and then they were back on the ice.

The Maroons put up a brilliant battle and there was little to choose between the two clubs.

Example of *Detroit Times* article.
—*Detroit Times* photo/Courtesy of *The Detroit News*

BIG THIRD PERIOD
GIVES DETROIT 2ND IN A ROW

1935–1936 NHL STANLEY CUP SEMI-FINALS, GAME 2:
DETROIT RED WINGS AT MONTREAL MAROONS

Detroit Times, March 27th 1936 (Thurs. 3/26/36)
(Reprinted with the permission of *The Detroit News.*)
By Leo Macdonell

Jubilant, the glamorous Red Wings were home today needing only one more victory over Maroons to clinch the National League championship and continue on in their gallant fight for the Stanley Cup.

Brilliant on attack and impregnable on defense, Red Wings in Montreal last night shut out Maroons, 3–0, the Detroiters' second shutout victory on Forum ice where heretofore this season they failed to win a game over the team that won top honors in the International division.

Turning back Maroon in another marvelous exhibition of goal tending, the amazing Normie Smith ran his string of 12 consecutive periods in which he batted and kicked out every puck fired at him by desperate Montreal players.

Never in modern hockey had Montreal fans witnessed such brilliance in sustained net minding, and the smiling blonde goalie from Detroit, once a Maroon player himself, was accorded a demonstration as the dropped on the final game of the series to be played on local ice.

Enthralled by Smith's superman display in the nets, fans were comparing him to the great Georges Vezina, generally rated greatest of all goalies and revered here.

With the shifting of the scene all remaining games with Maroons will be played in Olympia, startling Sunday night.

Three Detroit marksmen shared with Smith honors in the team's second triumph of the series with goals that were fashioned in the final period.

Syd Howe and Herbie Lewis produced two of them in sensational manner. That by Howe came midway in the heat with the aid of Johnny Sorrell, the former swinging down the middle of the ice bore his way through Stewart Evans and Cy Wentworth to finish beautifully by flipping the puck safely past the helpless Lorne Chabot.

LEWIS GETS A SOLO

The goal by Lewis was a solo and even more spectacular. With Maroons trapped in the Detroit zone, Larry Aurie and Lewis broke away all alone.

Just after they had crossed the blue line Aurie fell to the ice, leaving Lewis to go on alone, which he did in a dramatic manner. As the charging Lewis neared Chabot, the Maroon goalie, with a great lunge, dived out to block the shot.

As he came Lewis stopped suddenly, still clinging to the puck, whirled around and came back a second time to punch home the rubber with the big Montreal goaltender far out and leaving behind a yawning net.

It was one of the coolest bits of play that oldtimers here remember.

Then with less than a minute to go, Aurie scored with the assistance of Marty Barry and Lewis. While not so theatrical as the others the play was as effective. Chabot got a piece of the rubber but it dropped to the line and bounced inside.

THIRD LINES START

A surprise was handed the big crowd when both third lines took the ice for the opening faceoff of the game, and they were on only seconds when Chabot almost let Wally Kilrea's backhanded shot get away from goal.

From the start there was action with Maroons in a do or die spirit hurling four-man rushes into Detroit territory and as they did McDonald was penalized for charging Marker.

With this advantage [the] Maroons increased the heat. Montreal's first lines going into action. On the first rush Ward narrowly missed a goal.

Trapping Maroons in Red Wing territory, Goodfellow rushed and drilled a terrific shot that all but drove Chabot to the back of the net.

As Goodfellow came back he was elbowed in the face by Conacher.

With a change in lines Hec Kilrea broke away and raced in fast from right wing and made Chabot come far out of his net to smother a shot.

When more new faces appeared on the ice, Blinco weaved his way smartly through the Detroit defense for a shot that made Normie Smith stretch across to the corner of the cage in a swell stop.

PILUP—NO GOAL

Again the Maroons rushed and Evans was in for a shot at close range. Smithy again taking care of the shot. There was a pileup at the mouth of Detroit's goal and the crowd roared, thinking Maroons had scored.

It was not a tally, however, and Stewart faced off the centers in a corner of the rink.

As play moved to the other end, Howe tore down left wing for an angle shot that boomed off Chabot's pads. Robinson carried it back and was stopped at the Red Wing blue line.

Snaring the puck in center ice Marker whirled and dashed across the line with the crowd yelling "come on Goose," but a hurried shot was wide of the net.

A few seconds later Marker was sent off for slashing Sorrell, old teammate at Detroit, and five Red Wing forwards pressed vigorously to convert the advantage.

Marker had hardly left the ice when Sorrell threatened with a shot from right wing and Howe's slow roller almost beat Chabot. Just before the Maroon player returned, Aurie almost clicked after stealing the puck from Evans.

Again the third lines were matched when the second period opened and the "greenies" put on great skating shows, but with no serious scoring threats.

Once Marker came flying down and was dumped hard by McDonald.

With a switch in players the famed first lines clashed and there was action galore with Maroons carrying the fight. As the pressed savagely, Ward broke through and blazed a shot from left wing, close in, and hit the post.

It was a close call for Goalie Smith.

LOTS OF BUMPING

In a flareup, Ward bounced Young heavily into the boards and McDonald spilled Hooley Smith hard. There were no penalties. More replacements and the battle carried on, recharging with heat.

With Goodfellow off for cross checking Marker, the Maroons enjoyed the first break of the period, and with it they hurled five-man rushes into the Detroit sector.

Breaking away in a spectacular sprint. Howe made a sensational dash in which he weaved around both Ward and Hooley Smith and was then tripped by Ward.

The trip prevented what appeared to be a score in the making, but no penalty box, the crowd poured debris on the ice and there was a brief delay while attaches cleared the ice.

WINGS GANG CHABOT

Four forwards and Goodfellow ganged in an effort to convert and Sorrell was in close for a shot, Chabot saving miraculously, and the skinny Detroiter falling into the cage.

This was the only threat during Ward's absence.

With a new deal in players, Cain batted Gracie's puck for what would have been a counter had not Normie Smith been alert.

When play shifted to the other end, Kelley took Wally Kilrea's pass for a hard shot at Chabot. Back and forth the play surged with much scrambling and few threats.

As Shields was banished for hooking Lewis, the Red Wings once again enjoyed an edge in man power and pressed with five forwards, but Montreal's defense stiffened and the Wings failed to cash in on their opportunity.

SHIELDS SHOOED OFF

When Shields was ordered off for tripping Howe, Maroons, protested vigorously. After the trip, Shields fell too, and remained on the ice as if hurt, but recovered enough to out a whoop when he learned he had been penalized.

The crowd joined him as he skated angrily to the bench.

As the Wings pressed their new advantage in manpower, Blinco broke away and passed to Evans, who drilled a blazing shot from left wing which Normie Smith kicked out beautifully.

The Red Wings didn't get a shot with Shields off. Shortly after this, the period ended.

As the marathon plunged into the third period, Norman Smith picked off Ward's shot at the corner of the net and Chabot bounced one off his broad shoulders on Lewis' drive.

The period was steaming up to boiling pitch when Stewart decided to call a halt and sent Barry and Ward to the cooler for roughing. Thus the battle continued with abbreviated lineups.

NORTHCOTT MISSES

Hooley Smith swept around left wing and Northcott came in fast off the other wing and just missed the Hooler's pass as he sizzled across at the feet of the anxious Normie Smith.

Cutting off a Red Wing pass in center ice, Conacher drove a long, hard shot that brought Normie Smith to his knees, following which Blinco rifled a shot that the Red Wing net minder batted away from the corner.

Trottier was penalized for slashing Hec Kilrea over the head as the tempers of the frantic Maroons flared and oncemore the scarlet-clad Detroiters had a big chance and five forwards were tossed on the ice by Adams.

This time the power play worked. Howe, starting a sensational rush from his own zone, carried over the blue line and squeezing between Evans and Wentworth rifled the puck high in the corner at Chabot's right, a beautiful achievement that claimed the admiration of disappointed Montreal fans.

Sorrell earned an assist on the play and himself almost scored before Montreal was at full strength again as the Wings unfolded an amazing team passing try for another tally.

MAROONS DESPERATE

With seven minutes of the period left to play, the desperate Maroons threw five forwards on the field of battle.

Breaking away, Lewis and Bruneteau teamed prettily. Bruneteau came in off right wing alone but missed the net, and as the play surged to the Detroit sector Bruneteau was boarded and hurt and left the ice.

There were four minutes left when Bowman was ruled off for charging into Blinco and with it came Maroons'-great chance to tie.

In quick succession, Hooley Smith and Blinco drove menacing shots at Normie Smith, the Detroiter making remarkable saves that brought acclaim from the local fans.

Then came Lewis' brilliant goal and in the last minute the one by Aurie.

The Lineups:

DETROIT		MONTREAL
Smith	G.	Chabot
Young	R.D.	Wentworth
McDonald	L.D.	Evans
Barry	C.	Smith
Aurie	R.W	Ward
Lewis	L.W	Northcott

Scoring:

FIRST PERIOD:	Scoring—None.
	Penalty—McDonald, Marker, Shields.
	Goal Saves—Smith 9, Chabot 8.
SECOND PERIOD:	Scoring—None.
	Penalty—Goodfellow, Ward, Shields.
	Goal Saves—Smith 9, Chabot 10.
THIRD PERIOD:	Scoring—Howe (Sorrell) 9:48, Lewis 18:58, Aurie (Barry, Lewis) 19:20.
	Penalty—Barry, Trottier, Bowman, Ward.
	Goal Saves—Smith 13, Chabot 11.

BOWMAN'S GOAL BEATS
MAROON TEAM, 2–1

1935–1936 NHL Stanley Cup Semi-Finals, Game 3:
Detroit Red Wings vs. Montreal Maroons

Detroit Times, March 30th 1936 (Sun. 3/29/36)
(Reprinted with the permission of *The Detroit News.*)
By Leo Macdonell

National Hockey League champions!

Smashing their way to a tremendous victory over Montreal Maroons, 2 to 1, and climaxing an outstanding three game sweep that rocked the hockey world, the Red Wings today had added new honors to the long list of Detroit conquests in sports.

By their great victory in Olympia last night in the presence of more than 12,000 delirious puck pounding fans, the cyclonic Red Wings took their place alongside the Tigers of baseball—the Lions of football—Joe Louis of the prize ring—Gar Wood of the motorboat lanes—and other winners.

Now, pointed for the Stanley Cup in the world's hockey championship finals, the Red Wings rest on their laurels to date, awaiting eagerly the outcome of the series between the Toronto Maple Leafs and New York Americans.

It will be one or the other of these teams that furnishes the opposition in what promises to be the greatest of all hockey championship matches.

Beating Maroons in the third and final game of hockey's most remarkable series, the Red Wings roared down the ice lanes at Olympia to their second league championship, matching the achievement of two years ago when they defeated the Maple Leafs.

WINGS REPEAT UPSET
VICTORY SCORED 2 YEARS AGO
OVER LEAFS

Victory over the Maple Leafs in that memorable series, like that over Maroons, was an upset. In each instance Jack Adams' gallant ice athletes tore the dope apart.

It was fate that picked Scotty Bowman out of the galaxy of Red Wing stars to make the winning goal. The hard luck guy of the Detroit club for a good share of the season, in the current se-

Ebbie Goodfellow.
—*Detroit Times* photo/
Courtesy of
The Detroit News

ries [he] hit his stride and in the third period last night Scotty clicked off the goal that did the business.

To make the achievement dramatic, he scored half lying and sitting on the ice, battling home a puck that he had snared from Marty Barry, who had relayed a pass from Larry Aurie.

Just the period before, Johnny Sorrell had scored his first goal of the series to match a score chalked up by Gus Marker in the opening period. Incidentally, Marker is a former Detroit player.

When Marker scored midway in the opening heat he snapped a great record which was being piled up by Normie Smith, whose sensational goal-minding sticks out as the greatest achievement in the series.

Up to Marker's goal, Smith had gone 243 minutes 32 seconds without being scored on in the three-game set, one game of which, of course, broke all records in going 176 minutes 30 seconds.

While Olympia has housed bigger crowds, the game last night set a new record for total receipts in $31,665.50, due of course, to the increase in prices.

MAROONS MOB SMITH AND
SHOWER HIM WITH
CONGRATULATIONS

As Red Wings skated off the ice winners of their second league championship, wild scenes prevailed last night, a deluge of debris flooding the ice.

While Maroons rushed here and there on the ice to congratulate their rivals, the huge crowd stood in the seats—men roaring and women shrieking their joy.

Normie Smith was fairly swamped with Maroons who raced toward the Detroit goal to slap his back and shake his hand. His brilliant work in the nets in the three games was more popular, perhaps, with an opposing team than the victory of any goalie in history. His is a former Maroon player and popular with the Montreal players.

The warmest greeting he received was from Lorne Chabot, Montreal goalie, who like Smith turned in one of the greatest performances any man ever has achieved in the nets. The Smith-Chabot duel in the marathon game in Montreal has gone down in hockey history as the most titanic of all net-minding struggles.

With all that was at stake, the game was remarkably clean—the cleanest game ever played in a playoff, perhaps. But two penalties were called, one on Peter Kelley in the first period and the other on Joe Lamb in the second. There was none in the final stanza.

LIONEL CONACHER FIRES LONG ONE AT DETROIT NET BUT SMITH SAVES

Seconds later Conacher rushed the puck into Detroit's territory for a long shot at the cage, only to have Smith make the save.

The third lines were only seconds on the ice when Sorrell skated in fast for what looked like a goal. With the ice open between him and Chabot the fleet Johnny moved into scoring position and fired.

It looked a sure goal, but the big Maroon goalie, with catlike action surprising in a man to ponderous, slid far out for a sensational save.

The roar of the crowd sunk into a gasp and then a hand for the goalie's marvelous save.

Then came Marker's score, the first of the game and what eventually proved to be the only tally for the Maroons.

To score, Marker came feet down the middle of the ice to snare a pass from Gracie from off left wing and flipped the puck into the net high in a corner. He had Normie Smith helpless, moving in unguarded to feint the Detroit goalie to one side and slap home the puck.

The score came with a suddenness that stunned the Detroit fans who were congregated to witness a kill.

Immediately after Kelley was penalized for tripping the same Marker, but Detroit's defense stiffened and Maroons failed to get a shot on goal during the Red Wing player's absence.

MAROONS' GOAL PUTS ON THE HEAT AND LIVELY SKIRMISHING FOLLOWS

Maroons had scored the first big goal; the heat was on.

Flaming the two teams tore into each other like a pack of bulldogs meeting up with strange Airedales.

They tore into each other with a vengeance with no quarter asked. It was a fight to finish with no holds barred—as were the games in Montreal.

As players were changed, Barry, slickest of the stick-handlers, playing brilliant hockey but still trying for his first goal, skated in smartly and bounced the puck off Chabot's chest. Sweeping in behind, Goodfellow moved in like a tornado and almost scored with the rebound.

It was a close call for the Montreal net-minder and the fans dropped back limp in their seats.

Again Barry and Goodfellow rushed in another cyclonic swing down the ice that had the frenzied fans on their toes. They came in with tremendous strides, this time Barry almost clicking with Ebbie's pass that came skimming across the ice from right wing. The harassed Chabot had to move like lightning to save and it was a brilliant achievement.

The Montreal goalie had given another demonstration of workmanlike netminding.

Trapping Maroon forwards, Pettinger and Howe broke away on their way down the ice with a change in personnel. They had jut rushed the blue line when the gong sounded the end of the period.

SORRELL SWOOPS IN AND HIS SHOT ALMOST PRODUCES TYING SCORE

Trailing for the first time in the series, [the] Red Wings were fighting viciously with the opening of the second period. With the opening face-off they rushed with determination.

As they pressed Sorrell, lanky and fast, suddenly came soaring down left wing and fired wickedly to all but beat Chabot. It was a great save by the veteran.

Almost instantly, Chabot again faced another menacing movement in which Wally Kilrea provided the threat, skating in close for a shot that forced Chabot to turn quickly to his left to sweep the disc out of danger.

No ordinary goalie could have turned the trick.

The inspired Marker turned in the only other threat before there was a change in players, swooping in to all but click his second goal of the night.

Normie Smith smiled as he turned aside the threat.

With the first lines on the ice Lewis broke away and was in alone on Chabot, the Red Wings' biggest chance thus far and a sure tally had not the capable Chabot dived far out for another sensational stop.

Chabot rose to his feet slowly and dusted off his pad as the crowd gave him a hand. It was the achievement of a great goalie.

Off went the first lines and others took their places as the puck grind went around and around.

Would the Red Wings tie the score?

Was this their Waterloo. The fans were wondering. They had heard tales of great goings on up in Montreal. Were they to be in on the first defeat? There was a flareup!

DEMAND PENALTY AS CONACHER CROSS CHECKS BUCKO MCDONALD

The game started to boil and the crowd yelled for a penalty as Conacher, the veteran, cross-checked McDonald, the kid phenom. Players tumbled here and there on the ice and the delirious fans shrieked and roared.

It was another do-and-die vicious struggle between two great hockey teams.

Taking the disc from center ice Pettinger, poke-checking fool, swept in like a deer and almost beat Chabot in a play that brought another roar from the stands. Nerves jangled, the fans were screaming for a goal—screams that caused renewed efforts on the part of Red Wings, as eager for victory as the fans.

To continue the series meant nothing to the Red Wings—in money or any other way.

Here Trottier, hard-working Maroon, broke away and pounding his way down the ice rifled a shot that all but brought another Montreal score. Normie Smith saving magnificently.

Another storm of applause was loosened like the smashing of floodgates.

As the third lines skated off they were given a tremendous ovation by the crowd. A second or two later McDonald followed and he, too, was accorded tumultuous acclaim.

Fresh players took the ice—and steamed the already roaring contest to a mighty pitch. Each side attacked with increasing fury. Determined defenses turned back the rushes with equal fury.

Here came the great moment for the home team—and home fans.

Both teams were fighting viciously—when suddenly out of a scramble came Wally Kilrea, breaking away with flying feet and sweeping down left wing in a sensational dash.

Abreast of the flying Kilrea was Sorrell racing down middle ice.

Behind them they had left Maroons forwards. They were off for a goal!

Would they score?

Maroon defensemen and Chabot had turned back plays of a kind—many times before.

Kilrea was turned into a corner and Sorrell moved in the corner of the net. Out of the corner came the speeding puck, a beautiful pass and true to the mark. It was on Sorrell's stick and the next moment in the cage.

The score was tied and pandemonium broke loose. Fairly rocking the huge sports building, the crowd roared its joy in tremendous fashion.

As Lamb tripped Barry in center ice, the crowd yelled for a penalty, which was not forthcomming until [the] Red Wings lost possesion of the puck in accordance with the rules.

Four Detroit forwards combined with Goodfellow in the power play but as they ganged, their attacks met by a wily Montreal defense that turned back every assault. The Wings failed to get a shot during Lamb's incarceration.

AURIE RUSHED IT, BARRY PASSED AND BOWMAN COMPLETED THE JOB

Trying for a corner, Gracie boomed a shot off Smith's pads, a shot that resounded through the huge building. Then came Evans with two quick rushes and shots on Smith.

Desperate, the Maroons tossed everything they had into the conflict. And Ward, like Evans, threatened with a hard shot.

It was here where lightning struck—blotting out Montreal's chance to retain the Stanley Cup—as play proved eventually.

Bowman's goal was the clincher, coming in dramatic fashion as have most of the Detroit goals in the momentous series. Tumbling to the ice, Bowman was sitting when he batted home the puck that proved the winning goal.

Aurie had rushed the puck across Maroons' blue line

and passed to Barry, who in turn relayed the rubber to Bowman, who had come down the middle of the ice to join in the play.

It was Bowman's fourth goal of the season and the Detroit defenseman was accorded a great hand.

Maroons, now trailing, pressed like madmen. Trottier was in and almost scored and, trapping enemy players in the Detroit sector, Hec Kilrea twice broke away for shots, following which Howe, too, almost cashed in.

A change of players came and with it four and five-man rushes were hurled down the ice by the terror-stricken Maroons. Each second was tolling them out of the Stanley Cup playoffs.

Maroons were still fighting with their last drop of hockey blood, and in a scramble around the net. Near goals were made by Cain and Lamb, Normie Smith being forced to turn in Houdini saves.

As play surged to the other end, Sorrell drove wickedly from wing and just missed the corner of the net. And again Sorrell skated in fast with his lanky legs burning the ice. Again he was beaten by Chabot's fine save.

The first lines collided again midway in the final period and with each threat by the ace performers the hockey-nuts crowd let loose.

The fans screamed like mad when Ward broke through and was on his way for what looked like a certain Montreal goal, but Sorrell, ghost-like, swept in from the fog to poke the puck out of danger.

"Thanks, kid," Smith shouted at Sorrell.

Back up the ice the puck pounders roared and across the Montreal blue line swept the red-clad demons. Too eager, Lewis let fly the puck from Barry's pass and missed a half-open net.

Fleet Hec Kilrea, once winner of the National League skating championship, twice swept down in cyclonic stride. Maroon defensemen cut short his first dash. On the other Chabot smothered his shot.

CROWD PLEADS WITH RED WINGS TO HOLD OFF MAROON ATTACKS

"Hold 'em, Red Wings," the crowd begged.

These were history-making moments and desperate hockey players played desperate hockey. Sticks flew high and players tumbled over the ice.

Maroons, more desperate, tossed five forwards into the fray. It was their last chance.

Young and McDonald, who had done yeoman service, skated off the ice and new Detroit defensemen took their places.

The terrific struggle continued.

"Hold 'em, Red Wings!" The cry was chorused from one end of the rink to the other.

Marker came down fast but Gracie was offside and the whistle blew for a faceoff. Again Marker raced the rubber, but lobbed it into a corner. Gracie rushed in fast, reclaiming the disc and almost scoring.

"Hold 'em, Red Wings!" screamed the crowd.

It was like football Saturday at the University of Michigan Stadium.

Maroons rushed and in a jiffy Goodfellow had the puck. The big fellow rushed with long space-eating strides and shot a pass intended for Hec Kilrea. The pass was cut off.

Five Maroon forwards pressed savagely.

Four minutes to go!

The lines were changed and Wally Kilrea swept left wing and almost scored. Chabot made a marvelous save.

Three minutes to go!

Fresh troops to the front!

Five Montreal forwards battled Detroit's first line. They rushed and Goodfellow snared the puck and golfed it to the other end—and the great crowd gave a sigh of relief.

Two minutes to go!

Trapped, the Red Wings are left behind and Robinson almost scored. Boy, it was close! Only a miraculous save by Norman Smith averted a Montreal goal.

One minute to go!

"Hold 'em, Red Wings!" the crowd was still begging.

The teams were faced-off in a Detroit corner—too close to the Red Wing not to satisfy the nerve-frazzled customers.

Thirty seconds!

The puck is driven out of danger by Goodfellow.

Fifteen seconds!

Howe shoved the puck out of danger pas Blinco.

The bell!

BUCKO MCDONALD
FIRES FIRST SCORE HOME

1935–1936 NHL STANLEY CUP FINALS, GAME 1:
DETROIT RED WINGS VS. TORONTO MAPLE LEAFS

Detroit Times, April 6th 1936 (Sun. 4/5/36)
(Reprinted with the permission of *The Detroit News.*)
By Leo Macdonell

Striking early and with lightning effect, [the] Red Wings in Olympia last night swept to a smashing triumph over Toronto Maple Leafs, 3 to 1, thereby drawing first blood in the Stanley Cup finals—world series of hockey.

Brilliant on attack and hurling back the savage thrusts of frantic and always dangerous opposition, the inspired Red Wings soared to their fourth straight playoff victory attuned to the roars of 12,763 hysterical fans who witnessed the thrill-drenched spectacle.

Fate once again, as it did to Mud Bruneteau and Scotty Bowman in the series with Mntreal Maroons, touched its magic want to new members of Detroit's red-clad champions as the colorful Bucko McDonald, Syd Howe and Wally Kilrea turned in the goals that put the Wings one game to the good in the three-out-of-five series for the ice sport's greatest honor.

All scoring was crammed into the first period in eight minutes of blazing puck-pounding that had the great crowd plunged into wild excitement.

MCDONALD AND HOWE SCORE EARLY WITH DETROIT TEAM A MAN SHORT

The first goals scored by McDonald and Howe, came within a minute of each other with Larry Aurie off the ice on a tripping charge. The fascinating McDonald, demon of body-checkers turned into a scoring threat, accounted for his marker in a thrilling solo after he had snared the rubber in center ice, raced it into scoring position and fired deadly past the bewildered George Hainsworth, veteran of many championship campaigns.

The red light flashed McDonald's goal at 4 minutes and 53 seconds, with customers still being seated, and its blaze was the signal for a tremendous outburst from a hockey-mad crowd that came for thrills and got them early.

The roar of the crowd was still resounding through huge Olympia when Howe added the second tally, likewise a theatrical achievement in which Doug Young, captain of the Red Wings, collaborated.

Taking Young's pass in center ice, Howe dashed in from right wing and with beautiful stick handling beat the Toronto defense and fired the disc into the net on Hainsworth's short side. It was a beautiful bit of work, Howe not having more than a few inches space between the goalie's pads and the post through which to drill the shot.

The red light pitched the already delirious fans into another outburst, only in greater volume, the mammoth congregation as one leaping to its feet with men roaring and women shrieking.

WALLY KILREA SCORES THIRD ON PLAY STARTED BY BRUNETEAU

The building fairly shook with the demonstration, and Howe was all but squeezed to bits by joyful teammates.

And as the battle flamed with first one team and then the other surging down [the] ice in threats that kept the fans in a whirl came Wally Kilrea with the third Detroit counter which, like the others, was a spectacular deed.

And once again the crowd was plunged into hysteria, with the flashing of the light.

Young Bruneteau, who has played brilliantly in the play-offs and was the hero of the record game in Montreal, aided Kilrea in as smart hockey as has been seen on Olympia ice. Snaring the puck Bruneteau broke down center ice with Johnny Sorrell at his left and Kilrea at his right.

As they moved through center ice Bruneteau faked a pass to Sorrell, pushed the rubber skimming over the ice to Kilrea and Wally raced in to click.

Even Toronto's lone goal that came 10 seconds later and was scored by Buzz Boll failed to dampen the enthusiasm of the customers. Assisting in the Maple Leaf tally were Bill Thoms and Charley Conacher, the latter starting the play and Thoms relaying the pass.

Thus the score was 3 to 1 at the end of the period, at which it remained to the end of the breath-taking, hair-tingling contest in which the Leafs were whipped but went down fighting as gamesters do.

NORMIE SMITH AGAIN STANDS OUT IN WINGS' BRILLIANT DEFENSE

Storming the Detroit goal, [the] Maple Leafs in the in the second and third periods tried desperately to come level with the Red Wings but [the] Wings defense was too stout and refused to yield even to the pressure of four and five forwards at a time.

Again Normie Smith, sensation of the playoffs, was a shining light in the nets, batting and kicking out pucks in a manner phenomenal to add to his brilliant achievements against the Maroons.

When the glittering becapped blonde skated from his net at the end of three periods of magnificent goal-tending only two goals had been scored on him in four games, truly remarkable in high tension hockey.

With Smith all Red Wings shared honors in the glorious victory. Those who failed to get in on the point-making did yeomen service in checking the colorful Maple Leafs into defeat.

The game was remarkably free from penalties, considering all at stake, only three players being sent to the box. Besides Aurie's lapse in the opening period, Jack Shill and Red Horner of the Leafs were banished later in the game.

It was a grand exhibition throughout with plenty of thrills that whetted the appetite for the second big tussle which comes at the same arena Tuesday night. The third game will be played in Toronto Thursday.

To lanky Sorrell, the speedster, went the honor of driving the first shot on goal, a long poke from the blue line just after the opening whistle.

When play moved to the other end of the ice Art Jackson, younger brother of Busher Jackson, raced in from left wing at terrific speed and threw a great scare into the crowd when he nearly scored. After the shot the Toronto kid tumbled and skidded into the boards.

At first it was thought he might be hurt but he jumped quickly to his skates and was down the ice again.

With the first change of forward lines Detroit's crack first trio, including Barry, Lewis and Aurie, faced Primeau, Davidson and Busher Jackson.

They were on the ice but a short time when Aurie drew his penalty for tripping Red Horner, and four forwards and Andy Blair pressed to convert the advantage in manpower. It was an advantage with reverse English, with Detroit scoring.

Trapping Toronto players in the Detroit sector, McDonald scored, breaking away from center ice with Blair in hot pursuit. As Blair caught up to McDonald the Detroit youngster fired from about 15 feet out, catching the corner of the net at Hainsworth's left.

To count his marker Howe raked Young's pass in center ice, after the rubber had slid through Blair's legs, and raced down right wing. As he neared the cage he was met by a Toronto defenseman. Whirling prettily, Howe eluded the Leaf and moved in to find his mark, drilling the disc into the short side.

PETTINGER THREATENS AND THEN MR. FINNIGAN CAUSES BIG SCARE

A few seconds later tall Pettinger, whose stick-handling was a feature of the game, almost scored. Then came a threat by Finnigan, a Toronto member who plays good hockey but gets little ink in the newspapers.

Finnigan was in on Smith all alone and only a remarkable save by the Detroit goalkeeper prevented a Toronto goal. And twice more Finnigan had shots on goal before there was a change in players.

The crowd had hardly recovered from the first two goals when Wally Kilrea came through with his contribution to the victory. To score, Kilrea circled Horner with Bruneteau's pass and steamed the puck into the cage as Hainsworth looked on helplessly.

Boll's goal, seconds later, boomed off Smith's pads and dropped into the net.

Flushed with this success, Maple Leafs battled with renewed vigor but their challenges were met with stiff resistance on the part of a Detroit team that refused to give ice.

With two minutes of the period left to play, a revamped Toronto line that included Boll, Thoms and Conacher faced Detroit's first line. The change had hardly been made when Aurie forced Hainsworth to make a sensational stop.

Trailing two goals, [the] Maple Leafs attacked fiercely as the second period opened and a long blast by Art Jackson and a try by Kelly threatened. Seconds later Bruneteau was in alone with Wally Kilrea's slick pass, but Hainsworth dived far out of his coop to smother the shot.

With a switch in personnel Barry drilled a hard shot that made Hainsworth reach across the net to bat it away with his glove. Again Barry was in and this time the Toronto guardian almost fumbled the save into a goal at the corner of the net.

BOLL FIRES A ROUSING SHOT WHICH WORRIES RED WING GOALIE

With another change in lines Boll, always a threat, cannonaded a wicked shot off Smith's pads that all but took the breath away from the Detroit goalie. The noise of the impact resounded through the big building.

Hard and close checking prevailed as the teams roared up and down the ice. Once in a scramble in front of the Detroit net, Art Jackson just missed scoring for the Leafs. The boys were setting a fast pace.

Once again Detroit's first line was on the ice, this time facing Primeau, Shill and Conacher. Barry Aurie and Lewis teamed in a pretty swing, but Lewis' shot was wide of the net. As the teams surged to the other end of the rink Conacher roughed McDonald with his stick and the crowd roared disapproval.

Just after that incident Shill almost clicked and then was sent off for playing without a stick. With this break [the] Wings pressed with five forwards. As they did, Lewis nearly scored in a scramble in which half dozen players piled on one another at the mouth of the Toronto cage.

When they were unscrambled, the light flashed but Referee Stewart ruled no goal—the puck wasn't over the line when play was stopped—and there was a faceoff in a corner of the rink. The Wings did not threaten again during Shill's incarceration.

With three minutes left in the heat, Pettinger, Howe, and Hec Kilrea took the ice, matched with Thoms, Finnigan and Boll. The trios battled savagely with few scoring threats however.

A long shot by Aurie opened the third period following which Aurie and Barry were trapped in Toronto territory [while] Clancy and Primeau rushed the puck to the Detroit end. They were driven into a corner, however, by Detroit's defensemen.

Another change in players had been made when Horner steamed down the ice for a shot and seconds later Finnigan drove a wicked poke off right wing, Smith making a spectacular stop. Throwing four and five men into Red Wing territory, the Leaf's were attacking viciously.

HORNER'S THREAT IS FOLLOWED BY NEAR-CLASH WITH HOWE

In a scramble Horner once again threatened, Howe aiding Smith in guarding the net. Just after that the fiery redhead was banished for tripping Howe. Hot words were passed between Horner and Howe and Referee Smith stepped between the players.

The crowd let out a whoop as Horner skated to the penalty box.

With Toronto short-handed, the Wings pressed vigorously but the Maple Leafs stiffened and hurled back the attacks. Horner had just emerged from the coop when Wally Kilrea broke away with McDonald's pass and Hainsworth had to slide out fully 20 feet to prevent a score.

Pep Kelly broke away and was flying down right wing when caught from behind and checked by the speedy Bruneteau. In another rush, Harvey Jackson stickhandled brilliantly for a shot in front of the net, Smith turning in a sparkling save.

Five Leafs were laboring in Detroit's zone when Pettinger broke away with Conacher in pursuit. Hec Kilrea came tearing down the middle but Clancy cut off Pettinger's pass intended for Hec at the mouth of the net.

With replacements midway in the period, Horner was greeted with terrific booing as he returned to the ice.

YOUNG MAKES STIRRING DASH BUT BLAIR CHECKS HIM IN TIME

Young raced down the ice in a spectacular dash, but missed the net when checked by Blair, and when the ice pounders returned to the other end Art Jackson nearly scored with a shot at the corner of the cage. Sorrell broke away, but was run down by the same Jackson.

Tearing down left wing, Conacher rifled one of his bullet shots that made Smith move quickly. As Toronto tossed five men into their zone, Detroit players were compelled to golf the puck to lessen the tension.

As the game faded into its final moments, Thoms broke away with day's rebound off the boards and Smith saved nicely. Just before the final bell, Boll was in for a shot and Smith again sparkled.

WINGS HANG UP RECORD IN CRUSHING LEAFS

1935-1936 NHL STANLEY CUP FINALS, GAME 2: DETROIT RED WINGS VS. TORONTO MAPLE LEAFS

Detroit Times, April 8th 1936 (Tues. 4/7/36)
(Reprinted with the permission of *The Detroit News*.)
By Leo Macdonell

They were still digging Goalie George Hainsworth out of puck-flooded nets as triumphant Red Wings, pluming themselves, early today left for Toronto after crushing Maple Leafs, 9 to 4, to set new scoring records for modern hockey in the worst defeat ever handed a team in the Stanley Cup championship playoffs.

With the roars of 12,500 frenzied fans still pounding in their ears in the wake of their second straight victory in last night's amazing and blazing spectacle in Olympia, the Red Wings were on their way to the Canadian city for the third and what they hope will be the final game of the series.

One more victory will bring to Detroit its first Stanley Cup, and add to the city's long list another sport champion.

Victory tomorrow night would also complete an astounding sweep of six straight games and the world's hockey championship with a record of not having been beaten in the playoffs. It would add three games to three won over Maroons.

Incidentally, victory last night ran the flying Red Wings string of wins to seven, including victory over Blackhawks in winning the American sectional title and one over New York Americans in the final game of the regular season.

WINGS' SCORING ORGY SETS NEW RECORD IN PLAYOFFS

When the two teams in their unprecedented orgy last night turned Olympia into a mad house with 13 goals poured into the nets with machine-gun rapidity, a constant whistling of rubber bullets that had the bewildered Maple Leafs in a panic, they eclipsed what the same Toronto team previously had achieved in coming from behind to lick Boston in the current playoffs. The score in that game was 8 to 3.

Toronto also figured in the previous record total in a cup final, established when they twice turned back New York Rangers 6 to 4, three years ago.

Johnny Sorrell, lean and lanky money player with the sharp eye, combined two goals and two assists to lead the Red Wings in their wild scoring bee in which all but four members of the team accounted for one or more points.

At his heels were Marty Barry, who scored his first goal of the series and combined it with two assists for three points and Syd Howe, who got three assists.

With two goals each, Gordon Pettinger, another of the lean and lanky club, and the amazing Bucko McDonald were tied with Sorrell in the sniping department.

Others to score in the avalanche of goals that buried the helpless Hainsworth, veteran of veterans, were Wally Kilrea, again outstanding, and Herbie Lewis.

LEAFS PARCEL THEIR FOUR GOALS OUT ONE TO A MAN

Four Maple Leafs shared in a wide distribution of the visiting team's four goals, including Bill Thoms, Buzz Boll, Joe Primeau and Bob Davidson. As in the first game of the series the great Charley Conacher, greatest of shots, was held pointless.

While, comparatively, four goals seem big in the Detroit goalkeeper's sensational record in the playoffs, Normie Smith turned in another brilliant game in which he turned back the threats of four and five-man rushes that were hurled at him in quick succession as frantic Leafs left Hainsworth to his own resources to press for goals.

As against Maroons and in the first Toronto game, Smith starred, batting and kicking out goal-labeled shots that brought groans from the huge assemblage.

Striking early and cyclonic as they did in the first tussle between the two, [the] Red Wings flooded the Toronto net with three goals inside of 10 minutes and 5 seconds, plunging the throng into a hysteria from which it never recovered as goal after goal was exploded into the nets.

When Boll scored Toronto's first goal, the two teams had totaled four markers in 12 minutes and 15 seconds. 20 seconds less than the time used in accounting for four goals in the game Sunday.

MAPLE LEAFS' DEFENSE LEAKY

As Sorrell moved around like some will-o-the-wisp and the stick-handling Pettinger swung into action to combine their talents with other Red Wings, three tallies were tossed into the Toronto cavern as that team's leaky defense yielded to the pressure of a relentless Detroit attack.

Only a part of the scoring can be charged to Hainsworth. Only a super-goalie could have withstood those attacks without help other than a papier-mache front put up by his mates.

Blind fury was not enough to stop the smooth and polished red-clad whirling dervishes that made monkeys out of what was once regarded as hockey's greatest aggregation.

The spectacle of young McDonald, two years out of the amateurs, and the scrappy Wally Kilrea and others unknown until this season, pomping over and around the leafs, provided a treat of treats for those who witnessed the sight.

As the two teams plunged into battle at the opening whistle, Sorrell took the first shot on goal, a long blast which Hainsworth batted away from the corner.

It was Sorrell who took the next poke and on his rebound that Wally Kilrea scored to give the Red Wings a lead with less than two minutes played, the first of what was to prove to be an avalanche of goals.

To pave the way for this lightning bit of work, Sorrell raced down left wing and shot from the boards. Kilrea ssweeping in from nowhere and from eight feet out drilling the puck into the net at Hainsworth's left. The Toronto goalie was caught flat-footed, bewildered and standing rooted to one spot.

BOWMAN HELPED BARRY ON PLAY

It was less than three minutes later when Barry added the second counter, another blazing play that swept the Maple Leafs off their feet.

Bowman made the play. He rushed the puck down the middle of the ice and dropped it back to Barry, who

smartly tossed the rubber as Hainsworth came out of the net.

As the lines changed Hainsworth turned in a beautiful save that robbed Howe of a goal. And as the ice pounders moved to the other end Smith made two sensational saves on Blair, who was in close unguarded.

In another Toronto rush Davidson almost scored.

On his second appearance on the ice Sorrell again threatened, and just following, Clancy was penalized for holding Johnny. Five Red forwards pressed for more blood, which came soon after when Lewis picked the puck out of Hainsworth's lap to count on Sorrell's rebound.

And before Clancy got out of the box, Barry and Horner were sent to the box for tossing sticks into each other's faces. As the belligerents took their seats they were given a few words of advice by Referee Stewart.

With Barry and Clancy in the box, Boll scored for Toronto taking some of the joy out of the Detroit feast. Boll clicked midway in the period on a pass from Thoms in a beautiful play, knifing through Goodfellow and Bowman and beating Smith with an ice skimmer as Smith came out to save.

SMITH STOPS A FAST ONE

Throwing caution to the rafters, [the] Maple Leafs hurled tremendous rushes down the ice and kept Smithy bobbing from one side of the cage to another. Thoms almost scored and so did Finningan, the Detroit netminder saving spectacularly.

As the desperate Leafs came flying down the ice in a great rush, McDonald was banished for tripping Harvey Jackson. Enjoying its first big break, Toronto attacked furiously but without results. They were hurled back by Detroit's sturdy defense until Bucko came out.

From right wing Conacher rifled a bullet shot that made Smith go down fast to clear, and seconds later Thoms took Finnigan's pass and almost clicked.

McDonald had just returned to the ice and snared Hec Kilrea's pass when he scored Detroit's fourth tally. The two Wings broke away and McDonald skated in close and completely fooled Hainsworth, the puck whizzing through the veteran goalie's legs.

Just after, Horner sailed down right wing to the tune of a roar of boos and fired on goal from the boards, an easy save for the Red Wing net guardian.

As the second period opened, Primeau just missed a

loose puck on Smith's doorstep and when play surged to the Toronto end Lewis bounced a long shot at Hainsworth.

As the lines changed, Thoms and Boll had shots on goal, Smith just getting a piece of Thoms' high shot for the corner with his gloved hand. Hainsworth made an identical save seconds later on Bowman.

With Horner in the brig for the second time, Sorrell scored twice within a few seconds, but only the second one counted. On the first try the puck skidded into the net off Barry's leg and was disallowed by Stewart.

WINGS' FORWARDS PLAY BRILLIANTLY

Then came another, this one legitimate, in a brilliant team play in which Howe and Barry figured. The play was started by Barry, who passed to Howe, the latter relaying the disc to Sorrell. The latter pivoted and flicked the rubber into the net back-handed. It was a glittering play that brought new roars from the crowd.

Just after Horner was released, Pettinger added Detroit's sixth marker of the night, less than two minutes after Sorrell's goal. Trapping Maple Leafs in the Toronto zone, Young broke away with the puck, rushed it into the enemy's sector and shot it over to Howe. The latter overskated and dropped the puck to Pettinger, who swooped in from right wing to score, amid tumultuous cheering.

When he cross-checked Aurie, Shill was thumbed off the ice and again the Maple Leafs were in desperate starts, with the goal-hungry Wings clawing for more gore.

Trailing five goals, the Maple Leafs attempted little in the way of defense and Finnigan raced in for a shot. A little later, Boll, in all alone, was robbed by Smith in a dramatic save by the Detroit goalie.

With Shill out, Horner almost scored with Primeau's rebound.

At 14 minutes, Primeau took Shill's pass at the mouth of the goal and scored, a pretty play, to slice Detroit's big lead by a point.

Two rushes to the Toronto end with Sorrell and Wally Kilrea almost clicking, and seconds later Davidson was sent off for tripping McDonald.

HEC AND PETE BOTH THREATEN

With this edge in manpower, the Red Wings attacked furiously, using four forwards and Young. In a scramble in front of Hec Kilrea nearly counted. And with Davidson still in the box players were changed and Kelley just missed a Red Wing marker.

Out of the box, Davidson, unnoticed, swept down right wing and was in all alone for what looked like a Toronto goal but Smith saved on another marvelous play, sliding out far to smother the shot.

Four and five-man rushes were thrown into the Detroit zone as the frantic Leafs pressed and pressed, providing the unusual sight of 11 players, for minutes at a time, crowded into one end zone.

With one minute of the period left, Red Wings changed lines and Pettinger, Howe and Hec Kilrea took the ice. They faced Thoms, Boll and Conacher. Toronto's three outstanding players combined for the first time in the game.

Tearing down left wing at break-neck speed, Boll fired the first shot on goal in the third heat, a cannon shot that Smithy bounced off his chest.

There was a change in lines before Red Wings turned in a shot on goal. When it came it was off Lewis' stick, a comparatively easy save.

AURIE AND BARRY ARE STOPPED

Just after that Aurie crashed through Toronto's defense and was in all alone, but Hainsworth came out of his net to make a nice stop.

Barry broke away, eluded three Toronto players and in center ice crossed from left to right wing. He swept in for a shot and Hainsworth almost lost the puck, which was headed for the top cornier on the near side.

And McDonald nearly scored with a terrific blast from the boards, Hainsworth getting his stick to the ice just in time. Horner tripped Lewis in center ice with Referee Smith watching but no penalty was called.

With another change in personnel came Detroit's seventh goal, a brilliant goal by Sorrell, with the assistance of Bruneteau and Wally Kilrea. Kilrea seized Bruneteau's pass in center ice, rushed the rubber over the line and after twisting himself through Horner and Blair, passed over to Johnny, who was coming in off left wing all alone.

As he swooped in on the harassed Hainsworth, Sorrell fired from about 15 feet out, finding the corner of the net.

Two minutes later Thoms scored from in front of the net in a play started by Davidson and in which Boll took part.

And a little over two minutes after that came Detroit's eighth tally when Hainsworth, coming out after a loose puck chased by Hec Kilrea, left an open net. As the pair raced for the rubber Pettinger came in fast and took Hec's pass to at the puck into the cavern before Hainsworth could scramble back.

Two fine saves by Smith robbed Blair and Shill, the one on Shill being a honey.

As lines changed, Aurie stick-handled prettily in front of the Toronto net to pave the way for another near score, and a moment later took Barry's pass for another peg at Hainsworth.

With four minutes to go, Davidson raced in and, picking up Finnigan's pass at the goal mouth, counted for Toronto's fourth marker, Harvey Johnson figuring in the play.

And later, McDonald tallied his second goal of the night. To score, Bucko, after filching the puck from Blair, raced in to shoot from 10 feet out. Hainsworth took a dive and the puck hopped over the goalie's legs.

RED WINGS		MAPLE LEAFS
Smith	G.	Chabot
Young	R.D.	Day
McDonald	L.D.	Clancy
W. Kilrea	C.	Davidson
Sorrell	R.W	H. Jackson
Bruneteau	L.W.	R.Kelly

ALTERNATES:	Red Wings—Goodfellow, Bowman, Barry, Lewis, Aurie, Pettinger, Howe, H.Kilrea, Kelley.
ALTERNATES:	Maple Leafs—Primeau, Shill, Conacher, Thoms, Boll, Finnigan, A. Jackson, Blair, Horner.
REFEREES:	Bill Stewart and A. G. Smith
FIRST PERIOD:	Scoring—W.Kilrea (Sorrell),1:30; Barry (Bowman), 4:25; Lewis (Sorrell, Barry, Aurie) 10:05; Boll (Thoms) 12:35; McDonald (H.Kilrea) 16:55. Penalties—Clancy (holding), Barry and Horner (high sticks), McDonald (tripping).
SECOND PERIOD:	Scoring—Sorrell (Howe,Barry),7:15; Pettinger (Howe, Young), 9:10; Primeau (Shill), 14:00. Penalties—Horner (tripping), Shill (cross-check), Davidson (tripping).
THIRD PERIOD:	Scoring—Sorrell (W.Kilrea, Bruneteau), 7:30; Thoms (Bolls, Davidson), 9:40; Pettinger (H. Kilrea), 12:50; Davidson (Finnigan, H. Jackson),16:10; McDonald, 17:15. Penalties—None.

STOPS BY GOALIES:				
Smith	10	9	10–29
Hainsworth	10	7	6–23

LEAFS TIE WITH THREE GOALS LATE IN THIRD AND BOLL WINS IN OVERTIME

1935–1936 NHL STANLEY CUP FINALS, GAME 3: DETROIT RED WINGS AT TORONTO MAPLE LEAFS

Detroit Times, April 10th 1936 (Thurs. 4/9/36)
(Reprinted with the permission of *The Detroit News.*)
By Leo Macdonell

TORONTO, April 10.—Forty-two seconds from the Stanley Cup!

The cherished hopes of 10 years were all but realized by the Red Wings here last night when in those few brief seconds, Fate, the Great Meddler, tossed in a last minute reprieve for [the] Toronto Maple Leafs.

And [the] Maple Leafs like the midnight express, came roaring out of the well known black of midnight in hockey's most stupendous, colossal and—well, just swell—finish to tie and go on and whip Detroit, 4 to 3, in overtime.

Just swell for some 14,000 hysterical Torontonians who rocked Maple Leaf Gardens like the Gardens have never before been rocked and left stunned a brave band of Detroit fans who saw nothing funny in the finish.

The story book ending crossed the dope and made bitter the entertainment for many of the Red Wing followers—though none of them gainsay that [the] Maple Leafs did not display great courage, and if courage rates over superior talent, [the] Leafs are more than entitled to the nod they got here last evening.

As a result, [the] Red Wings, their hopes for a brand new, shiny record for consecutive wins in Stanley Cup play blasted higher than one kite over another, must win from the Leafs Saturday if they hope to be out of the hockey trenches by Easter.

The Saturday battle will be on the same location with a fifth game if necessary, and Allah forbid, at Olympia in Detroit next week, come Tuesday.

BOLL SCORES WINNING GOAL IN 31 SECONDS OF EXTRA PERIOD

Frank Thorman Boll, known as "Buzz" and turned 26 as of March last, is the lad who turned things topsy turvy for the Red Wings, when in 31 seconds of overtime he rifled home the puck that spelled victory for Toronto and made wild with joy the great congregation.

Young Boll, the toast of Toronto today and a chap who hails from far away Saskatchewan province, scored with the help of Red Horner and Art Jackson.

It was redheaded Horner, who up to last evening had a low rating in Toronto hockey circles, who fed Boll the pass that turned the trick, Buzz shooting from about 15 feet out, and the puck steaming into the net low and at Normie Smith's right.

Smith was helpless.

To deadlock the count in the third period Toronto came from behind and scored three goals in eight minutes and six seconds of the fiercest offensive hockey seen in playoff games, a tremendous rally that wiped out what appeared to be sure victory for the Wings and a stranglehold on the trophy.

Two of the three goals

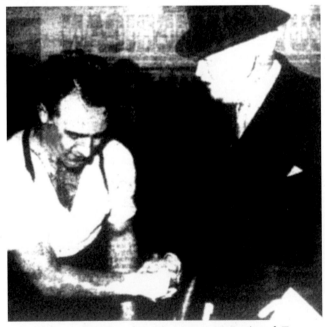

Pep Kelly shakes hands with Mayor McBride of Toronto after the Maple Leaf's "Miracle Win" in Game 3.
—*Detroit Times* photo/Courtesy of *The Detroit News*

came off the stick of Regis (Pep) Kelly, young Toronto hero, inside of four minutes after Joe Primeau had broken the Toronto drought with another shutout victory seemingly in sight for Smith, Detroit's goalie, and still great in defeat.

NORMIE SMITH HAS 22 SAVES DURING STORMY THIRD SESSION

In that blazing third period, Smith was sprayed with 22 shots that he stopped, most of them difficult and forcing Normie to rise to great heights to ward off defeat earlier in the heat.

Kelly's tying goal in the fading seconds of the third period was achieved with the help of Joe Primeau, a veteran who came into his rights last night.

A couple of minutes before Primeau had clicked with the help of Bob Davidson, Harvey Jackson and Horner.

To Scotty Bowman, playing in his home town, went the honor of scoring the first Detroit tally, incidentally the finest scoring achievement of the night. It came midway in the opening period with the assistance of Gordon Pettinger.

Mud Bruneteau's second Detroit goal was notched in the early part of the second period and was one of those freakish things in which the young Detroit star shot from center ice and the puck bounced crazily and careened into the net off George Hainsworth's stick.

Syd Howe, aided by Pettinger and Wally Kilrea, accounted for the third Red Wing goal after the mid-mark was passed in the third period and the Detroiters had apparently swept up the contest.

SORRELL GETS FIRST SHOT ON GOAL AS RIVALS BEGIN THEIR BATTLE

A long hard shot from off-left wing by Sorrell that banged off Hainsworth's stick inaugurated the battle after Referee Stewart had sounded the opening whistle.

Thoms retaliated with a drive on Smith after taking Finnigan's pass as play surged to the other end. When they pounded back to Toronto territory Bruneteau whacked a drive off Hainsworth's pads.

The game flamed as the Detroit first line of Barry, Lewis and Aurie took the ice, facing Primeau, Davidson, and Conacher. Barry and Lewis rushed, but Herbie's shot was wide of the net.

McDonald rushed spectacularly, spilling Clancy, but was chased into a corner. With a Toronto rush Primeau poked a long shot was wide of the net.

At this juncture, Goodfellow and Bowman replaced Young and McDonald. Lewis just missed Aurie's pass at the goal mouth and in a swing around right wing at the other end of the ice Davidson blasted a terrific shot on which Smith made a great save.

The crowd roared as Horner spilled Goodfellow at the Toronto blue line just after there was a new change of forward lines. And shortly after Kelly made Smith go to his knees.

Midway in the period came Bowman's goal that sent the Red Wings off to flying lead. Taking Pettinger's pass in the Detroit sector, where Toronto forwards were trapped, Bowman paved the way for his marker with a sensational dash down the ice after eluding Blair, who came out to meet him.

As Bowman swung in from left wing he stick-handled in beautifully, feinted Hainsworth out of the cage and drilled the puck in behind the hapless Maple Leaf goalie, a smart piece of work for the Toronto born Detroit player.

A moment later Finnigan drilled a hard shot that to the crowd looked to be in the net, and there was a demonstration in the stands. The disc, however, was caught in the twine on the outside of the net and the roars died out instantly.

CONACHER HUMILIATED

With the crowd's cheers in his ears Conacher started one of his spectacular drives only to be humiliated by having Barry steal the puck from him at the Toronto player's own blue line.

Davidson and Lewis collided in a corner and tumbled to the ice as the fans jumped to their feet sensing a scrap which didn't materialize. Blair brought them to their pins again when he almost scored with a great drive from right wing. Smith had to move fast to make the save, a nice bit of work on the part of the Detroit net minder.

Three minutes of the period were left when, with another switch in players, Smith saved sensationally on Finnigan, stretching his right leg far to the corner to kick out the threatening rubber.

As the two players fell to the ice, Conacher piled on top and Lewis the butt end of his stick on top of the head as Toronto fans looked on incredulously.

The starting lineups again faced each other as the teams plunged into the second period and were not long on the ice when Sorrell fired from the side boards for a shot on goal.

BRUNETEAU'S FREAK SHOT

The period was only one minute and six seconds old, when Bruneteau scored Detroit's second goal with a freak shot that must have set some sort of a record for distance in a playoff final.

The shot, lifted from center ice, fully 10 feet in front of the Toronto blue line, bounced on its way to the net and as it did Hainsworth stepped out to stop what seemed to be an easy save. The rubber bounced and Hainsworth nicked only a piece of it and the disc was deflected into the net. The crowd was stunned.

When a little later Aurie shot another long shot the crowd clapped loudly in derision as Hiansworth saved. As play moved down the ice, Smith made brilliant stops on Harvey Jackson and Thoms. The latter looked to have a sure goal as he raked Clancy's pass at the mouth of the net.

McDonald rushed in a dramatic dash, but his long shot from just inside the blue line was wide. Hainsworth, goat of the series, was accorded an acclaim when he saved miraculously in robbing Sorrell of a goal after the Detroiter had rifled a vicious drive from the boards. The force of the shot drove the Toronto goalie to the ice, where he sprawled.

Just after the lines were changed, Barry rushed, only to be checked at the blue line. On a second try, Marty dropped a long and easy save in Hainsworth's lap.

LEAFS'S RUSHES ARE CHECKED

Red Wings checked close and Toronto rushes were stopped and the puck iced out of danger, with the Red Clads seemingly waiting for breaks. As one came Aurie was in all alone with Barry's pass and Hainsworth was forced to dive out far to smother the shot.

Then trapping the Detroit forwards, Horner rushed for a shot at Smith. Wally Kilrea swept around left wing for a shot which Hainsworth again came far out to save.

Bowman snared a loose puck in his own zone, stick-handled around Finnigan in center ice, raced down the boards to move around Conacher smartly and sneak his way to the front of the cage for a shot which Hainsworth speared.

In the next Detroit rush, Barry raced in from right wing for another threat that made the harassed Hainsworth move

quickly. When play shifted to the other end Art Jackson was in for a threat that Smith took care of nicely.

Sidestepping McDonald, Davidson circled the Detroit net and passed to Harvey Jackson, who was robbed by another spectacular Smith play. The rubber was headed for the corner of the cage when Normie deftly shot his left arm in the air to deflect the puck over the net.

As the puck missed Jackson pounded the ice angrily with his stick.

Shill moved in fast and dropped the puck at Smith's doorstep, but there was no help in sight and a grand opportunity was wasted. As the boys pounded to the other end of the ice, Goodfellow all but knocked over Hainsworth with one of his terrific cannon shots.

The players were scrambling in the Detroit end near the net as the bell sounded the end of the heat.

LEAFS GANG UP ON OUR NORMIE

Conacher was on the Toronto defense, paired with Day, as the teams came out for the third period. [The] five Leafs ganging in the Detroit zone almost scored. Smith turning in one of his grand saves. As the Leafs pressed Conacher fell and the crowd yelled for a penalty on Sorrell, but it was not forthcoming.

As McDonald broke away in center ice, he was held by Day, who was sent to the box for a penalty, and five Detroit forwards joined in the power play in a tremendous effort to add to the team's lead. With Toronto short-handed, Aurie took Howe's pass for a long and harmless shot from the blue line that Hainsworth stopped with his feet.

With Toronto short-handed, Aurie took Howe's pass for a long and harmless shot from the blue line that Hainsworth stopped with his feet.

Taking the puck from a faceoff in his own territory, Hec Kilrea rushed the length of the ice and after being dumped by Horner, recovered the puck and almost scored with a smoking shot from right wing.

Sweeping in from right wing, Sorrell was in all alone with Wally Kilrea's pass for what looked like a marker, but Hainsworth skated out and bounced the shot off his chest.

With a change in lines, Toronto hurled five men down the ice and there a wild scramble in which Smith batted out a half dozen Toronto shots in a spectacular manner. This was the home team's best effort of the night up to the time and the crowd roared its approval.

ALL TUMBLE INTO THE NET

Sorrell and Wally Kilrea teamed in a sensational rush with three Leafs in pursuit and as they neared the Toronto net, the puck skimmed into a corner and three players tumbled into the net with Hainsworth.

Just after that, McDonald was penalized for tripping Boll and the Maple Leafs enjoyed their first big chance of the night. Four forwards and Clancy ganged in an effort to break the Toronto drought.

Battling furiously, Leafs stormed Smith's cage with frequent scrambles in front of the net. Out of one of these Aurie golfed a puck to the Toronto end and when Clancy shot it back there was a faceoff at the Detroit blue line.

Snaring a loose puck inside the blue line, Conacher tore off a wicked shot that brought Smith to his knees. As the Detroit net guardian dropped Primeau swept in and almost clicked on the rebound.

The crowd was suffering agonizing moments as the frantic Leafs sought to score and Primeau almost counted, but McDonald came out of the coop before there was another threat.

Detroit's young defense star was hardly on the ice when Howe batted home Pettinger's pass to give the Wings a 3–0 lead. Pettinger started the play, racing around. Blair with Wally Kilrea getting into the play.

HARVEY JACKSON NEARLY TALLIES

Harvey Jackson stick-handled his way through Detroit's defense and whipped a hard shot from about 15 feet out, Smith turning the rubber aside with his shoulder in a fast move. It was close to a goal.

Throwing all Leafs but Hainsworth into the Detroit area, the trailing Toronto clan pressed savagely until finally they broke the ice, Primeau scoring from in front of the net after Davidson passed out from the boards in the wake of a rush by Horner.

Flushed with this success, the inspired Leafs increased the fury of their attack, abandoning all defense. Five minutes to go and Kelly rushed spectacularly down right wing with Finnigan's pass to rifle a sizzling shot that found its mark hard in the corner at Smith's right for a Toronto goal. Smith didn't have a chance on the shot.

The goal plunged the great crowd into a wild demonstration. Goodfellow broke away trailed by Harvey Jackson, who cut off Ebbie's pass and as play returned to the other end, Davidson burned a shot off Smith's pads.

The Reds and Blues scrambled around the net and Smith bobbed from one side to the other like a jackrabbit. From the blue line came a burning shot off Conacher's stick. Smith turned in a magnificent save.

Two minutes to go and Finnigan rushed down right wing and was stopped at the blue line. Maple Leafs game to the end, pressed the fight.

There was an offside near the Detroit blue line and McDonald golfed the puck. [The] Leafs rushed, but the rush was spent near the blue line.

OFF GOES ROOF AS KELLY SCORES

One minute to go, Young smothered Conacher's try as the seconds were tolled off by the Garden clock.

Forty two seconds to go—and the roof came off the building as Kelly scored to tie the count. The goal came on a faceoff in which Primeau won the draw and Kelly snared his mate's puck and jammed it inside of Smith at the corner of the net.

Thirsting for more goals, the Leafs pounded away at Smith and just before the game was plunged into overtime the Detroit goalie kicked and batted away goal ticketed shots by Conacher and Kelly.

HOW RED WINGS
BEAT TORONTO TO WIN CUP

1935–1936 NHL STANLEY CUP FINALS, GAME 4:
DETROIT RED WINGS AT TORONTO MAPLE LEAFS

Detroit Times, April 12th 1936 (Sat. 4/11/36)
(Reprinted with the permission of *The Detroit News.*)
By Leo Macdonell

TORONTO, Ont., April 11.—The Holy Grail at last.

The Red Wings tonight, after a wait of 10 years, were the champions of all hockey.

Beating Toronto Maple Leafs, 3–2, before 14,728 fans, the largest crowd in Maple Leafs' Garden this season, in a blazing and hard-fought game, the Red Wings captured their first Stanley Cup and added another high honor to the long list of sport titles boasted by the Dynamic City.

When they defeated [the] Maple Leafs here, the Wings won the series three games to one and made unnecessary a fifty game in Detroit Tuesday.

The game was played before a roaring crowd of frenzied fans who in the fading moments of the thrilling contest pictured another grandstand finish similar to that in the first game here in which the Leafs turned in the miracle of the season.

WINGS COME FROM BEHIND AFTER
LEAFS SCORE FIRST

To win the game, a gang of Red Wings had to come from behind and overhaul a one-goal lead enjoyed by Toronto at the end of the first period. And in the final moments of the third period, Normie Smith again rose to supreme heights to ward off the terrific attacks of a frantic opposition.

Smith did it superbly—batting and kicking out pucks in uncanny fashion as the mammoth crowd roared and groaned with each threat and each stop. The "Blond Beauty of the Nets" came out of the series the standout.

Two Red Wings, who up to tonight had not scored a point, shared with Smith's greatness—Ebbie Goodfellow, the veteran, and Peter Cameron Kelly, the Detroit freshman. They scored two of the Stanley Cup champions' three goals.

Incidentally, it was Goodfellow who drove home the goal two years ago that beat the Maple Leafs and gave the Wings their first league championship in the fifth game in Detroit in that memorable series.

Marty Baarry tallied the other counter for the Wings to add to that smart young man's already fine record. Herbie Lewis, turning in one of his finest performances, aided in the markers clicked by Barry and Kelly.

Joe Primeau and Bill Thoms were the Toronto goal getters, the slick Primeau, outstanding among the Leafs, counting late in the opening period on a brilliant solo.

THREE BIG CHANCES

With Leafs off the ice, Detroit had three big chances in the opening heat and each time five forwards were thrown out onto the ice, but the power play refused to work.

But midway in the second heat came Goodfellow's goal, with the help of Johnny Sorrell, high point man of the playoffs for the Wings.

Forty-four seconds later, Barry counted to put the Red Wings in the lead, 2 to 1, which they held going into the final chapter, a period that was a blinger and kept the crowd in constant and tumultuous uproar.

But miracles don't happen twice in three days. [The] Red Wings wouldn't stand for it. They met rush with rush to earn victory brilliantly.

SECOND LINES START

The second lines, as in the other games, faced each other as the game swung into action. Pettinger, Howe and Hec Kilrea matched with Thoms, Boll and Finnigan.

With the first rush, Hec Kilrea swept down right wing and in on Hainsworth, but his shot missed the corner of the net, and in the next rush Horner was penalized for tripping Howe and Detroit enjoyed the first big chance.

Five Red Wings forwards were hurled onto the ice and

in the first attack Lewis was close in but missed the cage. As the Wings pressed, [the] Maple Leafs stiffened and Horner was out of the box before there was another threat.

With a change in lines, Primeau, Harvey Jackson and Conacher started together for the first time. They matched shots with Detroit's first line, Barry, Lewis and Aurie; and the tempo of the contest increased.

The change had hardly been made when big Conacher, like a great locomotive, steamed down the board and raced in close to almost score, throwing the huge crowd into its first thrill.

SMITH MOVES FAST

And a moment later Harvey Jackson tore down left wing and fired a wicked shot from the boards that made Normie Smith move fast.

As play moved into Toronto territory, Barry drilled a hard shot off Hainsworth's pads. As the third lines took the ice, Art Jackson and Kelly, trapping the Detroit forwards, rushed spectacularly. Kelly's shot missed the corner of the cage however. Boll rushed down the middle of the ice and was turned back at the blue line.

Just after, Blair broke through in a great spurt but offside was called.

Once more the first lines clashed and as they did, Lewis almost scored. As McDonald rushed for the first time in the game, the crowd roared as he was stopped by Clancy.

Young rushed the puck the length of the ice and drove a hard shot into Hainsworth's net and the red light flashed. But it was an offside play and the puck was called back.

Leaf and Red Wing aces battled furiously, but they were too well matched, and close checking held the threats to a minimum. Snaring the disc in center ice, Kelly raced down right wing and missed the net. Seconds later Day was sent off the ice for holding Wally Kilrea, and again five Detroit forwards ganged.

As the Wings pressed into the Toronto zone, Blair broke away all alone and tore off a terrific shot from just inside the blue line on which Smith turned in a remarkable save.

FANS SURPRISED

As Smith fell down after making the stop, the fans, believing the Toronto player had scored, let out a tremendous whoop, but the puck had skidded off Smith's stick into a corner of the rink. Davidson and Howe pushed one another around as the fans yelled, but their behavior was not serious enough to call for a penalty.

At this juncture came a goal by Primeau in a sensational rush from his own zone down right wing and scoring from off the wing, a wicked drive that whistled by Smith and almost tore the twine at the right of the Detroit goalie.

The goal pitched the mob into a great demonstration, which continued as the Toronto center skated off with a change of players.

RULED NO GOAL

A little later Pettinger scored in a scramble in front of the Toronto net, but it was ruled that the Detroit man had carried the puck into the net on a pass from Howe.

Then came another Toronto penalty—Harvey Jackson being banished for spilling Pettinger. The Toronto player was still languishing in the coop when the period ended.

Harvey Jackson, with only 49 seconds of his term to serve was out of the box before there was a scoring threat in the second period ended.

The period was only a minute old when Day fired a blistering shot that made Smith move fast, a pretty save. Red Wings pressed and Howe weaved in close for a shot which Hainsworth cleared with ease. Again the first line took the ice for another of their duels.

Barry rushed and was turned back by Blair. Lewis cut across the right wing with the disc and was chased into a corner, following which Conacher and Haarvey Jackson teamed for a rush. Conacher missed a drive from the boards. The big train followed with another dash and missed the corner of the net.

Aurie broke through and had a nice chance, but missed the net.

As the game flared, Conacher and Goodfellow mixed with fists and were separated by Referee A.G. Smith. They got only minor penalties.

Wally Kilrea joined them for tripping Boll, and Blair was added to the list when he dumped Young, filling the coop with four players. This left but three players on a side, other than the goalies.

BOLL MISSES

As Maple Leafs rushed, Boll almost scored, and immediately after Smith robbed Primeau on a beautiful save.

The rivals waged fierce war up and down the ice and in one of the rushes Primeau crashed into the net with Smith and was hurt. He left the ice under his own power but limped.

Smith had to be untangled from the side of the cage,

where his skates were caught in the twine. With both teams at full strength once more Thoms broke through but his shot was hurried and he missed the net.

They battled in center ice and snaring a loose puck Blair rushed over the blue line only to be turned aside by the Detroit defense. Art Jackson moved in fast and almost beat Goodfellow to a loose puck on Smith's doorstep.

EBBIE SCORES

Just after this, Goodfellow pounced on the puck in his own sector and raced it spectacularly down the ice where he lost it momentarily but Sorrell picked it up and passed to Goodfellow, who walked in on Blair and Horner to beat Hainsworth cold for Detroit's first goal.

Forty-four seconds later Barry accounted for the second Red Wing tally on a smart play in which he raked Lewis' pass and moved in from left wing to shove the rubber past Hainsworth on the far side.

From Detroit fans came loud roars as first one and then another goal was turned into the net to give the Wings the lead.

Howe just missed Pettinger's pass at the corner of the net as he swept in from nowhere and in the next Toronto rush Thoms broke through with a pass from Finnigan for what looked like a sure goal but Smith dove out in a great play to smother the shot.

Just after Smith came out to make another fine save, this time robbing Art Jackson, who drilled a burning shot from far out. Young and Sorrell rushed and Sorrell swept in from right wing, his shot missing the net. Harvey Jackson, stealing the puck from Aurie, circled the net and almost caught a corner for a goal.

In a great sprint Conacher moved around the net but as he did Goodfellow came fast across the ice to cut off a shot at Smith's right corner.

BOLL STOPPED

With the opening of the third period Howe blazed a long shot on goal, following which Clancy rushed the puck and was stopped at the Detroit blue line. Boll likewise was stopped there as he tried it and Thoms shot from the line, the puck whistling over smith's head.

Taking Clancy's pass in the Toronto area, Boll raced down the boards and swept around McDonald for a shot on goal, Smith making a nice save. This was Toronto's first shot on goal in the stanza.

To beat Howe and Pettinger on two more threats, Hainsworth was tested, moving fast to avert danger.

McDonald was in and threw a scare into the Toronto camp. Swirling around the net Conacher passed out to Primeau, who missed a beautiful chance to tie the score from 10 feet, the puck going over the net and hitting the screen.

Again Conacher and Primeau teamed and Smith stopped miraculously Primeau's steaming shot.

Clancy and Primeau rushed but they were checked. Goodfellow checked Harvey Jackson inside of [the] blue line. The two lines were given a big hand as they left the ice for replacements.

With the change, Finnigan came down with the puck but was stopped by Young. Trapping four Toronto players, Wally Kilrea was in on a shot. Thoms rifled Finnigan's pass, all but burning a hole in Smith's pads.

Kelly took Aurie's place on the line with Barry and Lewis, and the change had hardly been made when Kelly scored from in front of the net with Lewis' pass.

The goal was very apparent for the light did not flash. Stewart didn't miss it and the goal was counted over the protests of the Leafs. Just after, Clancy was in and Smithy saved. The desperate Maple Leafs rushed again and Primeau almost scored, Smith turning in a marvelous save, sitting down.

One minute and 12 seconds after Kelly's goal Thoms snared the puck in center ice, skated in like a bolt of lightning and fired from 15 feet out, the puck steaming past Smith knee high.

Sensing another finish like that in the first game here the crowd was in an uproar.

Frantically the Leafs fought to come level with the Wings. They fought viciously with each rush, fiercer than the one before. There was a temporary lull as the lines were changed.

Six minutes to go.

Primeau drove Smith to his knees. Young broke away with Barry's pass and was in on Hainsworth all alone only to lift the rubber over the top of the net.

Barry, too, swept away and missed a nice chance with nobody around him, Hainsworth coming far out of the net to save.

Five minutes to go.

Kelly missed the net with Art Jackson's pass. Young golfed the puck out of danger. McDonald tumbled Conacher to the ice in a vicious check.

Three minutes to go.

Howe rushed a shot and almost scored on a rebound. Hainsworth made two grand stops on Kelly and Wally Kilrea.

Two minutes to go.

Lines changed. Goodfellow iced the puck into Toronto territory.

One minute to go.

Toronto again changed players and renewed the attack. They batted in center ice.

Two seconds to go.

They faced off.

THE BELL!

ADAMS LISTS
HIGHLIGHTS OF WINGS' TRIUMPH

Tues. April 14th 1936, *Detroit Times*
(Reprinted with the permission of *The Detroit News*)
By Jack Adams

Manager of the Red Wings, World's Champion Hockey Team Leo Macdonell wanted a dozen highlights on the play of the Red Wings in their flight to the Stanley Championship. That's a tough order. I don't know of less than a million.

I am glad that I had some part in bringing another championship to Detroit to be listed with the great triumphs of Mickey Cochrane and his Tigers, Potsy Clark and the Lions and the others who have brought fame to the best city in the world.

But the following are my 12 biggest thrills of the series:

1. Modere Brunetreau's goal that won the long game against the Maroons. (First game in Montreal that went 176 minutes 30 seconds for a new record.)
2. Normie Smith's goal keeping.
3. Great showing of Wally Kilrea. (Kilrea, one of the new men, was brought up this year from [the] Olympics.)
4. Douglas Young's playing on defense in the Montreal Series.
5. Bucko McDonald's body checking in the first game in Montreal.
6. Herbie Lewis' marvelous checking of Charley Conacher of the Maple Leafs, who scored no goals and only one assist in the cup finals.
7. The goals made by Syd Howe and Herbie Lewis in the second game at Montreal.
8. Johnny Sorrell's consistently fine play.
9. The look on Mr. Norris' face (James Norris Sr.) when fans sang "He's a Jolly Good Fellow" in the Hotel Royal York after he received the cup from President Calder.
10. Young's cutting off of Thoms' perfect pass meant for Buzz Boll with his stick after a great dive in the first game with the Leafs. The entire complexion of the game might have been changed had that pass been completed.
11. McDonald's goal against Leafs in the first game of the final series. It was one of the prettiest scoring plays I ever saw.
12. First 10 minutes of the first and second games with Toronto.

Jack Adams (left) and Leo Macdonell legendary writer for the *Detroit Times*, talk during a Red Wings practice session.
—*Detroit Times* photo/Courtesy of *The Detroit News*

FURTHER READING

BOOKS

Enders, Eric. 100 Years of the World Series, Barnes and Noble Publishing, 2003.

Bak, Richard. Ty Cobb: His Tumultuous Life and Times; Taylor Publishing Company (Dallas, Texas), 1994.

*Incredible book about Cobb. Many of the short quotes about Cobb and his influences on Cochrane and Gehringer came from this book.

Bak, Richard. The Detroit Red Wings, the Illustrated History; Taylor Publishing Company (Dallas, Texas), 1997.

*This book is highly recommended for those seeking to understand the origins of the Detroit Red Wings in more detail.

Falls, Joe. The Detroit Tigers an Illustrated History; Walker & Company, (New York), 1989.

Falls, Joe. Baseball's Great Teams, Detroit Tigers; MacMillian Publishing Company, (New York), 1975.

Fischler, Stan and Shirley. The Great Book of Hockey; Publications International, (Illinois), 1996.

Fischler, Stan. Those Were The Days. Dodd, Mead & Co. 1976.

Hardy, Stephen. "Urbanization and the Rise of Sport" in Major Problems in American Sport History ed.: Steven A. Riess (Boston, 1997).

Levine, Lawrence W. (1977) in Chris Mcade. "Joe Louis as Emerging Race Hero in the 1930's" in Major Problems in American Sport History ed.: Steven A. Riess (Boston) 1997.

Margolick, David. Beyond Glory; Alfred A. Knopf (Random House), (New York), 2005.

*Margolick has done an incredible job in describing the origins of Joe Louis and his struggles against racial prejudices in 1930's America.

Murray, Mike (Editor), Albert, Tom (Photo Editor) Arthur, Dan (Researcher) Stumbo, Anita (Design and Typography). Lions Pride: Sixty Years of Detroit Lions Football; Taylor Publishing Company (Dallas, Texas), 1993.

Whittingham, Richard. What a Game They Played; Harper and Row Publishers, (New York), 1984.

ARTICLES

Jerry Green. "Motor City Memories: Oldest Former player Presnell recalls early days in Detroit," Herald-Dispatch (Gannett News Service).

Bob Greene. "Some Rays of Light in a Darkened World: Sports and the Jewish Community in Depression-Era Detroit," in Michigan Jewish History. Vol. 39 fall 1999.

Joe Grimm. "The next best thing to playing shortstop!;" in Chronicle, The Quarterly Magazine of the Historical Society of Michigan, Spring 1984, Vol.20, No.1.

Ring Magazine, 50 Greatest Heavyweights of All-Time, 1998.

Ring Magazine, 100 Hardest punchers of All-Time, 2003.

Tony Yanik. "1903—The Year That Made Detroit; in Chronicle, The Quarterly Magazine of the Historical Society of Michigan, Spring 1984, Vol.20, No.1.

Reach Official American Baseball Guide, 1936.

INTERNET RESOURCES

Brian DeCaussin. "Bengals Are Champions! A look back at the 1935 Detroit Tigers." Tigers Central, www.tigerscentral.com

Bill Dow. "Cochrane a good model for Pudge." Detroit Free Press, 2004, www.freep.com

Editorial, "How the Great Depression changed Detroit." Detroit News Online, www.detnews.com

Jenny Nolan. "The Brown Bomber—The Man Behind the Fist." Detroit News Online, www.detnews.com.

Doug Warren. "Lions, Bears and the First Thanksgiving," Lions Insiders. www.lionsfans.com (Aug. 2, 2003)

Patricia Zacharias. "Detroit, the City of Champions." Detroit News online, www.detnews.com.

Patricia Zacharias. "Schoolboy Rowe, the Tigers Southern Gentleman." Detroit News online, www.dctnews.com.

FOR GENERAL INFORMATION

www.DetroitTigers.com
www.ChicagoCubs.com
www.NHL.com
www.TorontoMapleLeafs.com
www.MontrealMaroons.com
www.DetroitLions.com
www.NewYorkGiants.com
www.RedWings.com
www.JoeLouis.com
www.MaxBaer.org
www.Wikipedia.com

NEWSPAPERS

Amsterdam News   *Detroit Times*
The Detroit News   *Kalamazoo Gazette*
Detroit Free Press   *New York Times*

NEWSPAPER WRITERS

Detroit Wire Service
  Earl Hilligan
Detroit Times
  Bud Shaver
  Bob Murphy
  Leo Macdonell
  Edgar Hayes
  John C. Manning
The Detroit News
  John E. McManis
  H.G. Salinger
  Harry Leduc
  Jack Cuddy

George Stark
Lloyd Northard
Fred Cousins
Detroit Free Press
  Doc Holst
New York Writers
  Paul Gallico
  Damon Runyon
  Jimmy Cannon
  Grantland Rice
New York Times
  John Drebinger

PERSONAL ACKNOWLEDGEMENTS

Even if I had a hundred golden tongues, and a hundred golden mouths with which to speak from, I wouldn't be able to thank all of the people in my life enough for their influences, friendships, love, and contributions. I follow the lead of my favorite poet and pray to the muses for help in attempting an impossible endeavor; that of thanking all those who have impacted me in my personal and professional life. I undertake this endeavor knowing full well that even with my greatest effort, I must fail. But I do so anyway, humbly and thankfully; first and foremost to God the creator, for his all embracing and ever-present touch. To my mother, Charlotte Burgett-Howell, my soul, greatest protector, tutor, and confidant, to her I owe my life. The Lord most assuredly blessed me with the gift of being born from a woman as wonderful as she. My Father next, Christopher Avison, for my life, for his protection during my most vulnerable age, and for teaching me to harness my passions instead of letting them consume me. Most similar are we, and through your tutelage have shown me the power of words and the importance of studying history. John Howell, my Dad. From the first moment you came into my life you taught me the values of truth, sincerity, integrity, and you taught me how to look the world and other men straight in the eye. Never once have you treated me as anything less than your son, and for all these reasons, I shall be eternally grateful. Connie Avison for her ever-present kindness and gentle disposition.

My brothers and sisters: Curtis Avison, Catherine Williams, Cameron Howell, Patrick Avison, Tiffany Avison, Ryan Stetler, and Charles Williams. My niece Jaiden, I love you all dearly, much more than words can describe.

I have been most fortunate for the family God has surrounded me with.

My Grandpa (Lawrence) and Grandma (Helen Virginia) Avison, the epitome of class and culture. My aunts and uncles: Judy Avison, Virginia (Ginger) Rank, Lance Avison and David Rank for all of your guidance and profound influence over the years,

Grandpa (Don) and Grandma (Joanne) Burgett, in a word, Love. In a world that tosses the word around haphazardly, they have demonstrated it in so many ways that a new definition is necessary. The current of love be-

tween these two extraordinary people is present in tangible form on the faces of all of their children, childrens children, and childrens children children. Including my aunts and uncles: Pam and Steve Bonner, Mary and Owen Baker, Don and Jane Burgett, Leslie and Trina Burgett, Tami and Dale Fite, Anna and Jim Randall. My cousins next, Scott and Jennifer Bonner, Brett and Tina Bonner, Therese and Dan Damman, (Scott, Brett, and Therese you were like the older brothers and sister that I never had and whether you know it or not, I have always looked up to you.) Brandon Baker, you're like a brother to me kid. Misty and Bill Hohmann, Don Jr. and Angela Burgett, Ben and Stacy Burgett, (Misty, Little Don, Ben, I loved every minute of the time we spent together as kids). Tori Fite, Hunter Fite, and Faith Fite, Taylor Randall, Blake Randall and Connor Randall, I love you all dearly. The same for the newest generation of my Grandpa and Grandma's children's children's children: Jessica Bonner, Eileen Bonner, Claire Mei-xing Bonner, Mason Lawson, Emily Lawson, Brett Bonner Jr., Gage Bonner, Nicole Burgett, Leslie Jr. Burgett, Jay Burgett, Danielle Burgett, Ricky Burgett, Wyatt Burgett, Elaina Henson, and Cora Sheffield. Billy Hohmann, Austin Hohmann, Emily Hohmann, Luke Burgett, Allison Burgett, Lillianna Burgett.

The Howell's. Strength, Pride, Honor. All are virtues common to this side of my family. Of the highest quality of people, My Grandpa Ken and Grandma Roz have set the bar high for their children and grandchildren. My aunts, Kay Howell, Koni Howell, and uncles Barry Howell, Kenny Howell, and Christopher Howell. My cousins, Jordan Howell, Adam Howell, Allison Howell, Kera Howell, and Colin Howell.

My Grandpa Paul and Grandma Joy Verhey for always treating me like one of their own, and their children, Dale and Carol Verhey, along with my cousin Nick Verhey.

I have also been blessed by God for the quantity and quality of people that I have met in my life. My memory escapes me from my early childhood but the Burch's, Brian and David were among my closest. In Kalamazoo, in the order we met, I thank you all: Kevin Bush, Ryan Bush, Mike Grella, Brad and Joey Giddings, Ryan Earwood, Rob Gray, David, Christa, Angie, and Linda Nitz, Rebecca Ender,

Jacob Ellis and his family, Jerry Woodfield and his family, Jeremy McReynolds, Little Mark, Coach Wesley, John Soisson Jr., Kevin Janssen, Nathan Diamond, Timothy Liggins, Ryan Daam, Austin Ward, David Birdsall, Meghan Fry, Collin Wilcoxin, Mike Hampton, Dallas Shannon, Jared Dellario, Jeff Gallagher, Vince Anderson, Todd Korabik, Greg Jefson, Melissa Osborn, Brian Roy, Adam Scheidt, Jeff Schettner, Stephanie Boltjes, Mike McMorrow, Father Mike Osborn, Father Brian, Kevin Downing, Frank Downey, Drew Girard, John (L.J.) Northrop, Troy Daily, Chad Spencer, Josie Smith, Mary and Bill Gephart, Jeremy (Rome) Gephart, Ryan (Peeps) Gephart, Jeremy Hunter, Russ Northrop, Michelle Northrop, Julie Northrop, Laurie and Jeff Howe, John Northrop Jr., Melissa Millard, Jenny Spencer, Amy Siminske, William Bush, Ivory Joe Stewart, Karen Dyskiewicz, Matt (oke) Grieser, Laura Hunter, Jennifer Earwood, Collin and Krista Daily. Bob "Sarge" Hunter. Rachel, Christine, Jason and Joe Dolhay. Alicia Kay. Gus, Josie, Patty and Maeleigh Cooke.

My Mackinac Island friends who have helped me to understand the world from the island perspective. My main man and fellow bon' vivant John Nash of whom enough good things cannot possibly be said. Vince and Dan O'Brien, Avi Ratica, John Kissane, Mike Buonocore, Eoghan Byrne, John Starzyk, Jesse Medina, Matt Yosten, Michelle Dean, Jim Eber, Tim Russell, Mary McGuire, Connor Quinlan, Peggy Siebrahnt, Louise Trembath, Gareth (Giggs) Bohan, Jimmy Cicala, Archie Horn, Justin Adams, Aidan Heeney, Tony (Heavy T) Doud, Claudia Garrett, Dan Burrell, Mike (Worm) Schirmer, Zelda Nash, Howard Samuels, Desroy Jones, Rohan Reid, Fitzroy,Glenroy, Gladstone Lynch, Harold Jonas, Gonzo Albornoz, Karl Roland Thalacker, and Slade Jones.

Kim Reilly has been one of the most influential women in my whole life. Enough cannot be said for her and her parents, Eileen and Terry. They have demonstrated a most uncommon amount of generosity even in a country that is known for its hospitality.

My Scottish pals next. A braver, prouder, more excellent race of people, God has never blessed the earth with, and I am lucky to be able to count several among them as my dearest of friends. Mike Fraser, Tony Carrigan, and Mikey Brown, for welcoming a strange Yank when you could just as easily have turned your backs. Jimmy (M Ol' Man) Patton, Blair Patton, Joe and Jerry (the sparks), Davy the spark, Andy and Liam Jack, Shugg, and Stephen Reilly. Tom, my main man at the Star and the best harmonica player on earth. My Edinburgh Wolves American Football family, especially: Doug and Kat Adamson,Don Edmondson, Craig (Chip) Lyall, Campbell Lewis, Alistair May, David Glendinning, Duncan Tanner, Darren (hightower) Robb, Gavin (it ain't livin if you ain't skydiving) Hume, Gordon (Goggs) Erskine, Ben Hutton, Stuart Galloway, Stuart Young, Deek Donaldson, Johnny Bannerman, Alex (Frenchie) Theys, Big Lee, Alan Price, Alan Melville, Kenny Mackay, James Collins, James (stiffler), David (Magic) Malloy, Jim Scott, Emile Reynolds, Kudzi Chidziva, Neil Warren, Salim Ahmed, Jamie Harkins, Stuart Niven, Colin Scott and Paul Jeffreys.

To the Silver Band Boys hunt club; May a silver banded arrow always find its mark.

To the following friends that I have met since moving back to Michigan; Angela Hohmann, Dan, Jean, and Jason Carolan; Aleshia Ritchie, Tim Ritchie, Eileen Browning, Paul Newbrough, Rhonda and Tim Morris, Jennifer Rader; Thank you.

Last but definitely not least. My Aunt Florence Thoms, Aunt Marie Zimmer, and Great Great Aunt Laura Burgett.

I undertook this acknowledgement knowing full well that it may take on the appearance of an extended Oscar speech and I hope the reader will forgive the length and know that it was purely an attempt to thank many of the people that have impacted my life.

PRODUCTION
ACKNOWLEDGEMENTS

A great many people have had their hand in making this project a reality. First and foremost my parents John and Charlotte Howell sacrificed much and were a constant source for morale, advice, and support from start to finish.

My brother Curtis Avison. Contributed more than any other in the actual production phase. His expertise in photos, photoshop, scanning, art, and many other miscellaneous aspects were absolutely critical. I can honestly say that without his help this book would not physically have been possible.

My Uncle Dave and Aunt Ginger Rank. Dave for his contribution of a grant for this project, and Ginger for her constant advice, I don't think two weeks went by over the course of the past year that your advice did not help in some way.

My brother Cameron Howell. Cameron was ever present through every moment of this project and helped me through the day to day highs and lows. His gift of a pencil sharpener though humble, was extremely thoughtful and being the best pencil sharpener I've ever used, was responsible for the grinding of an entire forest worth of pencils.

My cousins Scott and Jennifer Bonner. Contributed a significant loan toward this project. When things were looking dark in the early stages of this project you both came through in a big way. Your laid back demeanor and enthusiasm for the project truly helped me turn the corner. Scott's technical help towards my constant computer woes, was also invaluable.

My Grandma Virginia and Grandpa Lawrence Avison contributed with a loan as well. For this and so many other things, Thank You.

Valerie Robinson. The very first professional that I talked to in the very early stages of this project. Valerie was an invaluable help for technical advice.

Mary and Bill Gephart for their generous loan, you may have saved the entire project.

Alan Feldman. A private collector, Mr. Feldman's collection is simply extraordinary. Through his information and the use of many pieces of his collection this project was made possible. He doesn't get enough credit for the role he's played along the years towards the creation of many books and T.V. shows or his preservation of the very important pieces of Detroit sports memorabilia. But to you Alan, I speak for many people when I say thank you for your efforts toward the preservation of Detroit's sports heritage.

Therese and Dan Damman. Therese for your work on the biography. Dan for your legal advice. Both of you for your unceasing support.

Rhonda Morris. Thank You for the use of your computer throughout the course of the project. Without it, this project would not have been possible.

Lance and Judy Avison. Judy for her editing help, and both of you for the extended use of your car. It was absolutely imperative that I had a vehicle to drive and you made sure that I had one.

My thanks to the following people and organizations for their roles in this book: Kevin Bush and Jeremy Hunter for helping bring this story to my attention; Dr. Linda Borish for her guidance during the original thesis project; Dr. Fred Dobney for his help on the original manuscript; Dr. Rebekah Farrugia for her copyright advice; Barb Gunia and Susie Kenyon at San Serif for their Art Layout; Chrissy Gorzen for her early advice; Kristen Karpinski for her editing help; Tom Gilbert at the Associated Press for his extensive amount of help; Deanna Caldwell and the Detroit Lions for making my life so much easier; Gina Britley, Alice Pepper, Ruthie Miles and the *Detroit Free Press* for their invaluable contributions; Jan Lovell, Linda Culpepper and *The Detroit News*, without your help this book surely would not have been possible; the Detroit Tigers, Detroit Red Wings, Ilitch Holdings and their representative Sharon Arend, thank you so much for your photo contributions; John Horne, Freddie Berowski and the Baseball Hall of Fame for the photos and finding the answers to several difficult questions; Martha Mahrle, Rob Schneider, and Greg Colton at Graphic Sciences Inc. for their microfilm services; Kelly Karnesky and Kelly Wurn for their outstanding photographic work; Craig Campbell and the Hockey Hall of Fame for all of your help; Anne Marie Bedard at the Port Huron Library, thank you so much, your help was invaluable at one of the most critical moments; Vicky Hurley at the Marysville Library, a constant help in various aspects throughout this project, and Dr. William Anderson, Director of Arts and Libraries for the State of Michigan, thank you.

Charles Avison, a native and life-long resident of Michigan, has lived in numerous cities across the state. Born in Alma he attended schools in Mt. Pleasant (Sacred Heart Academy), Rockford (Our Lady of Consolation), New Baltimore (Our Lady of Immaculate Conception), Anchor Bay (Anchor Bay Middle School), Kalamazoo (St. Monica), and graduated from Hackett Catholic Central High School in Kalamazoo.

A student of history, Charles attended Kalamazoo Valley Community College, Grand Rapids Community College, and the University of Edinburgh (Scotland), before graduating from Western Michigan University in 2005 with a Bachelor of Arts Degree in Liberal History. He remains dedicated to the study of history, philosophy, and art, especially where it concerns Western Civilization.

Charles currently resides in the Detroit Metropolitan area, where he founded and operates Diomedea Publishing.